FOCUS

FOCUS ON VOCABULARY

Thematischer Wortschatz in Texten

von Steve Williams

Welcome to *Focus on Vocabulary*!

Dieses Buch richtet sich an Schülerinnen und Schüler, die sich auf das Abitur oder die Fachhochschulreife vorbereiten. Es kann aber auch bereichsübergreifend als Hilfsmittel zur Verbesserung des Englischwortschatzes eingesetzt werden.

Dieses Buch ist kein Wörterbuch und keine rein rezeptive Wortschatzliste! *Focus on Vocabulary* bietet ein kontextualisiertes Wortschatztraining: Vokabeln werden in **85 informativen Texten** präsentiert. Diese sind in **7 Themenfelder** gegliedert, die die wichtigsten Themen für das Abitur und die Fachhochschulreife abdecken.

Wörter, die im Text markiert sind, werden in der Liste auf der rechten Seite genauer erläutert. Sie finden dort Anmerkungen zur Aussprache und Übersetzung. In der dritten Spalte finden Sie weiterführende Hinweise zur Wortverwendung, typischen Fehlern und verwandten Begriffen, damit Sie Ihren Wortschatz vergrößern und vertiefen können.

LANGUAGE BOX

Hier werden ausgewählte idiomatische Ausdrücke, Wortfamilien und weitere Übersetzungsmöglichkeiten präsentiert. Unterstrichene Wörter oder Phrasen sind im Text verwendet worden.

CHECKPOINT *In English, please!*

Ein Checkpoint nach jedem Text hilft Ihnen, Ihren Lernerfolg zu überprüfen.

TEST YOURSELF
Auf jedes Themenfeld folgen vier Seiten Übungen, anhand derer Sie einschätzen können, wie gut Sie den Lernwortschatz verinnerlicht haben. Sie können Ihre Antworten auf S. 204–214 überprüfen.

 Auf scook.de finden Sie zu jedem Text **interaktive Online-Übungen**, womit Sie den neuen Wortschatz festigen können.

AUDIOS online Alle Texte sind auf scook.de als **Audiodateien** verfügbar.

Im **Index** können Sie alle Vokabelwörter schnell und bequem finden.

Wir wünschen Ihnen viel Freude und Erfolg mit *Focus on Vocabulary*!

Folgende Abkürzungen und Symbole werden im Buch verwendet:

AE	American English
BE	British English
ABBR	abbreviation
ADJ	adjective
ADV	adverb
INFML	informal
N	noun
V	verb
≈	synonym
◁▷	antonym/opposite
≠	does not mean
!	Careful! Mistakes are often made here.

e.g.	(Latin) exempli gratia = for example
etc.	(Latin) et cetera = and so on
etw	etwas
i.e.	(Latin) id est = that is, in other words
jd	jemand
jdm	jemandem
jdn	jemanden
jds	jemandes
p.	page
pl	plural
pp.	pages
S.	Seite
sb	somebody
sth	something
vgl.	vergleiche

CONTENTS

A Free time

Leisure activities

How do young people use their free time nowadays? Older adults frequently criticize them for sitting around doing nothing. Do they have a point?

Leisure patterns are changing and the leisure activities of today's youth are different to ten years ago. As you might expect, there is greater use of electronic devices for communication and entertainment. However there are other, less obvious changes. *Leisure Behaviour of Young People*, a study by the German Institute for Economic Research, has found that organized educational activities are replacing informal activities. Over 60% of 16-year-olds in the study did some kind of structured extracurricular activity on a regular basis, compared with less than 50% ten years ago. Over 20% of teenagers volunteer in their community or for a charity at least once a week (ten years ago: 11%).

CHECKPOINT   *In English, please!*

a Erwachsene kritisieren häufig die Jugend von heute.
b Elektronische Geräte haben unsere Freizeitaktivitäten verändert.
c Wir engagieren uns ehrenamtlich für eine Wohltätigkeitsorganisation.

Expressions with 'hobby'

to **take up a hobby** ein Hobby anfangen; anfangen, etw (in der Freizeit) zu tun
to **pursue a hobby** einem Hobby nachgehen, sich (in der Freizeit) mit etw beschäftigen
to **do sth as a hobby** etw als Hobby betreiben, etw (in der Freizeit) tun
it's a hobby of mine das ist ein Hobby von mir, das mache ich in meiner Freizeit

Word family 'criticize'

to **criticize sb for sth** jdm wegen etw kritisieren
criticism Kritik
critic Kritiker/in
critical (of sb/sth) kritisch (jdm/etw gegenüber)

leisure activity [ˈleʒər æktɪvəti]	*Freizeitbeschäftigung*	≈ **leisure pursuit** [ˈleʒə pəsjuːt]
to **criticize sb for sth** [ˈkrɪtɪsɪz]	*jdm wegen etw kritisieren*	→ *Kasten links*
to **do nothing** [ˌduː ˈnʌθɪŋ]	*nichts tun*	≈ to **be idle**
youth [juːθ]	*Jugend*	≈ **young people**
electronic device [ɪlekˌtrɒnɪk dɪˈvaɪs]	*elektronisches Gerät*	
obvious [ˈɒbviəs]	*offensichtlich, klar*	≈ **clear, apparent**
behaviour [bɪˈheɪvjə]	*Verhalten*	v to **behave** *sich verhalten*
educational [ˌedʒuˈkeɪʃənl]	*Bildungs-, Weiterbildungs-*	v to **educate** N **education**
to **replace** [rɪˈpleɪs]	*ersetzen*	N **replacement** *Ersatz*
structured [ˈstrʌktʃəd]	*strukturiert*	≈ **organized** ◑ **informal**
extracurricular [ekstrəkəˈrɪkjʊlə]	*außerhalb des Lehrplans, außerunterrichtlich*	◑ **curricular, classroom**
on a regular basis [ɒn ə ˌreɡjələ ˈbeɪsɪs]	*regelmäßig*	≈ **regularly** ◑ **occasionally**
to **volunteer** [ˌvɒlənˈtɪə]	*ehrenamtlich tätig sein, sich ehrenamtlich engagieren*	N **volunteer** *(Person)*
charity [ˈtʃærəti]	*Wohltätigkeitsorganisation, guter Zweck*	ADJ **charitable** *karitativ, wohltätig*

Less time for friends

Rather than spending a lot of time hanging out with friends or daydreaming, today's teenagers are likely to take up a creative pastime such as art, music or drama, or do voluntary work or sport. Because of all the creative, structured activities that they are busy with, today's teenagers have a lot less time for informal socializing. Their friendships may be suffering as a result: ten years ago, 40% of teenagers went out with their best friend every day; now only 25% do so.

However, that doesn't mean that today's teens *only* do organized activities. Their favourite activity is still listening to music. It's by far the most popular way for young people to switch off and 'chill'. Nearly 90% of teens do this every day. Other popular unstructured leisure activities include watching TV, browsing the internet and using social media.

Nevertheless, the general pattern is clear: far from being lazy and sedentary, today's teenagers lead busy, active lives.

CHECKPOINT	*In English, please!*

a Meine Lieblingsbeschäftigung ist das Nutzen sozialer Medien.
b Ich habe zu viel zu tun, um mit meinen Freunden abzuhängen.
c Was sind deine Lieblingsbeschäftigungen außerhalb des Lehrplans?
d Ich beschäftige mich gern mit kreativen Hobbys wie Musik und Kunst.
e Weit davon entfernt, aktiv und vielbeschäftigt zu sein, führt er ein Leben im Sitzen.

Expressions with 'activity'

leisure activity Freizeitbeschäftigung
educational activities Weiterbildung, Bildungsaktivitäten, Unterricht
extracurricular activites außerschulische Aktivitäten
organized activities organisierte Aktivitäten

Slang terms teenagers use

to **hang out** (mit jdm) Zeit verbringen, abhängen
to **chill** chillen
to **post pics** Bilder (in den sozialen Medien) posten

to **spend time doing sth** [ˌspend ˈtaɪm]	*Zeit (damit) verbringen, etw zu tun*	*vgl.* to **spend money on sth** *Geld für etw ausgeben*
to **hang out with sb** [ˌhæŋ ˈaʊt wɪð]	*mit jdm abhängen, (freie) Zeit mit jdm verbringen*	**!** informal ≈ to **spend time with sb**, to **socialize with sb**
to **daydream** [ˈdeɪdriːm]	*(mit offenen Augen) träumen, Tagträumen nachhängen*	N **daydream** N **daydreamer** *(Person)*
to **be likely to do sth** [bi ˈlaɪkli tə]	*etw wahrscheinlich tun*	◀▶ to **be unlikely to do sth**
to **take up sth** [ˌteɪk ˈʌp]	*(mit) etw anfangen*	
creative [kriˈeɪtɪv]	*kreativ*	N **creativity**
pastime [ˈpɑːstaɪm]	*Freizeitbeschäftigung, Zeitvertreib, Hobby*	≈ **hobby** *vgl.* **craze, fad** *Modeerscheinung*
voluntary work [ˌvɒləntri ˈwɜːk]	*ehrenamtliche Arbeit*	≠ **paid work**
socializing [ˈsəʊʃəlaɪzɪŋ]	*Treffen (in der Freizeit)*	V to **socialize (with sb)**
to **go out with sb** [ˌgəʊ ˈaʊt wɪð]	*mit jdm ausgehen, sich mit jdm treffen*	*vgl.* to **go out on a date with sb** *mit jdm ausgehen, mit jdm ein Date haben*
to **browse the internet** [ˌbraʊz ði ˈɪntənet]	*im Internet surfen*	≈ to **surf the internet**
social media [ˌsəʊʃl ˈmiːdiə]	*soziale Medien*	*vgl.* **social media platform**
lazy [ˈleɪzi]	*faul*	N **laziness**
to **be sedentary** [bi ˈsedntri]	*viel (herum)sitzen*	≈ **inactive** ◀▶ **active**
to **lead a … life** [ˌliːd ə ˈlaɪf]	*ein … Leben führen*	
busy [ˈbɪzi]	*geschäftig, vielbeschäftigt*	*vgl.* **hectic** *hektisch*

Volunteering benefits the volunteer

Volunteering is 'in'. Around 20% of young Germans volunteer every week in their community and many choose to do a volunteering 'gap year' abroad after leaving school.

Many young people volunteer because they have a strong social conscience. They believe that they can make a difference to the lives of others. Volunteering often takes people out of their comfort zone and requires them to learn new skills or work together with people from different social or ethnic backgrounds. It is a good preparation for work or further study.

Volunteers abroad may have to adapt to living conditions which are much more basic than those back home. In working together towards a shared goal, volunteers often make friendships which last a lifetime. Volunteering can take people to new, unfamiliar countries around the globe, or show them new aspects of their own society.

Expressions with 'volunteer'/ 'voluntary'

voluntary position/job ehrenamtliche Stelle
voluntary/volunteer work ehrenamtliche/freiwillige Arbeit
volunteer programme Freiwilligenprogramm

Expressions with 'world'/'globe'

to **go around the world/globe** um die Welt reisen
to **go globetrotting** auf Weltreise gehen
to **see the world** sich die Welt ansehen, die Welt bereisen
to **the other side of the world/ globe** auf die andere Seite der Welt
to **travel the world/globe** die Welt bereisen

CHECKPOINT	*In English, please!*

a Wir überlegen, ein Jahr Auszeit zu machen, wenn wir von der Schule abgehen.
b Im Ausland zu arbeiten wird uns einer Herausforderung aussetzen.
c Die Freiwilligen kommen aus vielen unterschiedlichen sozialen Verhältnissen.
d Wir werden neue Fähigkeiten erlernen und uns an ungewohnte Lebensbedingungen anpassen müssen.

to **volunteer** [ˌvɒlənˈtɪə]	*ehrenamtlich tätig sein, freiwillige Arbeit leisten*	ADJ **voluntary**
to **benefit sb** [ˈbenɪfɪt]	*jdm nützen*	N **benefit**
volunteer [ˌvɒlənˈtɪə]	*ehrenamtliche/r Mitarbeiter/in, Freiwillige/r*	↔ **paid worker**
community [kəˈmjuːnəti]	*Gemeinde, Kommune*	vgl. **local/wider/international community**
gap year [ˈgæp jɪə]	*freies Jahr zwischen Schulabschluss und Studienbeginn*	vgl. to **go on/take/do a gap year** *ein Jahr Auszeit nehmen*
abroad [əˈbrɔːd]	*im Ausland*	**!** *Adverb, nicht Adjektiv*
social conscience [ˌsəʊʃl ˈkɒnʃəns]	*soziales Gewissen*	vgl. **conscientious** *gewissenhaft*
to **make a difference to sth** [dɪfrəns]	*etw verändern, etw für etw bewirken*	vgl. **Your help made all the difference.** *Eure Hilfe hat sehr viel bewirkt.*
to **take sb out of their comfort zone** [kʌmfət ˌzəʊn]	*jdn einer neuen Herausforderung aussetzen*	vgl. to **stay in one's comfort zone** *sich keiner Herausforderung aussetzen*
skill [skɪl]	*Fähigkeit, Kompetenz*	ADJ **skilful, skilled**
background [ˈbækgraʊnd]	*Herkunft, Verhältnisse*	vgl. **origin**
to **adapt to sth** [əˈdæpt]	*sich auf etw einstellen, sich an etw anpassen*	ADJ **adaptable**
living conditions [ˈlɪvɪŋ kəndɪʃnz]	*Lebensbedingungen*	vgl. **living standard** *Lebensstandard*
basic [ˈbeɪsɪk]	*einfach*	≈ **simple, rudimentary**
goal [gəʊl]	*Ziel*	≈ **aim, objective**
unfamiliar [ˌʌnfəˈmɪliə]	*fremd, neu*	N **unfamiliarity** *Fremdheit, Unvertrautheit*

Volunteering benefits the community

Charities which rely on volunteers are often short of money, and the services they offer might not be available without the unpaid work of volunteers. These charities greatly improve the quality of life of the elderly, the homeless and those with disabilities, for example. However, meaning well is not enough. Volunteering programmes need to be designed to be genuinely useful to the recipients; volunteers need adequate training. Some people criticize 'voluntourism': programmes which are designed to provide the participants with adventures, rather than being genuinely useful.

Finding a voluntary position in your community is not hard. Many non-profit organizations use volunteers. Volunteering abroad, on the other hand, requires a lot more thought and preparation. You can search online for overseas programmes. Think hard about your relevant skills and expect an application process just like for a paid job.

Volunteering opportunities

aged care Altenpflege
conservation Naturschutz
development aid Entwicklungshilfe
disability support Behinderten-
  betreuung, Hilfe für Behinderte
disaster relief Katastrophenhilfe,
  Nothilfe
event organization Veranstaltungs-
  organisation
youth work Jugendarbeit

CHECKPOINT   *In English, please!*

a Hilfsorganisationen wie wir sind auf freiwillige Helfer wie euch angewiesen.
b Alle Teilnehmer erhalten eine angemessene Schulung.
c Ich interessiere mich dafür, älteren Menschen und Menschen mit Behinderung zu helfen.
d Sie will eine ehrenamtliche Stellung bei einer gemeinnützigen Organisation finden.

charity ['tʃærəti]	*Hilfsorganisation*	ADJ **charitable**
to **rely on sb/sth** [rɪ'laɪ ɒn]	*auf jdn/etw angewiesen sein*	N **reliance**
to **be short of sth** [bi 'ʃɔːt əv]	*unter Mangel an etw leiden*	◆ to **have plenty of sth**
service ['sɜːvɪs]	*Dienst, Leistung, Dienstleistung*	*vgl.* **assistance** *Hilfe, Unterstützung*
unpaid [ˌʌn'peɪd]	*unbezahlt, ehrenamtlich*	≈ **voluntary**
the elderly [eldəli]	*ältere Menschen, Senioren*	≈ **aged** *(bes. Amtssprache)*
the homeless ['həʊmləs]	*Obdachlose*	ADJ **homeless** *obdachlos* N **homelessness**
disability [ˌdɪsə'bɪləti]	*Behinderung*	ADJ **disabled**
to **mean well** [ˌmiːn 'wel]	*es gut meinen*	ADJ **well-meaning** *wohlmeinend, gut gemeint*
programme ['prəʊgræm]	*Programm*	! *bei* AE *und Computer:* **program**
recipient [rɪ'sɪpiənt]	*Empfänger/in, Adressat/in*	V to **receive** N **receipt** *Empfang*
adequate ['ədɪkwət]	*ausreichend, angemessen*	≈ **enough**
participant [pə'tɪsɪpnt]	*Teilnehmer/in*	N **participation**
adventure [əd'ventʃə]	*Abenteuer*	ADJ **adventurous**
non-profit [ˌnɒn'prɒfɪt]	*gemeinnützig*	≈ **not-for-profit**
overseas [ˌəʊvə'siːz]	*Auslands-, in Übersee*	*auch Adverb:* to **go overseas** *usw.*
application process [ˌæplɪ'keɪʃn prəʊses]	*Bewerbungsverfahren*	*vgl.* to **apply for sth** *sich für/um etw bewerben*

B Health and well-being

Adolescence

Adolescence is a vulnerable time for everyone. We all have the same basic need to feel loved and accepted. After all, that's part of what makes us human. Adolescence is a stage in our lives when it may be particularly difficult to find this acceptance, as our bodies change and mature and we face new social situations and roles. As adolescents we try to find our place in the world and define ourselves. At this time, the opinions of our peers matter to us very much – we experience peer pressure. It's natural to feel insecure about our appearance and our social competence: our ability to find friends and attract a partner. Other adolescents, struggling with their own problems, may be unkind to us.

At the same time, we have to cope with media pressure. Media companies are doing their best to exploit our insecurities as a marketing opportunity. Adolescence can be tough!

Word family 'accept'

to **accept sb/sth** jdn/etw annehmen, jdn/etw anerkennen, jdn/etw akzeptieren
acceptance Anerkennung, Akzeptanz
acceptable akzeptabel, annehmbar
accepted anerkannt
unacceptable unannehmbar, inakzeptabel

Word family 'attract'

to **attract sb** jdn gewinnen, jdn anziehen
attractive anziehend, attraktiv
attraction Anziehung; Attraktion
unattractive unattraktiv, ohne Reiz

adolescence [ˌædəˈlesns]	Jugend, Adoleszenz	vgl. **puberty** Pubertät
vulnerable [ˈvʌlnərəbl]	verwundbar, prekär, anfällig	N **vulnerability**
human [ˈhjuːmən]	menschlich	N **humanity**
acceptance [əkˈseptəns]	Anerkennung, Akzeptanz	◀▶ **rejection** → Siehe auch Kasten links
to mature [məˈtʃʊə]	heranreifen, erwachsen werden	N **maturity**
to face sth [feɪs]	einer Sache gegenüberstehen, mit etw konfrontiert werden	◀▶ to **avoid sth**
social [ˈsəʊʃl]	sozial, gesellschaftlich	vgl. **society** Gesellschaft
role [rəʊl]	Rolle, Funktion	vgl. to **play a role**
peer pressure [ˈpɪə preʃə]	Gruppenzwang, sozialer Druck	vgl. **peer group** Gleichaltrige, Gleichrangige
insecure [ˌɪnsɪˈkjʊə]	unsicher	N **insecurity** Unsicherheit
appearance [əˈpɪərəns]	Aussehen, (äußere) Erscheinung	V to **appear**
social competence [ˈsəʊʃl kɒmpɪtəns]	soziale Kompetenz	ADJ competent
to attract sb [əˈtrækt]	jdn gewinnen, jdn anziehen	→ Kasten links
adolescent [ˌædəˈlesnt]	Jugendliche/r	auch ADJ heranwachsend, jugendlich
to struggle with sth [ˈstrʌgl wɪð]	mit etw ringen, mit etw zu tun haben	N **struggle**
unkind [ˌʌnˈkaɪnd]	unfreundlich, gemein, nicht nett	N **unkindness**
to cope with sth [ˈkəʊp wɪð]	mit etw zurechtkommen	≈ to **deal with sth**
to exploit sth [ɪkˈsplɔɪt]	etw ausnutzen, etw ausbeuten	N **exploitation**
insecurity [ˌɪnsɪˈkjʊərəti]	Unsicherheit	≈ **lack of self-confidence**

Body image

Modern media have changed our ideas of how we should look, with consequences for our body image and our self-esteem. In magazines and online, we see endless photos of models with flawless skin, fit bodies and perfect teeth. The film and music industries are full of unusually attractive people.

These media images present us with impossible ideals to live up to and are bad for our self-esteem and body image. The images often aren't even real – the models' normal human imperfections have been covered by make-up artists and photographers, or hidden by a graphic designer.

It's hardly surprising, then, if we are preoccupied with how we look. This can lead to a range of physical and mental health problems, including eating disorders, obsessive exercise, anxiety and depression. An obsession with body image may lead people to undergo unnecessary plastic surgery.

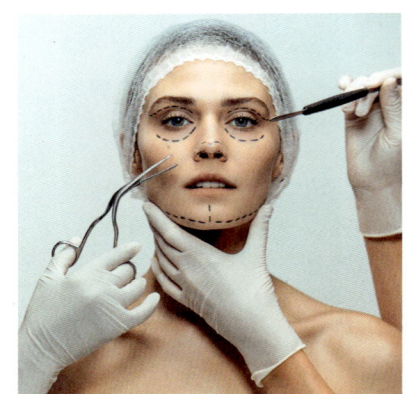

The prefixes 'un-', 'in-' and 'im-'
unacceptable unannehmbar, inakzeptabel
unattractive unattraktiv, ohne Reiz
unhealthy ungesund
unkind unfreundlich, gemein, nicht nett
unnecessary unnötig
unusual ungewöhnlich
inhuman unmenschlich
insecure unsicher
invulnerable unverwundbar
!**immature** unreif
!**imperfect** unvollkommen
!**impossible** unmöglich

CHECKPOINT

In English, please!

a Die meisten Models haben nicht wirklich makellose Haut.
b Sogar attraktive Menschen haben Makel.
c Es ist wichtig, Ideale zu haben, denen man gerecht werden muss.
d Er beschäftigt sich ständig mit seinem körperlichen Erscheinungsbild.
e Angst und Depressionen sind ernsthafte mentale Gesundheitsprobleme.
f Ihr geringes Selbstwertgefühl brachte sie dazu, sich einer Schönheitsoperation zu unterziehen.

body image ['bɒdi ɪmɪdʒ]	Körperwahrnehmung	vgl. **self-image** Selbstbild
self-esteem [ˌself ɪ'sti:m]	Selbstwertgefühl	≈ **self-confidence**
model ['mɒdl]	Model, Mannequin	N **modelling** (abstrakt)
flawless ['flɔ:ləs]	makellos	◁▷ **flawed**
fit [fɪt]	durchtrainiert	N **fitness**
to **live up to sth** [ˌlɪv 'ʌp tə]	einer Sache entsprechen, einer Sache gerecht werden	≈ to **measure up to sth**
imperfection [ˌɪmpə'fekʃn]	Unzulänglichkeit, Makel	◁▷ **perfection**
hardly ['hɑ:dli]	kaum	! ≠ **hard** hart, schwer
to **be preoccupied with sth** [prɪ'ɒkjupaɪd]	sich stark/ständig mit etw beschäftigen	N **preoccupation** (ständige gedankliche) Beschäftigung
eating disorder [ˌi:tɪŋ dɪs'ɔ:də]	Ess-Störung	to **have/suffer from an eating disorder** eine Ess-Störung haben/an einer Ess-Störung leiden
anxiety [æŋ'zaɪəti]	Angst	ADJ **anxious**
depression [dɪ'preʃn]	Depression(en)	to **suffer from depression** an/unter Depressionen leiden ADJ **depressed** deprimiert
to **undergo sth** [ʌndə'gəʊ]	sich einer Sache unterziehen	! **underwent**
plastic surgery [ˌplæstɪk 'sɜ:dʒəri]	Schönheitsoperation(en), plastische Chirurgie	≈ **cosmetic surgery**

Drugs – definition and use

A drug is any substance (other than food) that, when introduced to the body, causes a physiological and/or psychological change. The drug may be injected, smoked, eaten, drunk or absorbed through the user's skin.

Drugs may be taken for medical reasons. A medicine is a drug which is taken to cure or manage the symptoms of a disease or medical condition, or to prevent such a condition from occurring in the future. Such drugs may be available 'over the counter' or only via a prescription from a doctor.

Medicines need to be treated with respect and only used according to the instructions on the packet. Overdoses of many medicines can be dangerous, even fatal. Prolonged use of some medicines, e.g. painkillers, can also be habit-forming. For these reasons, the availability of most medicines is restricted.

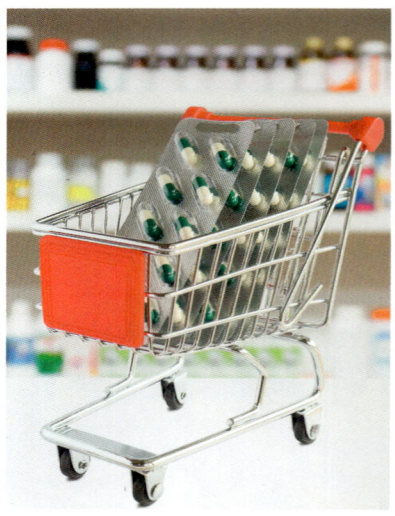

CHECKPOINT	*In English, please!*

a Dieses Arzneimittel sollte Ihnen helfen, mit Ihren Symptomen zurechtzukommen.
b Allerdings kann es psychologische Veränderungen verursachen.
c Kann ich es ohne Rezept kaufen?
d Nein, Sie benötigen ein Rezept Ihres Arztes.
e Seien Sie vorsichtig und nehmen Sie nicht zu viel: Eine Überdosis kann gefährlich sein.

Expressions with 'drug' (1)

gateway drug Einstiegsdroge
over-the-counter drug frei verkäufliches Arzneimittel
prescription drug rezeptpflichtiges Arzneimittel
recreational drug Freizeitdroge
hard drug harte Droge
soft drug weiche Droge
→ *Siehe auch Kasten S. 22*

substance ['sʌbstəns]	*Wirkstoff, Substanz*	*vgl.* **controlled substance** *verbotene Substanz*
physiological [ˌfɪziə'lɒdʒɪkl]	*physiologisch*	N **physiology**
psychological [ˌsaɪkə'lɒdʒɪkl]	*psychologisch*	N **psychology**
to **inject** [ɪn'dʒekt]	*injizieren, spritzen*	N **injection**
to **smoke** [sməʊk]	*rauchen*	N **smoker** *(Person)*
user ['juːzə]	*Konsument/in*	N **use** ! [juːs] *(abstrakt)*
medical ['medɪkl]	*medizinisch*	◆ **non-medical**
medicine ['medsn]	*Arzneimittel*	ADJ **medicinal** *arzneilich, medikamentös*
to **cure** [kjʊə]	*heilen, therapieren*	N **cure** *Therapie, Heilung*
disease [dɪ'ziːz]	*Krankheit, Leiden*	≈ **illness, sickness**
to **prevent** [prɪ'vent]	*verhüten*	N **prevention** ADJ **preventable**
over the counter [ˌəʊvə ðə 'kaʊntə]	*rezeptfrei, ohne Rezept*	ADJ **over-the-counter**
prescription [prɪ'skrɪpʃn]	*(ärztliches) Rezept, Verschreibung*	ADJ **prescribed** *verschrieben*
instructions *pl* [ɪn'strʌkʃnz]	*Anleitung, hier: Beipackzettel*	V to **instruct**
overdose ['əʊvədəʊs]	*Überdosis*	V to **overdose**
fatal ['feɪtl]	*tödlich*	≈ **deadly**
prolonged use [prəˌlɒŋd 'juːs]	*anhaltender Gebrauch, hier: längere Einnahme*	V to **prolong** *verlängern*
habit-forming ['hæbɪt fɔːmɪŋ]	*süchtig machend*	≈ **addictive**
availability [əveɪlə'bɪləti]	*Verfügbarkeit*	ADJ **available**
restricted [rɪ'strɪktɪd]	*eingeschränkt*	N **restriction**

Recreational drugs

As well as for medical reasons, drugs are also taken for recreational reasons: the aim is to change the user's mood or senses in a pleasurable way. The user may become temporarily more relaxed or more energetic through drug use, or may experience sensory changes (e.g. changes to their vision, hearing or sense of smell). These can be pleasurable or, in the case of a 'bad trip', frightening and disorientating.

Commonly used recreational drugs include caffeine, alcohol and tobacco. These drugs are all legal in European countries, and most other countries around the world, although the use of alcohol is banned or restricted in some countries. Other recreational drugs are illegal in most European countries. Governments justify these anti-drug laws by pointing out that these drugs are harmful to the health of users and to wider society. Some medicines can be misused as recreational drugs and may be highly addictive.

Word family 'addict'

addict Süchtige/r
addiction Sucht
addictive süchtig machend
to **get/become/be addicted** süchtig werden

The five senses

sight, vision Sehvermögen
smell Geruchsinn
hearing Gehör
taste Geschmackssinn
touch Tastsinn

The prefix 'mis-'

to **misbehave** sich schlecht benehmen
to **misjudge** (jdn/etw) falsch einschätzen
to **mislead** (jdn) täuschen, irreführen
to **mismanage** (etw) schlecht führen/ verwalten, (etw) herunterwirt- schaften
to **misrepresent** (etw) falsch darstellen
to **misunderstand** missverstehen
to **misuse** [mɪsˈjuːz] missbrauchen, falsch verwenden

recreational [ˌrekriˈeɪʃənl]	*Freizeit-*	↘ **recreation** *Erholung, Hobby*
mood [muːd]	*Stimmung, Laune*	ADJ **moody** *launisch, missmutig*
sense [sens]	*Sinn, Sinneswahrnehmung*	ADJ **sensory** *Sinnes-, sensorisch*
pleasurable [ˈpleʒərəbl]	*angenehm*	N **pleasure**
energetic [ˌenəˈdʒetɪk]	*energiegeladen*	◀▶ **tired, lethargic**
frightening [ˈfraɪtnɪŋ]	*erschreckend, fürchterlich*	*vgl.* **frightened** *verängstigt*
disorientating [dɪsˈɔːriənteɪtɪŋ]	*desorientierend, verwirrend*	ADJ **disorientated** *desorientiert, verwirrt*
caffeine [ˈkæfiːn]	*Koffein*	*vgl.* **decaf(feinated)**
tobacco [təˈbækəʊ]	*Tabak*	*vgl.* **cigarette**
to **ban** [bæn]	*(gesetzlich) verbieten*	N **ban (on sth)** *Verbot (von etw)*
to **restrict** [rɪˈstrɪkt]	*einschränken, begrenzen*	N **restriction**
to **justify** [ˈdʒʌstɪfaɪ]	*rechtfertigen, begründen*	N **justification**
anti-drug law [ˌænti ˈdrʌg ˌlɔː]	*Drogengesetze*	◀▶ **pro-drug**
harmful (to sb/sth) [ˈhɑːmfl]	*schädlich (für jdn/etw)*	◀▶ **harmless**
addictive [əˈdɪktɪv]	*süchtig machend*	≈ **habit-forming**
		→ *Siehe auch Kasten links*

Debate about recreational drugs

There is debate and controversy about how dangerous individual drugs are. Some drugs such as cannabis are widely considered to be 'soft' drugs which are unlikely to lead to addiction or cause major harm to the user, if they are used in moderation. Expert opinion may support this point of view.

However, others – including other medical experts – claim that the evidence shows these 'soft' drugs to be more dangerous than commonly believed. There is also concern that the so-called soft drugs may be 'gateway' drugs to 'hard' drugs such as heroin.

An argument for legalization of recreational drugs lies in the failure of the long-running 'War on Drugs' to reduce drug use in countries such as the USA, which have harsh punishments for drug possession and drug dealing. By making it harder for users to obtain a drug, governments may actually make it a more profitable and attractive product for organized crime.

Expressions with 'drug(s)' (2)

drug dealer Drogenhändler/in, Dealer/in
drug dealing Drogenhandel
drug possession Drogenbesitz
drug use Drogenkonsum
drug user Drogenkonsument/in
to **take/use drugs** Drogen konsumieren
to **get high on drugs** sich mit Rauschgift zudröhnen
to **be on drugs** Rauschgift nehmen, auf Droge sein
→ *Siehe auch Kasten S. 18*

CHECKPOINT   *In English, please!*

a Es gibt eine Kontroverse über die Legalisierung von Cannabis.
b Auch weiche Drogen können große Gesundheitsschäden verursachen.
c Es gibt keine Belege dafür, dass sie gefährlich sind, wenn sie in Maßen konsumiert werden.
d Reduzieren harte Strafen für Drogenbesitz den Drogenkonsum?

controversy [ˈkɒntrəvɜːsi]	*Streit, Kontroverse, Diskussion*	ADJ **controversial** [kɒntrəˈvɜːʃl] *umstritten, kontrovers*
addiction [əˈdɪkʃn]	*Sucht*	N **addict** *(Person)* → *Siehe auch Kasten S. 20*
to **cause harm (to sb)** [ˌkɔːz ˈhɑːm tə]	*Gesundheitsschäden verursachen*	≈ to **harm sb** ADJ **harmful** ◆ **harmless**
major [ˈmeɪdʒə]	*erheblich, schwerwiegend*	◆ **minor**
in moderation [ɪn ˌmɒdəˈreɪʃn]	*in Maßen, maßvoll*	◆ **without moderation, excessively**
expert opinion [ˌekspɜːt əˈpɪnjən]	*Expertenmeinung*	vgl. **expertise** *Sachkenntnis*
to **support** [səˈpɔːt]	*stützen*	≈ to **give weight to, to back up**
evidence [ˈevɪdəns]	*Hinweise, Belege, Indizien*	ADJ **evident**
gateway drug [ˈgeɪtweɪ drʌg]	*Einstiegsdroge*	
legalization [ˌliːgəlaɪˈzeɪʃn]	*Legalisierung*	vgl. **decriminalization** *Legalisierung*
failure [ˈfeɪljə]	*Misserfolg, Wirkungslosigkeit*	◆ **success**
war (on sth) [wɔː]	*Krieg (gegen etw)*	vgl. to **declare war on sb/sth**
harsh [hɑːʃ]	*streng, hart*	◆ **lenient** N **harshness**
punishment [ˈpʌnɪʃmənt]	*Strafe(n), Bestrafung*	≈ **penalty** V to **punish sb**
possession [pəˈzeʃn]	*Besitz*	V to **possess, to be in possession of** N **possessor** *(Person)*
profitable [ˈprɒfɪtəbl]	*rentabel, einträglich*	≈ **profit-making**
crime [kraɪm]	*Kriminalität*	ADJ **criminal** N **criminal**

Alcohol – Europe's drug of choice

Alcohol is the 'drug of choice' for many adult Europeans. It is legal, inexpensive and widely available. There is almost endless variety in the alcoholic drinks available, ranging from beers and wines to fortified wines and spirits.

Moderate social drinking helps people to relax and unwind after a busy day. It increases our enjoyment of a meal and acts as a 'social lubricant', helping to create a relaxed atmosphere. For many, it is an important and enjoyable part of European culture.

Binge drinking, by contrast, is anti-social. It involves consuming an excessive amount of alcohol in a short time, resulting in intoxication and loss of self-control. Many young people see binge drinking as a 'rite of passage' to adulthood. Excessive drinking at parties, nightclubs and bars leads to embarrassing drunken behaviour. Sadly, binge drinking can have far more serious consequences than just embarrassment. *(See box on page 26)*

(See box on page 26)

Word family 'alcohol'

alcohol Alkohol
alcoholic alkoholisch, alkoholhaltig
alcoholic *(Person)* Alkoholiker/in
alcoholism Alkoholsucht, Alkoholismus
non-alcoholic nicht-alkoholisch

The prefix 'self-'

self-centred selbstbezogen, egozentrisch
self-confident selbstsicher, selbstbewusst
self-confidence Selbstsicherheit, Selbstbewusstsein
self-control Selbstkontrolle
self-discipline Selbstdisziplin
self-esteem Selbstwertgefühl

CHECKPOINT   *In English, please!*

a Maßvolles Trinken in Gesellschaft schafft eine entspannte Atmosphäre.
b Komasaufen kann ernste Konsequenzen haben.
c Bei der Party trank er eine übermäßige Menge Alkohol.
d Sein Verlust an Selbstkontrolle war peinlich für seine Freunde.

alcohol [ˈælkəhɒl]	*Alkohol*	ADJ **alcoholic** → *Siehe auch Kasten links*
drug of choice [ˌdrʌg əf ˈtʃɔɪs]	*Droge der Wahl, bevorzugte Droge*	V to **choose**
available [əˈveɪləbl]	*erhältlich, verfügbar*	N **availability**
fortified wine [ˌfɔːtɪfʌɪd ˈwʌɪn]	*angereicherter/aufgespritzter Wein*	V to **fortify** *stärken*
spirits [ˈspɪrɪts]	*Spirituosen*	≈ **strong liquor**
moderate [ˈmɒdərət]	*maßvoll*	◑ **immoderate, excessive**
social drinking [ˌsəʊʃl ˈdrɪŋkɪŋ]	*Trinken in Gesellschaft*	*vgl.* to **drink socially**
to **relax** [rɪˈlæks]	*sich entspannen*	N **relaxation** ADJ **relaxed**
to **unwind** [ˌʌnˈwaɪnd]	*sich entspannen*	◑ to **get wound up, tense**
enjoyment [ɪnˈdʒɔɪmənt]	*Genuss*	V to **enjoy** ADJ **enjoyable**
social lubricant [ˌsəʊʃl ˈluːbrɪkənt]	*soziales Schmiermittel*	*vgl.* to **lubricate** *schmieren*
binge drinking [ˈbɪndʒ drɪŋkɪŋ]	*Komasaufen, Saufgelage*	*vgl.* to **go on a binge** *saufen gehen*
excessive [ɪkˈsesɪv]	*übermäßig, exzessiv*	N **excess**
amount [əˈmaʊnt]	*Menge*	N **quantity**
intoxication [ɪnˌtɒksɪˈkeɪʃn]	*Rausch, Trunkenheit*	ADJ **intoxicated**
loss [lɒs]	*Verlust*	V to **lose**
self-control [ˌself kənˈtrəʊl]	*Selbstkontrolle*	*vgl.* to **lose control, get out of control** *die Kontrolle verlieren*
rite of passage [ˌraɪt əf ˈpæsɪdʒ]	*Initiationsritus*	*vgl.* to **undergo a rite of passage**
drunken [ˈdrʌŋkən]	*betrunken, im Vollrausch*	*vgl.* to **get drunk**

What is a safe level of alcohol use?

The latest medical advice is that there is no safe level. There is a clear link between alcohol and various types of cancer, and excessive drinking is known to be very dangerous to young people up to the age of 25, whose brains are still developing. Drunk driving is another danger. A driver's judgement is impaired, even by small quantities of alcohol. Reactions are slower and coordination is poorer – at the same time that self-confidence and risk taking increase. This dangerous combination often leads to fatal accidents.

Like many other drugs, alcohol can be habit-forming and addictive. Alcoholism is a particularly destructive form of addiction. In the past, these concerns have led some Western countries, such as the USA, to experiment with the prohibition of alcoholic drinks. Prohibition failed to reduce alcohol abuse, instead creating an attractive black market.

In English, please!

CHECKPOINT

a Alkohol am Steuer führt oft zu tödlichen Unfällen.
b Ein beeinträchtigtes Wahrnehmungsvermögen führt zu erhöhter Risikobereitschaft.
c Selbst geringe Mengen Alkohol sind für Fahrer bedenklich.
d Für viele Menschen ist Alkoholkonsum abhängig machend.
e Alkoholmissbrauch ist zerstörerisch, aber ein Verbot ist nicht die richtige Antwort.

Excessive drinking can lead to …

accidental injury and death Unfallverletzung und Unfalltod
alcohol poisoning Alkoholvergiftung
drunk driving Alkohol am Steuer
hooliganism Rowdytum, Hooliganismus
sexual assault sexueller Übergriff, sexuelle Gewalt
unwanted sexual contact unerwünschter Sexualkontakt
violence Gewalt

Word family 'safe'

safe sicher, ungefährlich, unbedenklich
safely sicher, gefahrlos, vorsichtig
safety Sicherheit, Unbedenklichkeit
unsafe bedenklich, gefährlich
to **save** schützen, retten, sparen

level [ˈlevl]	*Grad, Niveau, Ausmaß*	≈ **degree**
advice [ədˈvaɪs]	*Empfehlung(en), Rat*	∨ to **advise** ! [ədˈvaɪz]
link [lɪŋk]	*Verbindung, Beziehung*	∨ to **link**
cancer [ˈkænsə]	*Krebs*	∨gl. **tumour**
brain [breɪn]	*Gehirn, Hirn*	∨gl. **mind** *Geist, Verstand*
drunk driving [ˌdrʌŋk ˈdraɪvɪŋ]	*Alkohol am Steuer*	ʒᴇ *auch:* **drink driving**
judgement [ˈdʒʌdʒmənt]	*Urteilsvermögen*	∨ to **judge**
to **impair** [ɪmˈpeə]	*beeinträchtigen, mindern*	∨ **impairment** *Beeinträchtigung, Minderung*
reaction [riˈækʃn]	*Reaktion*	∨ to **react (to sth)**
coordination [kəʊˌɔːdɪˈneɪʃn]	*Koordination*	∨gl. to **become uncoordinated** *unkoordiniert*
self-confidence [ˌself ˈkɒnfɪdəns]	*Selbstsicherheit*	ᴀᴅᴊ **self-confident**
risk taking [ˈrɪsk teɪkɪŋ]	*(erhöhte) Risikobereitschaft*	∨ to **take risks** *Risiken eingehen*
fatal accident [ˌfeɪtl ˈæksɪdənt]	*tödlicher Unfall*	∨gl. **fatality** *Todesfall*
habit-forming [ˈhæbɪt fɔːmɪŋ]	*abhängig machend*	∨gl. **drug habit** *Drogensucht*
destructive [dɪˈstrʌktɪv]	*zerstörerisch, destruktiv*	∨ **destruction**
prohibition [ˌprəʊˈbɪʃn]	*Verbot, Prohibition*	∨ to **prohibit**
alcohol abuse [ˈælkəhɒl əbjuːs]	*Alkoholmissbrauch*	∨ to **abuse** ! [əbjuːz]
black market [ˌblæk ˈmɑːkɪt]	*Schwarzmarkt*	∨ **black marketeer** *(Person)*

C Identity and relationships

The modern family

There is a traditional African saying, 'It takes a village to raise a child.' This means that the entire community provides a safe environment for children to grow up in. However, in our modern society, small, stable, close-knit communities of this kind rarely exist: modern life is more anonymous. Nevertheless, it is still true that children's upbringing is influenced by people outside their immediate 'nuclear family' of parents and siblings. These people include extended family such as grandparents, uncles, aunts and cousins and other relatives, unrelated family friends, neighbours and teachers. These people are our 'village'.

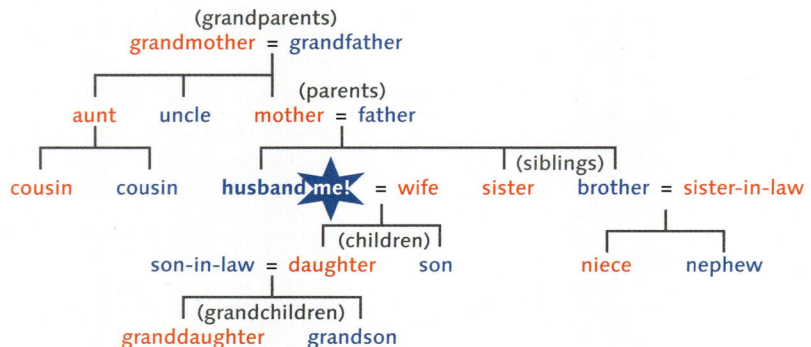

CHECKPOINT   *In English, please!*

a Greg wuchs in einer kleinen, engen Gemeinschaft auf.
b Zu seiner erweiterten Familie gehörten viele Tanten, Onkel, Cousins und Cousinen.
c Die Familie, Freunde und Nachbarn beeinflussten seine Erziehung.
d Er möchte ein sicheres, stabiles Umfeld für seine Kinder.

to **raise sb** [reɪz]	*jdn großziehen, jdn aufziehen*	≈ to **bring sb up**
community [kəˈmjuːnəti]	*Gemeinschaft, Gemeinde*	ADJ **communal** *gemeinsam, Gemeinschafts-*
to **provide** [prəˈvaɪd]	*bieten, bereitstellen*	N **provision** *Versorgung, Bereitstellung*
environment [ɪnˈvaɪrənmənt]	*Umfeld*	≈ **surroundings** *pl*
to **grow up** [ˌɡrəʊ ˈʌp]	*aufwachsen*	ADJ **grown-up**
society [səˈsaɪɪti]	*Gesellschaft*	
stable [ˈsteɪbl]	*stabil*	N **stability**
close-knit [ˌkləʊs ˈnɪt]	*eng, eng verbunden*	≈ **intimate, close**
anonymous [əˈnɒnɪməs]	*anonym, unpersönlich*	N **anonymity**
upbringing [ˈʌpbrɪŋɪŋ]	*Erziehung*	≈ **raising**
to **influence** [ˈɪnfluəns]	*beeinflussen*	N **influence** ADJ **influential** *einflussreich*
nuclear family [ˌnjuːkliə ˈfæməli]	*Kernfamilie, Kleinfamilie*	≈ **elementary family**
extended family [ɪkˌstendɪd ˈfæməli]	*erweiterte Familie*	*vgl.* to **extend beyond sth** *über etw hinausgehen*
relative [ˈrelətɪv]	*Verwandte/r*	≈ **relation**
unrelated [ˌʌnrɪˈleɪtɪd]	*nicht (miteinander) verwandt*	N **relation** *Verwandte/r*
neighbour [ˈneɪbə]	*Nachbar/in*	*vgl.* **neighbourhood** *Nachbarschaft, Viertel*

Family breakup

The modern family can be fragile. Many children will experience family breakup at least once during their childhood and adolescence. They may have to cope with the separation and divorce of their parents, and live in a single-parent family or become part of a blended family with a step-parent and step-siblings, followed later by half-siblings. Others may go to live with foster parents or adoptive parents if their biological parents are no longer alive or are unable to look after them.

The disruption of a child's nuclear family through marriage breakdown may be accompanied by sudden changes in their wider social network – their 'village' of relationships. A change of family home brings a change of neighbours, classmates and teachers. Unlike parents, none of these important people have a right of access to the child, so they may simply disappear from the child's life.

CHECKPOINT   *In English, please!*

a Ein Auseinanderbrechen der Familie ist für Kinder verstörend.
b Ann musste mit der Trennung und Scheidung ihrer Elter zurechtkommen.
c Sie lebte in einer Patchworkfamilie mit Stief- und Halbgeschwistern.
d Dann lebte sie bei Pflegeeltern.
e Plötzliche Veränderungen in unseren sozialen Netzwerken können schwierig sein.

family breakup [ˌfæməli ˈbreɪkʌp]	*Auseinanderbrechen der Familie*	v to **break up (with sb)**
fragile [ˈfrædʒaɪl]	*labil, zerbrechlich*	◊ **robust, strong**
childhood [ˈtʃaɪldhʊd]	*Kindheit*	◊ **adulthood** *Erwachsenenalter*
adolescence [ˌædəˈlesns]	*Jugend, Adoleszenz*	ADJ/N **adolescent** *(Person) heran-wachsend, jugendlich; Jugendliche/r*
separation [ˌsepəˈreɪʃn]	*Trennung*	v to **separate (from sb)**
divorce [dɪˈvɔːs]	*Scheidung*	v to **divorce, to get divorced (from sb)**
half-siblings pl [ˌhɑːf ˈsɪblɪŋz]	*Halbgeschwister*	vgl. **step-siblings** *Stiefgeschwister*
to **look after sb** [lʊk ˈɑːftə]	*sich um jdn kümmern, für jdn sorgen*	≈ to **care for sb**
disruption [dɪsˈrʌpʃn]	*Zerfall, Zerrüttung*	v to **disrupt** *stören, zerreißen* ADJ **disruptive** *verstörend, zerstörerisch*
marriage [ˈmærɪdʒ]	*Ehe*	v to **marry, to get married (to sb)**
breakdown [ˈbreɪkdaʊn]	*Scheitern*	v to **break down**
social [ˈsəʊʃl]	*sozial, gemeinschaftlich*	N **society** *Gesellschaft*
relationship [rɪˈleɪʃnʃɪp]	*Beziehung*	vgl. to **form a relationship with sb** *eine Beziehung zu jdm aufbauen*
classmate [ˈklɑːsmeɪt]	*Klassenkamerad/in*	≈ **fellow pupil**
right of access [ˌraɪt əv ˈækses]	*Umgangsrecht*	vgl. to **access sb** *Zugang zu jdm haben*
to **disappear** [ˌdɪsəˈpɪə]	*verschwinden*	N **disappearance**

Same-sex marriage

Marriage between partners of the same gender is now recognized in many countries. This reflects the view that homosexuality is natural, that sexual orientation cannot be chosen or influenced and that homosexual relationships are equal to and no less 'normal' than heterosexual relationships. This view is confirmed by science. The definition of marriage in all major English dictionaries is now gender-neutral.

Studies indicate that the children of same-sex couples fare just as well as the children of opposite-sex couples, and that gay and lesbian partners' emotional, physical and material well-being is improved when their stable, committed relationships are recognized by society as a whole. However, some groups continue to oppose same-sex marriage on religious or cultural grounds.

Nevertheless, the majority of countries around the world do not allow same-sex marriages to be performed and do not recognize the validity of same-sex marriages performed in other countries. In many countries, openly homosexual couples face persecution and imprisonment.

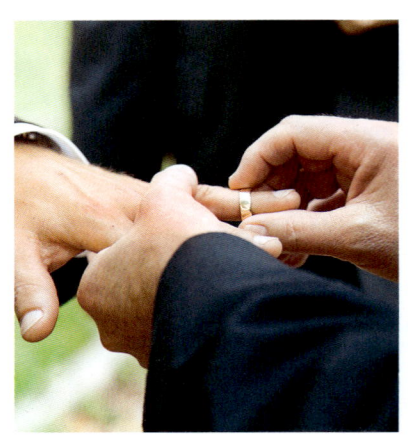

CHECKPOINT   *In English, please!*

a Dieses Land erkennt gleichgeschlechtliche Ehen an.
b Homosexuelle Beziehungen sind mit heterosexuellen Beziehungen gleichgestellt.
c Gleichgeschlechtliche Paare haben stabile, feste Beziehungen.
d Gesellschaftliche Anerkennung ist wichtig für das emotionale Wohlergehen.

same-sex [ˌseɪm ˈseks]	*gleichgeschlechtlich*	≈ gay, homosexual
gender [ˈdʒendə]	*Geschlecht*	≈ sex
to **recognize** [ˈrekəgnaɪz]	*anerkennen*	N recognition *Anerkennung*
homosexuality [ˌhɒməˌsekʃʊəˈælɪti]	*Homosexualität*	ADJ homosexual
sexual orientation [ˌsekʃʊəl ɔːriənˈteɪʃn]	*sexuelle Orientierung*	ADJ sexually oriented
heterosexual [ˌhetərəˈsekʃʊəl]	*heterosexuell*	N heterosexuality
gender-neutral [ˌdʒendə ˈnjuːtrəl]	*geschlechtsneutral*	N gender neutrality
couple [ˈkʌpl]	*Paar*	
sb fares well/badly [ˌfeəz ˈwel/ˈbædli]	*jdm (er)geht es gut/schlecht*	≈ to do well/badly
opposite-sex [ˌɒpəzɪt ˈseks]	*verschiedengeschlechtlich*	≈ heterosexual
gay [geɪ]	*schwul*	
lesbian [ˈlezbiən]	*lesbisch*	
well-being [ˈwel biːɪŋ]	*Wohlbefinden, Wohl*	≈ wellness
committed [kəˈmɪtɪd]	*(Beziehung:) fest*	V to **commit to sth** N **commitment** *Bindung, Verbindlichkeit*
to **oppose sth** [əˈpəʊz]	*etw ablehnen, gegen etw sein*	N opposition
on ... grounds [ɒn ˈgraʊndz]	*aus ... Gründen*	≈ for ... reasons
to **perform (a marriage)** [pəˈfɔːm]	*(eine Eheschließung) durchführen*	
validity [vəˈlɪdɪti]	*Rechtsgültigkeit*	≈ lawfulness, legality
persecution [pɜːsɪˈkjuːʃn]	*Verfolgung*	V to **face/suffer persecution** *verfolgt werden*
imprisonment [ɪmˈprɪznmənt]	*Haft, Freiheitsstrafe*	V to **imprison** *in Haft nehmen*

What is bullying?

Bullying is the use of violence, threats or verbal abuse to intimidate and dominate others. It is a distressing problem which causes stress and anxiety for the victim. Bullying can occur anywhere that people meet: for example in the home, in the workplace, at school, on the street, on the internet. Cyberbullying is particularly common, and may be anonymous, perhaps taking place under a false name.

Bullying may be motivated by personal dislike, but is just as likely to be caused by bravado (wanting to 'look big' in front of friends), cruel attempts at humour or even 'standing up for oneself'. The bully may be an insensitive or even sadistic person, but often is motivated by his or her own low self-esteem. In fact, the bully may not realize that what he or she is doing constitutes bullying, and may be surprised or even shocked when this is pointed out.

CHECKPOINT

In English, please!

a Mobbing beinhaltet nicht immer Gewalt oder Drohungen.
b Beschimpfungen sind quälend für das Opfer.
c Viele Menschen erleben Cybermobbing im Internet.
d Der Mobber war von geringem Selbstwertgefühl motiviert.
e Ihr Humor war gemein und unsensibel.
f Er wollte andere einschüchtern und dominieren.

The prefix dis-

disbelief Fassungslosigkeit, Ungläubigkeit
dishonesty Unehrlichkeit, Verlogenheit
dislike Abneignung
disorientation Orientierungslosigkeit, Verwirrung
to **disagree** anderer Meinung sein
to **disappear** verschwinden
to **dislike** nicht mögen, nicht leiden können
to **disobey** nicht gehorchen, (etw) missachten

bullying ['bʊliɪŋ]	*Mobbing*	! ≠ mobbing
violence ['vaɪələns]	*Gewalt*	ADJ **violent**
threat [θret]	*Drohung*	V to **threaten**
verbal abuse [ˌvɜːbl əˈbjuːs]	*Beschimpfung(en), Beleidigung(en)*	V to **abuse sb verbally**
to **intimidate** [ɪnˈtɪmɪdeɪt]	*einschüchtern*	N **intimidation**
to **dominate** ['dɒmɪneɪt]	*dominieren, beherrschen*	N **domination**
distressing [dɪˈstresɪŋ]	*verstörend, quälend*	≈ **upsetting**
anxiety [æŋˈzaɪəti]	*Angst*	≈ **worry**
victim ['vɪktɪm]	*Opfer*	◄► **perpetrator** *Täter/in*
cyberbullying ['saɪbəbʊliɪŋ]	*Cybermobbing*	N **cyberbully** *(Person)*
false name [ˌfɔːls 'neɪm]	*falscher Name*	≈ **fake name, pseudonym**
to **motivate** ['məʊtɪveɪt]	*motivieren, begründen*	N **motivation, motivator** *(Person)*
dislike [dɪsˈlaɪk]	*Abneigung*	V to **dislike**
bravado [brəˈvaːdəʊ]	*Imponiergehabe*	≈ **showing off**
cruel [kruːəl]	*grausam, gemein*	N **cruelty**
humour ['hjuːmə]	*Humor*	ADJ **humorous**
to **stand up for oneself** [ˌstænd 'ʌp fə]	*sich durchsetzen*	*vgl.* to **stand up to sb** *sich jdm widersetzen*
bully ['bʊli]	*Mobber/in*	*vgl.* **harasser** *Belästiger/in*
insensitive [ɪnˈsensətɪv]	*gefühllos, unsensibel*	N **insensitivity**
self-esteem [ˌself ɪˈstiːm]	*Selbstwertgefühl*	≈ **self-respect**
to **constitute** ['kɒnstɪtjuːt]	*darstellen, sein*	≈ to **be equivalent to,** to **be regarded as**

Help for victims of bullying

Victims often put up with bullying in the hope that it will stop. However, the bully may simply resort to worse behaviour or go on to victimize someone else, so this is not a good strategy.

One of the worst aspects of bullying is that often the victim blames him/herself and believes that being bullied is a sign of weakness. This is simply not true: the victim is not to blame, and there is no shame at all in seeking help. In fact, refusing to 'suffer in silence' is a sign of strength.

It is good to confide in friends in cases of bullying, but even more important to get the support of someone in authority, who is better able to make the bully change his/her behaviour. Many schools and workplaces offer counselling for victims of bullying. It is important to create a zero-tolerance attitude towards bullying in the organization.

Expressions with 'in'
in charge zuständig, verantwortlich
in authority in einer (offiziellen) Machtposition
to **be in control** Kontrolle ausüben

Word family 'shame'
shame Schande
to **shame sb** jdn bloßstellen
shameful schändlich, blamabel
shameless schamlos

CHECKPOINT

In English, please!

a Niemand sollte Mobbing hinnehmen müssen.
b Das Opfer kann nie etwas dafür.
c Es ist nichts Schändliches dabei, Hilfe zu suchen.
d Die Schule bietet Hilfe und Beratung für Mobbing-Opfer.
e Wir haben hier eine kompromisslose Haltung gegenüber Mobbing.

BULLY FREE SCHOOL ZONE

AHEAD

to **put up with sth** [ˌpʊt ˈʌp wɪð]	etw hinnehmen, etw ertragen	≈ to **tolerate sth**
to **resort to sth** [rɪˈzɔːt tə]	zu etw greifen, auf etw zurückgreifen	√gl. **as a last resort** als letztes Mittel
to **victimize sb** [ˈvɪktɪmaɪz]	jdn schikanieren, jdn Respressalien aussetzen	N **victimization**
to **blame sb** [bleɪm]	jdm die Schuld geben	√gl. to **take the blame** die Schuld auf sich nehmen
weakness [ˈwiːknəs]	Schwäche	ADJ **weak** ◀▶ **strength**
to **be to blame for sth** [bi tə ˈbleɪm]	etw für etw können, an etw schuld sein	◀▶ to **be innocent of sth**
shame [ʃeɪm]	Schande	→ Kasten links
to **seek help** [ˌsiːk ˈhelp]	Hilfe suchen	! **sought** (past)
to **suffer** [ˈsʌfə]	leiden	N **suffering** Leid, Leiden
silence [ˈsaɪləns]	Stille	ADJ **silent**
to **confide in sb** [kənˈfaɪd ɪn]	sich jdm anvertrauen	≈ to **tell sb sth in confidence** ADJ **confidential** vertraulich
support [səˈpɔːt]	Hilfe, Unterstützung	V to **support** ADJ **supportive** unterstützend
(sb) in authority [ɪn ɔːˈθɒrəti]	(jd) in einer (offiziellen) Machtposition	√gl. **an authority figure** eine Autorität(sperson)
counselling [ˈkaʊnsəlɪŋ]	Beratung	V to **counsel** N **counsellor** (Person)
zero-tolerance [ˌzɪərəʊ ˈtɒlərəns]	kompromisslos, Null-Toleranz-	√gl. to **tolerate** tolerieren

TEST YOURSELF

You can check your answers on pp. 204–205.

1 The _____ of European _____ are changing fast.

Freizeitbeschäftigungen; Jugend

2 We do organized _____ activities _____ .

Bildungs-; regelmäßig

3 During the summer holidays, I _____ for a charity at least once a week.

war ehrenamtlich tätig

4 Rather than doing structured activities, she prefers to _____ _____ daydreaming.

viel Zeit damit verbringen

5 Have you thought of _____ or doing a sport?

ein neues Hobby anzufangen

6 Although we like to switch off and 'chill', my friends and I _____ _____ .

führen ein aktives Leben

7 Are you thinking of _____ after you leave school?

ein Jahr Auszeit zu nehmen

8 Many young people today have a strong _____ .

soziales Gewissen

9 The voluntary job in India really _____ David _____ _____ .

setzte … einer erheblichen Herausforderung aus

10 The volunteers had to _____ the basic _____ _____ of the local people.

sich anpassen an; Lebensbedin-gungen

11 _____ like ours _____ volunteers in order to offer important services to the community.

Hilfsorganisationen; sind ange-wiesen auf

12 I would be really interested in working with the _____ .

Obdachlosen

38

meinten es gut	**13** The young volunteers _____, but their training was inadequate for the task.
Teilnehmerinnen u. Teilnehmer; Abenteuer	**14** The _____ in the programme had lots of exciting _____.
Bewerbungsverfahren; Auslands-	**15** Is there a complicated _____ for this _____ programme?
verwundbar; Adoleszenz	**16** We all feel _____ sometimes during _____.
menschlich; Anerkennung	**17** It's only _____ to seek _____ from the people around us.
Gruppenzwang; unsicher	**18** John experienced a lot of _____ from his friends, which made him feel _____.
makellos; Selbstwertgefühl	**19** Media photos of _____ models may not be good for our _____.
gerecht zu werden	**20** It's impossible for young people to _____ these beauty ideals.
beschäftigen sich ständig mit	**21** They _____ their social media photos.
Arzneimittel; bei längerer Einnahme	**22** Warning: this _____ may cause psychological changes _____.
rezeptfrei; Rezept	**23** Can I get this painkiller _____, or do I need a _____ from my doctor?
eingeschränkt; abhängig machend	**24** Its availability is _____ because it can be _____.

25 His experience of taking LSD was _____ and _____ .

erschreckend; verwirrend

26 Do you think these harsh new _____ are really _____ ?

Drogengesetze; gerechtfertigt

27 Where is the _____ that this drug can _____ to the user?

Belege; Gesundheitsschäden verursachen

28 There is _____ in the USA around harsh _____ for drug possession.

Streit; Strafen

29 Alcohol is Europeans' legal _____ .

bevorzugte Droge

30 There is a big difference between moderate _____ and _____ .

Trinken in Gesellschaft; Komasaufen

31 His _____ behaviour was a result of consuming _____ amounts of _____ .

betrunken; übermäßig; Spirituosen

32 _____ is dangerous because the driver's _____ will be _____ .

Alkohol am Steuer; Urteilsvermögen; beeinträchtigt

33 Alice _____ by her grandmother after her _____ died.

wurde großgezogen; Eltern

34 In traditional societies, the _____ usually provided a _____ for children to grow up in.

erweiterte Familie; sicheres Umfeld

35 Do you have much contact with your _____ and other members of your _____ ?

Nachbarn; Gemeinschaft

Verwandte; Erziehung	**36** Are _____ outside our nuclear family still important for our _____ ?

Verwandte; Erziehung

36 Are _____ outside our nuclear family still important for our
_____ ?

Auseinanderbrechen der Familie; Kindheit

37 She experienced _____ twice during her
_____ .

kümmerte sich um; Scheidung

38 Her father _____ her and her brother after the _____ .

Umgangsrecht

39 Her mother had _____ every second weekend.

geschlechtsneutral

40 The school was careful to use _____ language when
referring to the students' parents.

gleichgeschlechtlich; schwul

41 Ben's parents changed their ideas about _____ marriage after
learning that their son was _____ .

Mobbing; Gewalt

42 It was a clear case of _____ , even though there was no
_____ involved.

motivierte; gemein

43 I don't understand what _____ her behaviour: she isn't usually
_____ .

sich durchzusetzen; unsensibel

44 Telling victims of bullying to _____ isn't helpful
– it's just _____ .

Gib nicht dem Opfer die Schuld

45 _____ – she didn't cause the situation.

Null-Toleranz-

46 We have a _____ attitude towards this kind of behaviour.

leiden; suchten Hilfe

47 They refused to _____ in silence and _____
against the bully.

2 Education and work

A School and education

School systems in the UK

Each country in the United Kingdom has responsibility for its own school system. However, the systems are very similar to each other in England, Wales and Northern Ireland. The Scottish system is a little different.

In all countries of the UK, there are two stages of compulsory education: primary and secondary. In addition there is optional early years education. After compulsory education is completed, students may go on to further education at a college, or higher education at a university.

Most state schools in the UK are comprehensive schools, taking children of all abilities, but there are also grammar schools for the more academically able, academies which specialize in a particular subject area, e.g. media or technology, and faith schools, which are attached to religious groups.

Expressions with 'school'

- to **attend school** die Schule besuchen
- to **finish/leave school** den Schulabschluss machen, von der Schule abgehen
- to **drop out of school** von der Schule fliegen
- to **skip school** die Schule schwänzen

Expressions with 'lesson'

- to **skip a lesson** eine Stunde schwänzen
- to **take extra lessons** Nachhilfe nehmen/bekommen
- to **teach sb a lesson** jdm eine Lektion erteilen

CHECKPOINT   *In English, please!*

a Das britische Schulsystem ist anders als das deutsche System.
b Frühkindliche Bildung ist fakultativ.
c Die meisten staatlichen Schulen sind Gesamtschulen.
d Die meisten Schüler machen anschließend eine Weiterbildung oder eine Hochschulausbildung.

school system [ˌskuːl ˈsɪstəm]	*Schulsystem*	≈ **education system**
stage [steɪdʒ]	*Stufe*	≈ **level**
compulsory [kəmˈpʌlsəri]	*obligatorisch, Pflicht-*	≈ **mandatory** ◁▷ **optional, elective**
primary education [ˌpraɪməri edʒuˈkeɪʃn]	*Grundschule, Grundschulbildung*	≈ **elementary** ADJ
secondary education [ˌsekəndri edʒuˈkeɪʃn]	*Sekundarstufe, Sekundarschule, Sekundar-schulbildung*	≈ **high-school** ADJ
early years education [ˌɜːli ˈjɪəz edʒukeɪʃn]	*frühkindliche Bildung*	vgl. **nursery school, kindergarten**
further education [ˌfɜːðər edʒuˈkeɪʃn]	*Weiterbildung*	ABBR **FE**
college [ˈkɒlɪdʒ]	*Fachhochschule*	! AE **college = university**
higher education [ˌhaɪər edʒuˈkeɪʃn]	*Hochschulausbildung*	ABBR **HE** vgl. **tertiary education** *tertiärer Bildungsbereich*
university [ˌjuːnɪˈvɜːsəti]	*Universität*	INFML **uni**
state school [ˈsteɪt skuːl]	*staatliche Schule*	vgl. **state education** *öffentliches Bildungswesen*
comprehensive school [kɒmprɪˈhensɪv skuːl]	*Gesamtschule*	vgl. **comprehensive** *umfassend*
ability [əˈbɪləti]	*Begabung, Fähigkeit*	ADJ **able**
grammar school [ˈgræmə skuːl]	*Gymnasium*	! ≠ **gymnasium** *(Turnhalle)*
academically able [ækəˌdemɪkli ˈeɪbl]	*gut in der Schule*	N **ability**
academy [əˈkædəmi]	*Akademie*	vgl. **academic** *akademisch*
to **specialize in sth** [ˈspeʃlaɪz]	*sich auf etw spezialisieren*	N **specialization**
faith school [ˈfeɪθ skuːl]	*Konfessionsschule*	≈ **religious school**

UK education framework

UK law states that all children between five and 16, or in England 18, must be in full-time education. However, children do not have to be educated at school: parents may homeschool them. The National Curriculum provides a framework for school education in England and Wales, stating which subjects should be taught and what the course content should be. Most state schools follow it, but some independent schools, public schools and home educators design their own curricula. From 16 to 18, apprenticeships, traineeships and voluntary work are acceptable alternatives to school education.

Most students in the UK have to sit exams at the ages of 16 and 18. These are public exams: the papers are set and examined by independent examination boards according to strict marking criteria. The exams at 18 are important for students who want to go on to higher education. They are called A Levels (England, Wales, Northern Ireland) or Highers (Scotland). 'A' stands for 'Advanced'.

CHECKPOINT   *In English, please!*

a Eltern dürfen ihre Kinder zu Hause unterrichten.
b Sie müssen keinem strengen Lehrplan folgen.
c Der Rahmen legt fest, welche Fächer Schulen lehren müssen.
d Die Schüler legen am Ende ihrer Schulbildung Prüfungen ab.
e Hast du schon die Prüfungsergebnisse gesehen?

law [lɔː]	Recht, Gesetz	ADJ lawful, legal
full-time [ˌfʊl ˈtaɪm]	Vollzeit(-)	◊ part-time
to educate [ˈedʒukeɪt]	unterrichten	ADJ educated ausgebildet, gebildet
to homeschool [ˈhəʊmskuːl]	zu Hause unterrichten	N home schooling
curriculum [kəˈrɪkjələm]	Lehrplan	ADJ curricular
framework [ˈfreɪmwɜːk]	Rahmen	
subject [ˈsʌbdʒɪkt]	(Schul-)Fach	vgl. my best/worst subject mein bestes/ schlechtestes Fach
course content [ˈkɔːs kɒntent]	Lehrinhalt(e)	vgl. to take a course einen Kurs belegen
independent school [ɪndɪˌpendənt ˈskuːl]	unabhängige Schule, freie Schule	vgl. independence Unabhängigkeit
public school BE [ˌpʌblɪk ˈskuːl]	Privatschule (in GB)	! ≠ öffentliche Schule
home educator [ˌhəʊm ˈedʒukeɪtə]	Hauslehrer/in	vgl. home tutor Hauslehrer/in
apprenticeship [əˈprentɪʃɪp]	Ausbildung	N apprentice (Person)
traineeship [treɪˈniːʃɪp]	Praktikum, Volontariat	N trainee (Person)
voluntary work [ˈvɒlənt(ə)ri ˌwɜːk]	ehrenamtliche/freiwillige Arbeit	N volunteer (Person)
to sit an exam [ˌsɪt ən ɪgˈzæm]	eine Prüfung ablegen	≈ to take an exam
public exam [ˌpʌblɪk ɪgˈzæm]	staatliche Schulabschlussprüfung	vgl. school leaving exam Schulabschluss
examination board [ɪgˌzæmɪˈneɪʃn bɔːd]	Prüfungsausschuss	≈ exam board
to mark [mɑːk]	benoten	N marking Benotung, mark Note
advanced [ədˈvɑːnst]	fortgeschritten, höher	◊ basic

The US school system

Each of the USA's 50 states sets its own educational standards. Compulsory education begins between five and eight years of age and ends between 14 and 18, depending on the state. School education is split into elementary school, junior high school (middle school) and senior high school (high school). About 87 % of school-age children attend government-funded public schools, about 10 % attend private schools and about 3 % are homeschooled.

Children are usually split by age groups into grades. These start with kindergarten (five to six) up to 12th grade (17–18), which is the final grade of high school. The American school year begins in late August or early September, after a summer recess. Children usually move together from one grade to the next as a single class, regardless of their academic performance in the past year.

CHECKPOINT — *In English, please!*

a Ist deine Schule staatlich finanziert?
b Nein, ich besuche eine Privatschule.
c In welcher Klasse bist du?
d Nach den Sommerferien werde ich in der 12. Klasse sein.

UK and US school vocabulary

🇬🇧	🇺🇸	🇩🇪
mark/grade	score/grade	Note
year/form	grade	Klasse, Klassenstufe
school holiday	summer recess/break	Schulferien, Sommerferien
optional subject	elective (subject)	Wahlfach
secondary school	high school	Sekundarschule, Sekundarstufe
public school	(elite) private school	Privatschule
university	college/university	Universität

state [steɪt]	*Bundesstaat (der USA)*	≈ federal **state**
educational [ˌedʒuˈkeɪʃnl]	*schulisch, Bildungs-*	v to **educate**
standard [ˈstændəd]	*Norm*	v to **standardize**
elementary school [ˌelɪˈmentri skuːl]	*Grundschule*	≈ primary **school**
junior high school [ˌdʒuːniə ˈhaɪ skuːl]	*Mittelschule, Mittelstufe*	INFML junior **high**
senior high school [ˌsiːniə ˈhaɪ skuːl]	*Sekundarschule, Sekundarstufe*	N **seniority** *(höheres) Alter*
school-age child [ˌskuːl eɪdʒ ˈtʃaɪld]	*Kind im schulpflichtigen Alter*	vgl. **mandatory/compulsory school age** *Schulpflichtalter*
to **attend** [əˈtend]	*(die Schule) besuchen*	N **attendance** *(Schul-)Besuch*
government-funded [ˌgʌvənmənt-ˈfʌndɪd]	*staatlich finanziert*	≈ state-**funded**
public school AE [ˌpʌblɪk ˈskuːl]	*öffentliche/staatliche Schule*	≠ BE public **school** *(Privatschule)*
grade AE [greɪd]	*Klasse, Klassenstufe*	**8th grade** *8. Klasse* BE year, form
school year [ˈskuːl jɪə]	*Schuljahr*	vgl. **academic year**
summer recess [ˌsʌmə ˈriːses]	*Sommerferien*	≈ summer **break**
class [klɑːs]	*Klasse, Klassenverband*	
regardless of sth [rɪˈgɑːdləs əv]	*ungeachtet einer Sache*	vgl. **with regard to sth** *hinsichtlich einer Sache*
academic performance [ækəˌdemɪk pəˈfɔːməns]	*schulische Leistung(en)*	v to **perform**

The US school curriculum

Students study a range of compulsory subjects and electives. Their progress is assessed throughout the school year by the teaching staff, and report cards are sent to parents.

American schools place a lot of emphasis on extracurricular activities: educational activities which are not part of the curriculum but are supervised by the school. There are many such activities on offer, ranging from science and technology (e.g. robotics, astronomy) to the arts (drama, music, poetry, etc.), foreign languages and sports.

During high school, students (usually in 11th grade) may take one or more standardized tests (e.g. SATs or ACTs). Their scores in these tests along with their grade point average help to determine which, if any, colleges they can enrol at.

Higher education consists of college for undergraduates, and graduate school for those who already have a bachelor's degree. Around 38% of adult Americans over 25 have graduated from college.

'assess' – 'access'
to **assess** sth [əˈses] etw beurteilen, etw bewerten to **access** sth [ˈækses] auf etw zugreifen, Zugang zu etw haben **access** [ˈækses] Zutritt, Zugang

Word family 'supervise'
to **supervise** beaufsichtigen, betreuen **supervision** Aufsicht, Betreuung **supervisor** Betreuer/in, Vorgesetzte/r **supervisory** Aufsichts-

CHECKPOINT

In English, please!

a Deutsch ist an unserer Schule ein Wahlfach.
b Astronomie ist meine Lieblings-AG.
c Ich muss in der Prüfung eine hohe Punktzahl erreichen.
d Ich möchte mich bei einem guten College einschreiben.
e Meine Eltern haben beide einen Hochschulabschluss gemacht.

elective [ɪˈlektɪv]	*Wahlfach*	≈ **elective subject**
progress [ˈprəʊɡres]	*Fortschritte, Entwicklung*	v to **progress** ! [prəˈɡres]
to **assess** [əˈses]	*beurteilen, bewerten*	N **assessment**
teaching staff [ˈtiːtʃɪŋ stɑːf]	*Lehrkräfte, Lehrerkollegium*	≈ **teachers**
report card AE [rɪˈpɔːt kɑːd]	*Zeugnis*	v to **report** *berichten, melden*
to **place emphasis on sth** [ˈemfəsɪs]	*Wert auf etw legen*	≈ to **emphasize**
extracurricular activity [ekstrəkəˌrɪkjʊlə ækˈtɪvəti]	*außerschulische Aktivität, AG*	≈ **after-school activity**
to **supervise** [ˈsuːpəvaɪz]	*beaufsichtigen, betreuen*	→ *Kasten links*
standardized test [ˌstændədaɪzd ˈtest]	*standardisierte/einheitliche Prüfung*	N **standardization**
score [skɔː]	*Punktzahl, Ergebnis*	v to **score** (95%, etc.)
grade point average [ˌɡreɪd pɔɪnt ˈævərɪdʒ]	*Notendurchschnitt*	ABBR **GPA**
to **determine** [dɪˈtɜːmɪn]	*bestimmen*	≈ to **decide**
college [ˈkɒlɪdʒ]	*Hochschule, College*	ADJ **collegiate**
to **enrol** [ɪnˈrəʊl]	*sich einschreiben, sich immatrikulieren*	N **enrolment** AE **enroll, enrollment**
undergraduate [ˌʌndəˈɡrædʒuət]	*Student/in vor dem ersten Hochschulabschluss*	INFML **undergrad**
graduate school [ˈɡrædʒuət skuːl]	*Hochschule für höhere Fachsemester, Graduiertenkolleg*	*vgl.* **graduate** *(Person) Absolvent/in*
bachelor's degree [ˈbætʃələz dɪɡriː]	*Bachelor-Abschluss*	*vgl.* **Bachelor of Arts/Science (BA/BSc)**
to **graduate (from college)** [ˈɡrædʒueɪt]	*einen/den Universitätsabschluss machen*	N **graduation** *Abschluss*

B Work experience

From education to the workplace

When young people leave full-time education, they often face difficulties in finding a first job. Employers may ask for one or two years' experience even for junior roles. Many companies are reluctant to take on young people who have no workplace experience at all. How can young jobseekers gain that valuable experience?

An apprenticeship may be available in one's chosen field of work. Apprentices complete a combination of on-the-job training and classroom study. English-speaking countries do not generally have a comprehensive apprenticeship system like Germany's dual system of vocational training, covering hundreds of commercial and administrative, social, technical and craft professions. Instead, they may offer other forms of formal and informal on-the-job training, which may also lead to professional certification.

CHECKPOINT	*In English, please!*

a Diese Firma stellt keine jungen Leute ohne praktische Berufserfahrung ein.
b Lehrstellen sind in vielen technischen Berufen verfügbar.
c Meine Lehre ist eine Kombination aus Unterricht im Klassenverband und betrieblicher Ausbildung.
d Die Berufsausbildung in Deutschland ist übergreifend.

experience [ɪk'spɪərɪəns]	*(Berufs-)Erfahrung*	ADJ **experienced** *erfahren*
role [rəʊl]	*Funktion*	≈ **position**
to **be reluctant to do sth** [rɪ'lʌktənt]	*etw nur ungern tun*	◆ to **be keen/willing to do sth**
to **take sb on** [ˌteɪk 'ɒn]	*jdn einstellen*	≈ to **employ**, to **engage**, to **hire**
workplace ['wɜːkpleɪs]	*Arbeitsplatz*	vgl. **workplace experience** *praktische Berufserfahrung*
jobseeker ['dʒɒb siːkə]	*Arbeitssuchende/r*	vgl. to **seek work/a job** *Arbeit suchen*
apprenticeship [ə'prentɪʃɪp]	*Lehre, Ausbildung*	vgl. to **do/serve an apprenticeship**
field of work [ˌfiːld əv 'wɜːk]	*Fachgebiet, Tätigkeitsfeld*	≈ **area**
apprentice [ə'prentɪs]	*Auszubildende/r, Lehrling*	vgl. **apprentice technician, salesperson,** etc.
to **complete** [kəm'pliːt]	*(Ausbildung usw.) absolvieren*	N **completion** *Abschluss, Fertigstellung*
on-the-job training [ɒn ðə ˌdʒɒb 'treɪnɪŋ]	*betriebliche Ausbildung*	V to **train sb**, to **train as a ...**
classroom study [ˌklɑːsruːm 'stʌdi]	*Unterricht im Klassenverband*	V to **study sth** *etw lernen*
comprehensive [ˌkɒmprɪ'hensɪv]	*umfassend, übergreifend*	◆ **partial, limited**
vocational training [vəʊˌkeɪʃənl 'treɪnɪŋ]	*Berufsausbildung*	N **vocation** *Berufung*
commercial [kə'mɜːʃl]	*kaufmännisch*	N **commerce**
administrative [əd'mɪnɪstrətɪv]	*Verwaltungs-*	N **administration** (INFML **admin**)
technical ['teknɪkl]	*technisch*	N **technology, technician** *(Person)*
craft [krɑːft]	*Handwerks-*	vgl. **craftsperson, -man, -woman**
profession [prə'feʃn]	*Beruf*	ADJ **professional** *beruflich, professionell*
professional certification [prəˌfeʃənl sɜːtɪfɪ'keɪʃn]	*(offizieller) Berufsabschluss*	V to **certify** *(offiziell) bestätigen*

In-company training and internships

Larger companies often offer a graduate programme for candidates who have completed higher education. These programmes offer a combination of in-company training and real work tasks, often with a mentor for support. New employees may work for short periods in different departments, in order to get an overview of the company's operations. Competition for places is fierce.

An internship, on the other hand, is a temporary position, which may be paid or unpaid. It is usually considered different to a work experience placement, which is a planned part of a course of study, organized by the student's academic institution. Some internships may be open to school or university students, others just to graduates.

An internship offers the employer cheap labour and the chance to assess a potential future employee without making a commitment. It offers the intern the opportunity to get experience. When considering an internship, you should check that the company is offering a structured programme with planned learning opportunities and assessment.

Word family 'compete'

to **compete** konkurrieren
competition Konkurrenz, Wettbewerb
competitive konkurrenzfähig, wettbewerbsorientiert, (Preis:) günstig
competitiveness Wettbewerbsfähigkeit, Konkurrenzdenken
competitor Wettbewerber/in, Konkurrent/in

'experience' – 'an experience'

experience (*uncountable*) Praxis, Erfahrung
to **get experience** Erfahrung sammeln
to **have a lot of experience** viel Erfahrung sammeln
an experience (*countable*) Erlebnis
to **have a good experience** etwas Schönes erleben

graduate programme [ˈɡrædʒuət prəʊɡræm]	*Absolventenprogramm*	*vgl.* to **join the graduate programme**
candidate [ˈkændɪdət]	*Bewerber/in*	*vgl.* a **suitable/strong candidate**
in-company training [ɪn ˌkʌmpəni ˈtreɪnɪŋ]	*innerbetriebliche Ausbildung*	*vgl.* **(in-)company trainer**
support [səˈpɔːt]	*Hilfe, Betreuung*	v to **support**
department [dɪˈpɑːtmənt]	*Abteilung*	ADJ **departmental** *Abteilungs-*
to **get an overview of sth** [ˈəʊvəvjuː]	*einen Überblick über etw bekommen*	
operations *pl* [ˌɒpəˈreɪʃnz]	*betriebliche Tätigkeit(en), Betrieb*	ADJ **operational** *operativ, betrieblich*
competition [ˌkɒmpəˈtɪʃn]	*Konkurrenz, Wettbewerb*	→ *Kasten links*
fierce [fɪəs]	*hart, scharf*	! *Aussprache*
internship [ˈɪntɜːnʃɪp]	*Praktikum*	N **intern** *(Person)*
temporary [ˈtemprəri]	*befristet*	◀▶ **permanent**
paid [peɪd]	*bezahlt*	◀▶ **unpaid** v to **pay sb**
work experience placement [ˈwɜːk ɪkspɪəriəns pleɪsmənt]	*(Schul-/Ausbildungs-)Praktikum*	*vgl.* to **do work experience** *ein Praktikum machen*
course of study [ˌkɔːs əf ˈstʌdi]	*Ausbildung, Studium*	v to **study sth**
sth is open to sb [ɪz ˈəʊpən tə]	*jdm steht etw offen*	◀▶ to **be closed to sb**
labour [ˈleɪbə]	*Arbeitskräfte*	AE **labor**
to **assess** [əˈses]	*beurteilen, einschätzen*	N **assessor** *(Person)*
to **make a commitment** [kəˈmɪtmənt]	*eine Verpflichtung eingehen*	v to **commit (to sth)**
learning opportunities *pl* [ˈlɜːnɪŋ ɒpətjuːnətiz]	*Bildungsangebote*	*vgl.* to **have the/an opportunity to …**
assessment [əˈsesmənt]	*Beurteilung, Einschätzung*	≈ **evaluation**

Applying for a job

The first step in the job-seeking process is to find out about job vacancies. There are many places to look: sources of information about vacant positions include careers websites and newspaper advertisements, recruitment agencies and corporate websites.

Some positions may not be advertised but are known to people already working in the industry, even though this is often not considered ethical on the part of the employer. To find out about such positions, networking is an important job-seeking strategy.

The second step is to research your prospective employer thoroughly. Then you are ready to write your application. Traditionally, this involves preparing a CV and a covering letter, but these days it is common to have to fill in an online form too. You will usually be able to upload your CV and covering letter with your application.

CHECKPOINT   *In English, please!*

a Wie kann ich mich über offene Stellen informieren?
b Sehen Sie sich Karriere-Webseiten und Zeitungsannoncen an.
c Netzwerken ist eine weitere wichtige Strategie.
d Ich habe jede Menge Bewerbungen geschrieben und massenweise Online-Formulare ausgefüllt.
e Wie lade ich meinen Lebenslauf und mein Anschreiben hoch?

Expressions with 'career'

career advice Berufsberatung, Laufbahnberatung
career(s) advisor Berufsberater/in, Laufbahnberater/in
career break berufliche Auszeit, Laufbahnunterbrechung
career expectations berufliche Perspektive, Karrierevorstellungen
career opportunities Karrieremöglichkeiten, Aufstiegschancen
career path beruflicher Werdegang, Laufbahn
career prospects Berufsaussichten, Aufstiegschancen

Word family 'apply'

to **apply** sich bewerben, beantragen; anwenden
application Bewerbung, Antrag; Anwendung
applicant Bewerber/in, Antragssteller/in
applicable anwendbar, zutreffend

Synonyms for 'job' in advertisments

'We have a(n) … for an ambitious school-leaver.'
opening – position – post – vacancy

to **apply for a job** [əˌplaɪ fər ə ˈdʒɒb]	*sich um/auf eine Stelle bewerben*	*vgl.* to **apply to (a company, etc.)** *sich (bei einem Unternehmen usw.) bewerben*
job vacancy [ˈdʒɒb veɪkənsi]	*freie/offene Stelle*	*vgl.* to **fill a vacancy** *eine Stelle besetzen*
vacant position [ˌveɪkənt pəˈzɪʃn]	*freie/offene Stelle*	≈ **open position**
career [kəˈrɪə]	*Karriere, berufliche Laufbahn*	*vgl.* to **pursue a career in …** *Karriere in … machen*
advertisement [ədˈvɜːtɪsmənt]	*Anzeige, Annonce*	INFML **ad, advert,** V to **advertise**
recruitment agency [rɪˈkruːtmənt eɪdʒənsi]	*Personalvermittlung*	V to **recruit sb**
corporate [ˈkɔːprət]	*Unternehmens-*	N **corporation**
to **advertise (a position)** [ˈadvətʌɪz]	*(eine Stelle) ausschreiben*	
networking [ˈnetwɜːkɪŋ]	*Netzwerken*	V to **network,** N **network**
to **research** [rɪˈsɜːtʃ]	*recherchieren*	N **research** *Recherche*
prospective [prəˈspektɪv]	*potenziell*	N, USU PL **prospects** *Aussichten, Chancen*
application [ˌæplɪˈkeɪʃn]	*Bewerbung*	*vgl.* **letter of application** *Bewerbungs-schreiben* → *Siehe auch Kasten links*
to **prepare** [prɪˈpeə]	*erstellen, ausarbeiten*	N **preparation**
CV [ˌsiː ˈviː]	*Lebenslauf*	**curriculum vitae** *(Latein),* AE **résumé**
covering letter [ˈkʌvərɪŋ letə]	*Anschreiben, Begleitschreiben*	≈ **cover letter**
to **fill sth in** [ˌfɪl ˈɪn]	*etw ausfüllen*	≈ to **complete** AE to **fill sth out**
online form [ˌɒnlaɪn ˈfɔːm]	*Online-Formular*	≈ **web form, internet form**

CVs and covering letters

The CV format in English-speaking countries is different to the German format, and more flexible. It generally includes personal details, education and training, qualifications, work experience and referees' contact details. Include a brief description of personal interests which give a favourable impression of your character and accomplishments, e.g. sport teams. It is not usual to include a photograph. State your nationality and if you have a driving licence, mention that.

You should tailor the covering letter to the specific job. Follow this sequence: 1 Introduce yourself; 2 Explain which job you are applying for; 3 State why you are interested in the job and why you are suitable for it; 4 State that you look forward to hearing from the company and are available for interview. Use the correct format for a formal letter. Letters and CVs with grammatical or spelling errors will usually be rejected.

CHECKPOINT *In English, please!*

a Hast du für deinen Lebenslauf das deutsche Format benutzt?
b Nein, ich habe persönliche Angaben beigefügt, aber kein Foto.
c Schneiden Sie Ihren Lebenslauf auf die angebotene Stelle zu.
d Dieses Anschreiben hat mehrere Rechtschreibfehler.

UK and US job application vocabulary

🇬🇧	🇺🇸	🇩🇪
CV	résumé (or **resume**)	Lebenslauf
covering letter	cover letter	Anschreiben, Begleitschreiben
to **fill in a form**	to **fill out a form**	ein Formular ausfüllen
driving licence	driver's license	Führerschein
referee (= person)	reference (= report)	Referenzgeber, Referenz
surname	last name	Nachname

personal details *pl* [ˌpɜːsənl ˈdiːteɪlz]	*persönliche Angaben*	≈ **personal data**
qualification [ˌkwɒlɪfɪˈkeɪʃn]	*Abschluss, Qualifikation*	ADJ **qualified** *ausgebildet, qualifiziert*
referee [ˌrefəˈriː]	*Referenzgeber, Referenz*	*vgl.* **reference** *Referenz*
contact details [ˈkɒntækt diːteɪlz]	*Kontaktdaten*	v to **contact sb**
brief [briːf]	*knapp, kurz*	≈ **short, concise**
favourable [ˈfeɪvərəbl]	*gut, günstig*	AE **favorable** ≈ **positive**
impression [ɪmˈpreʃn]	*Eindruck*	v to **impress sb** ADJ **impressive**
accomplishment [əˈkʌmplɪʃmənt]	*Leistung, Erfolg*	ADJ **accomplished**
driving licence [ˈdraɪvɪŋ laɪsns]	*Führerschein*	AE **driver's license**
to **tailor sth to sth** [ˈteɪlə]	*etw auf etw zuschneiden*	≈ to **customize sth for sth**, to **adapt sth to sth**
suitable [ˈsuːtəbl]	*geeignet*	≈ **appropriate** → *Siehe auch Kasten links*
to **be available** [bi əˈveɪləbl]	*zur Verfügung stehen*	N **availability**
formal letter [ˌfɔːml ˈletə]	*förmlicher Brief, förmliches Schreiben*	◊ **informal**
grammatical [grəˈmætɪkl]	*Grammatik-, grammatikalisch*	N **grammar**
spelling error [ˈspelɪŋ erə]	*Rechtschreibfehler*	*vgl.* **typographical error** *Druckfehler* INFML **typo**
to **reject** [rɪˈdʒekt]	*ablehnen, aussortieren*	N **rejection**

Interviews

Employers may conduct a preliminary phone or video interview. This is usually part of the screening process to narrow down the field of candidates. Shortlisted candidates will be invited to a face-to-face interview. This may take place at the company, or a separate venue if a large number of candidates are being interviewed on the one day.

This may be a simple interview lasting 30 minutes to an hour. However, larger companies may invite candidates to a whole day of assessments, group interviews, psychometric tests and individual interviews. At these events there are usually opportunities to chat informally with the senior managers, and it is important to treat these 'informal' situations as part of the interview process, and impress the interviewers with your relevant questions, keen attitude, etc. There is usually a tour of the company and a chance to meet other employees and ask questions. Again, it is important to impress the staff with your keen attitude, even if they are not formally part of the interview process.

Word family 'impress'

to **impress** beeindrucken, imponieren
impression Eindruck
impressive beeindruckend, imposant
impressionable beeinflussbar

CHECKPOINT

In English, please!

a Wir möchten Sie zu einem Vorgespräch einladen.
b Wird das ein Video-Interview oder ein persönliches Vorstellungsgespräch?
c Das Vorstellungsgespräch wird ungefähr eine Stunde dauern.
d Es wird auch eine Beurteilung und ein Persönlichkeitstest stattfinden.
e Sie können sich zwanglos mit Führungskräften unterhalten.
f Es wird einen Firmenrundgang geben.

interview [ˈɪntəvjuː]	Vorstellungsgespräch	V to **carry out an interview**, to **interview** N interviewer, interviewee
to **conduct** [kənˈdʌkt]	durchführen	N conduct **!** [ˈkɒndʌkt] *Führung, Verhalten*
preliminary interview [prɪˌlɪmɪnəri ˈɪntəvjuː]	Vorgespräch	◀▶ final
screening process [ˈskriːnɪŋ prəʊses]	Auswahlverfahren	*vgl.* to **screen sb** *jdn einer Auswahl-prüfung unterziehen*
to **narrow sth down** [ˌnærəʊ ˈdaʊn]	etw (Auswahl) eingrenzen	◀▶ to **widen, expand**
field of candidates [ˌfiːld əf ˈkændɪdəts]	Bewerberspektrum, in Frage kommende Bewerber/innen	≈ **field of applicants**
to **shortlist** [ˈʃɔːtlɪst]	in die engere Auswahl ziehen	N shortlist
to **invite sb to sth** [ɪnˈvaɪt]	jdn zu etw einladen	N invitation
face-to-face [ˌfeɪs tə ˈfeɪs]	persönlich	*vgl.* to **speak face-to-face** *persönlich miteinander sprechen*
venue [ˈvenjuː]	Veranstaltungsort	≈ **place to meet**
assessment [əˈsesmənt]	Beurteilung, Einstufung	≈ **evaluation**
psychometric test [saɪkəˌmetrɪk ˈtest]	psychometrischer Test, Persönlichkeitstest	V to **test sb, sth**
informally [ɪnˈfɔːməli]	zwanglos, informell	N informality
to **impress** [ɪmˈpres]	beeindrucken	→ *Kasten links*
keen [kiːn]	begeistert, motiviert	N keenness ◀▶ lazy, apathetic
attitude [ˈætɪtjuːd]	Haltung, Einstellung	≈ **approach**
tour (of the company) [tʊə]	(Firmen-)Rundgang	*vgl.* **guided tour** *Führung*
employee [ɪmˈplɔɪiː]	Angestellte/r, Beschäftigte/r, Mitarbeiter/in	→ *Kasten S. 68*

C Working conditions

Workers' rights

In the 19th and 20th centuries, workers had to fight for basic rights that we often take for granted today. These included humane working hours, paid overtime, a minimum wage, paid annual leave, sick pay, redundancy payments and protection from unfair dismissal and discrimination. To win these rights, workers had to organize themselves into groups: individual workers could not hope to achieve much against the power of employers. These groups often took the form of trade unions.

Trade unions have played vital roles in protecting workers' rights, through advocacy, worker education and organized industrial action.

In the 21st century, many of these gains are under threat as work becomes increasingly flexible and globalized, and automation increases. Yet union membership is much lower than it has been in the past. After all, a flexible, global workforce is much more difficult to organize into a union.

CHECKPOINT

In English, please!

a Oft sehen wir Arbeitnehmerrechte als selbstverständlich an.
b Im 19. Jahrhundert bekamen nur wenige Arbeiter Krankengeld.
c Die Gewerkschaft will kürzere Arbeitszeiten und mehr Jahresurlaub.
d Manchmal sind Arbeitskampfmaßnahmen notwendig, um Arbeitsplätze zu schützen.
e Aufgrund der Automatisierung sind unsere Jobs bedroht.

Expressions with 'work'

at work bei der Arbeit, beschäftigt
to **be in work** Arbeit haben
out of work arbeitslos
to **get down to work** sich an die Arbeit machen
to **work full-time/part-time** Vollzeit/Teilzeit arbeiten
to **work freelance** freiberuflich arbeiten

Word family 'flexible'

flexible flexibel
flexibility Flexibilität
inflexible starr, unflexibel
inflexibility Starrheit, Inflexibilität

worker ['wɜːkə]	*Arbeiter/in, Arbeitnehmer/in*	≈ **working man/woman**
right [raɪt]	*Recht*	ADJ **rightful** *rechtmäßig*
to **fight for sth** ['faɪt]	*für/um etw kämpfen*	N **fight**
to **take sth for granted** [ˌteɪk fə 'grɑːntɪd]	*etw als selbstverständlich ansehen*	≈ to **assume/presume sth**
working hours *pl* [ˌwɜːkɪŋ 'aʊəz]	*Arbeitszeit(en)*	*vgl.* **40-hour week** *40-Stunden-Woche*
overtime ['əʊvətaɪm]	*Überstunden*	*vgl.* to **work overtime** *Überstunden machen*
minimum wage [ˌmɪnɪməm 'weɪdʒ]	*Mindestlohn*	
annual leave [ˌænjuəl 'liːv]	*Jahresurlaub*	*vgl.* to **take leave** *Urlaub nehmen*
sick pay ['sɪk peɪ]	*Krankengeld, Lohnfortzahlung im Krankheitsfall*	*vgl.* to **be off sick** *krankgeschrieben sein*
redundancy payment [rɪ'dʌndənsi peɪmənt]	*Abfindung*	*vgl.* to **be made redundant** *entlassen werden*
dismissal [dɪs'mɪsl]	*Kündigung*	V to **dismiss**
discrimination [dɪˌskrɪmɪ'neɪʃn]	*Diskriminierung*	V to **discriminate against sb**
trade union [ˌtreɪd 'juːniən]	*Gewerkschaft*	N **trade unionist** *(Person)*
advocacy ['ædvəkəsi]	*Interessenvertretung, Eintreten (für etw)*	V to **advocate for sth**
industrial action [ɪnˌdʌstriəl 'ækʃn]	*Arbeitskampfmaßnahmen*	*vgl.* **strike** *Streik*, **work-to-rule** *Dienst nach Vorschrift*
to **be under threat** [ˌʌndə 'θret]	*bedroht sein/werden*	≈ to **be threatened**
globalized ['gləʊbəlaɪzd]	*globalisiert*	N **globalization**
automation [ˌɔːtə'meɪʃn]	*Automatisierung*	V to **automate**
workforce ['wɜːkfɔːs]	*Arbeiterschaft, Arbeitnehmer pl*	≈ **staff, employees**

The gig economy

'Gig' is slang for a live musical performance. Musicians show up, play, get paid and leave. They don't usually have permanent contracts. This employment model now applies to many jobs outside the music industry: instead of permanent jobs, many people now have short-term contracts or work freelance. Instead of salaries, they may get one-off payments.

Typical jobs in the gig economy include food deliverers, couriers and some IT jobs. However, traditional trades such as self-employed electricians are also included, as are casual staff in retail outlets, etc. Online platforms have helped the gig economy to grow: apps can match people needing services with service providers.

There are some benefits for gig workers. These include flexible working hours and more control over their work-life balance. However, gig workers have little job security.

German 'Sicherheit'

safety Sicherheit *(Schutz vor Unfall und Gefahren)*
security Sicherheit *(Abwesenheit von Angriff und Bedrohung)*
certainty Gewissheit

Expressions with 'term'

long-term langfristig
medium-term mittelfristig
short-term kurzfristig
near-term zeitnah, kurzfristig
fixed-term befristet, mit fester Laufzeit

CHECKPOINT
In English, please!

a Bekomme ich einen unbefristeten Vertrag?
b Nein, wir möchten, dass Sie freiberuflich arbeiten.
c Das Geschäft beschäftigt viele Aushilfskräfte.
d Ich habe ein gutes Verhältnis zwischen Berufs- und Privatleben.
e Es gibt nur wenig Beschäftigungssicherheit, wenn man selbstständig ist.

economy [ɪˈkɒnəmi]	*Wirtschaft*	N **economics** *Wirtschaftswissenschaft*
to **show up** [ˌʃəʊ ˈʌp]	*erscheinen, antanzen*	≈ to **turn up**
to **get paid** [ˌget ˈpeɪd]	*bezahlt werden, (sein/ihr) Geld kriegen*	N **pay, payment**
permanent [ˈpɜːmənənt]	*unbefristet*	◀▶ **temporary**
contract [ˈkɒntrækt]	*Vertrag*	ADJ **contractual** *vertraglich*
short-term [ˌʃɔːtˈtɜːm]	*kurzfristig*	◀▶ **long-term, permanent** → *Siehe auch Kasten links*
freelance [ˈfriːlɑːns]	*freiberuflich*	N **freelancer** *(Person)*
salary [ˈsæləri]	*Gehalt*	*vgl.* to **pay sb a salary** *jdm ein Gehalt zahlen*
one-off [ˌwʌn ˈɒf]	*einmalig*	◀▶ **recurring, regular**
trade [treɪd]	*Branche, Gewerbe*	*vgl.* **tradesperson** *Gewerbetreibende/r*
self-employed [ˌself ɪmˈplɔɪd]	*selbstständig*	N **self employment**
casual staff [ˌkæʒuəl ˈstɑːf]	*Aushilfskräfte*	*vgl.* **permanent staff** *festangestellte /Mitarbeiter*
retail outlet [ˈriːteɪl aʊtlet]	*(Einzelhandels-)Geschäft*	≈ **retailer**
service provider [ˈsɜːvɪs prəvaɪdə]	*Dienstleister, Dienstleistungsunternehmen*	V to **provide a service** *eine Dienstleistung anbieten*
benefit [ˈbenɪfɪt]	*Vorteil, Nutzen*	V to **benefit (from sth)**
work-life balance [ˌwɜːk laɪf ˈbæləns]	*ausgewogenes Verhältnis zwischen Berufs- und Privatleben*	ADJ **balanced** V to **balance (sth against sth)**
job security [ˌdʒɒb sɪˈkjʊərəti]	*Beschäftigungssicherheit*	ADJ **secure**

Hot desking

Working conditions are changing, and employers are looking at innovative ways to reduce overheads such as the cost of premises.

Hot desking is one of these. It is the flexible sharing of office space between workers. Staff do not have their own office, workstation or desk: they simply work wherever they can find a suitable space. By sharing, employees make more efficient use of company space and resources. Workplaces with flexible schedules can find hot desking useful, as all the workers are not in the office at the same time.

Hot desking may be stressful and demoralizing for workers, as they have no permanent space for their things, and communication between team members may become difficult. As a result, some companies have abandoned the hot-desking experiment, as it has had a negative effect on productivity and staff morale.

CHECKPOINT   *In English, please!*

a Die Ideen der Arbeitgeber sind sehr innovativ.
b Die Arbeiter haben keine eigenen Arbeitsplätze.
c Sie müssen sich die Unternehmensressourcen effizient teilen.
d Die Mitarbeiter finden die Arbeitsbedingungen belastend.

Expressions with 'work(ing)'

work ethic Arbeitsmoral, Arbeits-ethos
work-life balance ausgewogenes Verhältnis zwischen Berufs- und Privatleben
working conditions Arbeitsbedingungen
working hours Arbeitszeit(en)
workplace Arbeitsplatz
workspace Arbeitsbereich, Arbeitsplatz
workstation Arbeitsplatz, Arbeitsbereich

working conditions pl [ˌwɜ:kɪŋ kənˈdɪʃnz]	*Arbeitsbedingungen*	*vgl.* **occupational health and safety** *Arbeitsschutz*
employer [ɪmˈplɔɪə]	*Arbeitgeber*	→ *Siehe Kasten S. 68*
innovative [ˈɪnəveɪtɪv]	*neuartig, neu, innovativ*	N **innovation**
overheads pl [ˈəʊvəhedz]	*Betriebskosten, Fixkosten*	≈ **operating cost**
premises pl [ˈpremɪsɪz]	*Geschäftsräume, Betriebsgelände*	! *Plural*
office space [ˈɒfɪs speɪs]	*Bürofläche(n)*	*vgl.* **office building, open-plan office**
staff [stɑːf]	*Mitarbeiter/innen*	V **to staff (an office, etc.)**
workstation [ˈwɜːk steɪʃn]	*Arbeitsplatz, Arbeitsbereich*	*vgl.* **cubicle** *Arbeitsplatz (Großraumbüro)*
suitable [ˈsuːtəbl]	*geeignet*	≈ **acceptable, satisfactory**
efficient [ɪˈfɪʃnt]	*effizient*	‹› **inefficient** N **efficiency, inefficiency**
resources pl [rɪˈsɔːsɪz]	*Ressourcen, Mittel*	*vgl.* **equipment** *Ausstattung, Geräte*
workplace [ˈwɜːkpleɪs]	*Arbeitsplatz*	≈ **place of work**
schedule [ˈʃedjuːl]	*Zeitplan, Zeiten*	≈ **timetable**
stressful [ˈstresfl]	*belastend*	‹› **relaxing**
demoralizing [dɪˈmɒrəlaɪzɪŋ]	*entmutigend*	N **demoralization**
communication [kəˌmjuːnɪˈkeɪʃn]	*Kommunikation*	V **to communicate**, ADJ **communicative**
to **abandon sth** [əˈbændən]	*etw aufgeben*	‹› to **continue (a practice)**
to **have a negative effect on sth** [həv ə ˌnegətɪv ɪˈfekt ɒn]	*sich negativ auf etw auswirken*	≈ to **affect sth negatively**
productivity [prɒdʌkˈtɪvəti]	*Produktivität*	ADJ **productive**
staff morale [ˈstɑːf mərɑːl]	*Arbeitsmoral (der Mitarbeiter)*	≈ **(team) spirit**

Unemployment and underemployment

Unemployment occurs when people of working age cannot find paid work. A high unemployment rate is considered bad for the social and economic well-being of a society. Unemployment rises when demand for goods and services falls or labour supply increases, but there may be many other underlying reasons for a scarcity of jobs. Underemployment happens when a worker is in a job which does not make good use of his or her skills or ability to work. It is more difficult to measure statistically than unemployment.

Many experts predict that unemployment and underemployment will both rise because of the increasing automation of the workplace. Even though automation will create new jobs (e.g. in maintaining the new machinery), it seems likely that the overall requirement for human labour will decrease both in manufacturing and service industries.

Synonyms for 'rise' and 'fall'

to **rise**
to **increase**
to **climb**
to **grow**

to **fall**
to **decline**
to **decrease**
to **drop**
to **sink**

CHECKPOINT   *In English, please!*

a Die Arbeitslosenquote (*rate*) sinkt.
b Die Nachfrage nach Waren und Dienstleistung steigt.
c Es besteht immer noch ein Mangel an guten Jobs.
d Nutzt Ihre Arbeit Ihre Fähigkeiten optimal aus?
e Nein, ich fühle mich bei meiner Arbeit unterbeschäftigt.

unemployment [ˌʌnɪmˈplɔɪmənt]	*Arbeitslosigkeit*	ADJ **unemployed**
underemployment [ˌʌndərɪmˈplɔɪmənt]	*Unterbeschäftigung*	ADJ **underemployed**
working age [ˌwɜːkɪŋ ˈeɪdʒ]	*erwerbsfähiges Alter*	
paid work [ˌpeɪd ˈwɜːk]	*bezahlte Arbeit*	*vgl.* **unpaid work, voluntary work** *unbezahlte/ehrenamtliche Arbeit*
social [ˈsəʊʃl]	*gesellschaftlich, sozial*	N **society**
economic [ˌiːkəˈnɒmɪk]	*wirtschaftlich*	N **economy** *Wirtschaft* N **economics** *Wirtschaftswissenschaft*
demand (for sth) [dɪˈmɑːnd]	*Nachfrage (nach etw)*	V to **demand**
supply [səˈplaɪ]	*Angebot*	V to **supply**
underlying reasons *pl* [ˌʌndəˌlaɪɪŋ ˈriːznz]	*tiefere Gründe*	◄► **superficial reasons**
scarcity (of sth) [ˈskeəsɪti]	*Mangel (an etw)*	ADJ **scarce** *rar, selten*
to **make (good) use of sth** [ˌmeɪk ˈjuːs əv]	*etw (optimal) nutzen*	≈ to **utilize**
skill [skɪl]	*Fähigkeit*	ADJ **skilled, skilful**
to **measure** [ˈmeʒə]	*messen*	N **measurement**
statistically [stəˈtɪstɪkli]	*statistisch*	N **statistics** *(Plural)*
to **maintain** [meɪnˈteɪn]	*warten, instand halten*	N **maintenance**
machinery [məˈʃiːnəri]	*Maschinen*	≈ **machines**
requirement [rɪˈkwaɪəmnt]	*Bedarf*	V to **require**
manufacturing industry [mænjuˈfæktʃərɪŋ ɪndəstri]	*produzierendes Gewerbe, Fertigungsindustrie*	V to **manufacture** N **manufacture**
service industry [ˈsɜːvɪs ɪndəstri]	*Dienstleistungsgewerbe*	

Types of <u>underemployment</u>

<u>Overqualification</u> happens when workers with a high <u>level</u> of education, <u>skill</u> or <u>experience</u> are <u>employed</u> in a job which does not fully use those <u>qualities</u>. An example is a foreign medical doctor who works in Germany as a supermarket cashier because her qualifications are not recognized there.

<u>Involuntary</u> part-time work happens when workers want to work full-time, but can only find part-time work. One example is a mother of young children, who would like to work full-time, but cannot get access to adequate childcare facilities. She therefore has to accept part-time work.

<u>Overstaffing</u> happens when companies <u>employ</u> more staff than they need to do the work which is available. An example is a hotel or restaurant in a popular tourist destination, where there is a lot of work to do in the tourist season, but less at other times.

CHECKPOINT *In English, please!*

a Hamids Abschlüsse wurden in Deutschland nicht anerkannt.
b Er hat ein hohes Bildungsniveau und mehrere Jahre Berufserfahrung.
c Zugang zu Kinderbetreuungseinrichtungen ist ein Problem für viele Arbeitnehmer.
d Teilzeitarbeit ist hier während der Feriensaison verfügbar.

overqualification [əʊvəˌkwɒlɪfɪˈkeɪʃn]	*Überqualifizierung*	ᴀᴅᴊ **overqualified** ᴨ **underqualification**
level [ˈlɛvəl]	*Niveau*	√*gl.* **high/low level**
experience [ɪkˈspɪəriəns]	*(Berufs-)Erfahrung*	√ to **experience**
quality [ˈkwɒləti]	*Eigenschaft*	≈ **attribute** [ˈatrɪbjuːt]
cashier [ˈkæʃɪə]	*Kassierer/in*	
qualification [ˌkwɒlɪfɪˈkeɪʃn]	*Abschluss, Qualifikation*	√ to **qualify (for sth)**
to **recognize** [ˈrekəgnaɪz]	*anerkennen*	ɴ **recognition** ᴀᴅᴊ **recognizable** *erkennbar*
involuntary [ɪnˈvɒləntri]	*unfreiwillig*	ᴨ **voluntary**
part-time work [ˌpɑːt taɪm ˈwɜːk]	*Teilzeitarbeit*	ᴨ **full-time work**
to **work full-time** [wɜːk ˌfʊl ˈtaɪm]	*Vollzeit arbeiten*	ᴨ to **work part-time**
to **get access to sth** [ˈækses]	*Zugang zu etw bekommen*	→ *Siehe Kasten S. 78*
childcare facility [ˈtʃaɪldkeə fəsɪləti]	*Kinderbetreuungseinrichtung*	√*gl.* **creche, nursery** *Kindertagesstätte*
overstaffing [ˌəʊvəˈstɑːfɪŋ]	*Personalüberschuss, Überbesetzung*	ᴨ **understaffing**
to **employ** [ɪmˈplɔɪ]	*beschäftigen*	→ *Kasten links*
available [əˈveɪləbl]	*erhältlich, verfügbar*	ɴ **availability**
tourist destination [ˌtʊərɪst destɪˈneɪʃn]	*Reiseziel, Urlaubsort*	≈ **holiday destination**
season [ˈsiːzn]	*Saison*	ᴀᴅᴊ **seasonal**

Universal basic income

Growing unemployment and underemployment could cause a range of social problems and also threaten further economic growth: if consumers have little money or are afraid they may lose their jobs, they won't buy goods and services. Ironically, the efficiency of modern automated industry may eventually cause the market to stagnate and contract.

If we accept that our society cannot fully employ everyone who could work, yet unemployment and underemployment have undesirable social and economic consequences, then one solution is to pay everyone a basic income which meets his or her needs. This is often referred to as a universal basic income (UBI). It makes paid work a lifestyle choice, rather than a necessity. A UBI is less expensive to administrate than unemployment benefit, and less open to abuse, because there is no means testing – every adult gets the same amount.

CHECKPOINT	*In English, please!*

a Die Arbeitslosigkeit bedroht das Wirtschaftswachstum.
b Wir haben Angst davor, unsere Arbeit zu verlieren.
c Ein allgemeines Grundeinkommen ist eine gute Lösung für dieses Problem.
d Arbeitslosengeld ist nur nach einer Bedürftigkeitsprüfung erhältlich.
e Würden Sie arbeiten, wenn es Ihr individueller Lebensentwurf wäre und nicht eine Notwendigkeit?

'lose' – 'loose'

to lose [luːz] verlieren
loose [luːs] locker, lose

Expressions with 'need'

need(s) Bedürfnis(se), Bedarf
to **need** benötigen, brauchen
to **feel a need for sth** ein Bedürfnis nach etw spüren
to **be in need of sth** etw (dringend) benötigen
needy bedürftig
neediness Bedürftigkeit

universal [juːnɪˈvɜːsl]	*allgemein*	N **universality** *Allgemeingültigkeit*
basic income [ˌbeɪsɪk ˈɪnkʌm]	*Grundeinkommen*	ADV **basically** *grundsätzlich*
to **threaten** [ˈθretn]	*bedrohen*	N **threat** ADJ **threatening**
growth [grəʊθ]	*Wachstum*	◀▶ **decline, contraction**
to **lose one's job** [ˌluːz wʌnz ˈdʒɒb]	*die Arbeit verlieren*	≈ to **be laid off, dismissed**
ironically [aɪˈrɒnɪkli]	*ironischerweise*	ADJ **ironic**, N **irony**
efficiency [ɪˈfɪʃənsi]	*Effizienz*	≈ **effectiveness** ADJ **efficient**
automated [ˈɔːtəmeɪtɪd]	*automatisiert*	V to **automate**
market [ˈmɑːkɪt]	*Markt*	V to **market** *vermarkten*
to **stagnate** [ˈstægneɪt]	*stagnieren*	ADJ **stagnant**, N **stagnation**
to **contract** [kənˈtrækt]	*schrumpfen*	≈ to **get smaller**, to **decline**
undesirable [ˌʌndɪˈzaɪərəbl]	*nicht wünschenswert*	V to **desire sth**
to **meet one's needs** [ˌmiːt wʌnz ˈniːdz]	*jds Bedürfnisse erfüllen*	≈ to **meet one's requirements**
lifestyle choice [ˈlaɪfstaɪl tʃɔɪs]	*individueller Lebensentwurf*	V to **choose**
necessity [nəˈsesəti]	*Notwendigkeit*	◀▶ **choice** *vgl.* **basic necessity** *Grundvoraussetzung, elementares Bedürfnis*
to **administrate** [ədˈmɪnɪstreɪt]	*verwalten*	N **administration** (INFML **admin**) N **administrator** *(Person)*
unemployment benefit [ʌnɪmˈplɔɪmənt benɪfɪt]	*Arbeitslosengeld*	≈ the **dole** INFML
means testing [ˈmiːnz testɪŋ]	*Bedürftigkeitsprüfung*	V to **means test sth/sb**

TEST YOURSELF

You can check your answers on p. 207.

1 _____ and secondary education are _____ in the UK. *Grundschul-; obligatorisch*

2 This academy _____ technology and science. *spezialisiert sich auf*

3 There are few _____ in this area: most schools around here are _____. *Gymnasien; Gesamtschulen*

4 Can schools design their own _____, or are the _____ _____ decided by the law? *Lehrpläne; Schulfächer und Lehrinhalte*

5 Harry has to _____ next year. *eine staatliche Schulabschluss-prüfung ablegen*

6 He plans to do an _____ after he _____ _____. *Ausbildung; den Schulabschluss machen*

7 The _____ in the USA begins after the _____. *Schuljahr; Sommerferien*

8 How old are US students when they are in 12th _____ – the final year of _____? *Klasse; Sekundarstufe*

9 Isn't it strange that '_____' in the UK means the same as '_____' in the USA? *Privatschule; Privatschule*

10 Please describe how _____ in your school. *schulische Fortschritte beurteilt werden*

11 The teachers have to _____ the students during _____. *beaufsichtigen; AGs*

Graduiertenkolleg; den Universitätsabschluss gemacht hast	**12** Will you go on to _____ after you _____ _____ college?
einen offiziellen Berufsabschluss; Berufsausbildung	**13** They will gain _____ at the end of their _____ .
stellen nur ungern ... ein	**14** Some companies _____ older jobseekers.
Funktion; betriebliche Ausbildung	**15** Does this _____ involve any _____ ?
Konkurrenz; Absolventenprogramm	**16** _____ for places on the _____ was fierce.
Praktikum; Arbeitskräfte	**17** Is this _____ a structured programme, or are the interns just cheap _____ ?
einen Überblick bekommen über; Abteilungen	**18** It is a good opportunity _____ the work in different _____ .
Personalvermittlungen; Berufsberatung	**19** Do _____ offer useful _____ ?
recherchieren; Bewerbung	**20** It's important to _____ a prospective employer before writing your _____ .
einen günstigen Eindruck; Leistungen	**21** Listing 'watching TV' as an interest doesn't give _____ of your _____ .
förmliches Schreiben; Grammatikfehler	**22** You should know how to write a _____ in English without _____ .

23 Please give a _____ explanation of why you are _____ this position.

knapp; geeignet für

24 We will _____ a video _____ as part of the _____.

durchführen; Vorstellungs-gespräch; Auswahlverfahren

25 The _____ really _____: I'd love to work there.

Firmenrundgang; hat mich beeindruckt

26 This candidate seems to have a _____, we should invite her back for a detailed _____.

motivierte Einstellung; Beur-teilung

27 If I have to do more than my usual _____, will I get paid _____?

Arbeitszeit; Überstunden

28 Workers in the USA may have less protection from unfair _____ and less _____ than in Germany.

Kündigung; Jahresurlaub

29 Is there a legal _____ in this country?

Mindestlohn

30 Even though she's ill, she has to _____ or she _____.

erscheinen; kriegt ihr Geld nicht

31 We are currently looking for reliable _____ for many of our _____.

Aushilfskräfte; Einzelhandels-geschäfte

32 There are many _____ for _____ workers with valuable skills and experience.

Vorteile; freiberufliche

33 Hot desking allows employers to use their _____.

Geschäftsräume; effizient

sich negativ auf die Produktivität auswirkt(e)	**34**	We abandoned it when we found that it _____ _____ .
Bürofläche; Ressource	**35**	_____ is an important and valuable _____ for companies.
Unterbeschäftigung; Arbeitslosigkeit	**36**	Do you think that _____ is as big a social problem as _____ ?
Angebot; Nachfrage	**37**	Wages are likely to fall when labour _____ is greater than _____ .
Dienstleistungsgewerbe; Fertigungsindustrie	**38**	There are more career opportunities in _____ than in _____ .
Überqualifizierung; (Berufs-) Erfahrung	**39**	_____ is a waste of an employee's education and _____ .
Vollzeit arbeiten; Personalüberschuss	**40**	She was no longer able to _____ because of _____ in her company.
Markt schrumpfte	**41**	We lost our jobs when the _____ .
Arbeitslosengeld; die Bedürfnisse eines Menschen zu erfüllen	**42**	Is _____ sufficient to _____ ?
Wachstum; nicht wünschenswert	**43**	Some economists believe that continual economic _____ is _____ .

3 Media and communication

A The internet

Web 1.0 (1990s)

The early web consisted largely of static websites which only allowed passive viewing of content. Limited bandwidth meant that images needed to be used carefully, otherwise pages would load slowly, which was annoying for end users, most of whom had slow and unreliable connections. Web pages were therefore largely text-based.

Many companies felt that a web presence would be beneficial for their marketing and customer service, as enthusiasm for the newly introduced internet and World Wide Web grew. However, often they had little idea about why they needed a website, or what to do with it.

Website design was very individual and often amateurish, with poor use of fonts, backgrounds and layout. Before web designer became an established profession, some websites were designed by book and magazine designers, who had no training in creating pages for the screen. Others were designed by computer programmers, who could write easily in HTML code, but often had no design skills at all. These factors reduced the user-friendliness and accessibility of many early websites.

Computer language

button Schaltfläche, Button
cursor Eingabemarke, Cursor
file Datei
folder Ordner
inbox Posteingang
operating system Betriebssystem
outbox Postausgang
search engine Suchmaschine
window Fenster
to **click sth** etw anklicken
to **delete** löschen
to **enter** eingeben
to **log in/out** sich ein-/ausloggen
to **save** sichern

CHECKPOINT   *In English, please!*

a Diese Webseite lädt sehr langsam.
b Das ist nervig. Enthält sie viele Bilder?
c Nein, sie ist überwiegend textbasiert, aber meine Verbindung ist ziemlich langsam.
d Das schlechte Layout mindert die Zugänglichkeit der Website.

static ['stætɪk]	*statisch*	◑ **dynamic**
to **view** [vjuː]	*sich ansehen, betrachten*	N **view**
content ['kɒntent]	*Inhalt*	! *Aussprache*
bandwidth ['bændwɪdθ]	*Bandbreite*	*vgl.* **broadband connection** *Breitbandanschluss*
image ['ɪmɪdʒ]	*Bild*	*vgl.* **graphic** *Grafik*
to **load** [ləʊd]	*laden*	*vgl.* to **upload** *hochladen*, to **download** *herunterladen*
end user ['end juːzə]	*Benutzer/in, Anwender/in*	*vgl.* **user interface** *Benutzeroberfläche*
connection [kə'nekʃn]	*Verbindung, Anschluss*	v to **connect**
web page ['web peɪdʒ]	*Webseite*	≠ **website** *Website*
text-based ['tekst beɪst]	*textlastig, textbasiert*	≈ **textual**
web presence ['web prezns]	*Webauftritt, Webpräsenz*	≈ **online presence**
design [dɪ'zaɪn]	*Gestaltung, Design*	*vgl.* **web designer**
amateurish ['æmətərɪʃ]	*laienhaft, dilettantisch*	◑ **professional**
font [fɒnt]	*Schrift(art), Zeichensatz*	≈ **typeface**
background ['bækgraʊnd]	*Hintergrund, Fond*	◑ **foreground**
layout ['leɪaʊt]	*Aufbau, Gestaltung, Layout*	v to **lay sth out**
user-friendliness [ˌjuːzə'frendlɪnes]	*Nutzerfreundlichkeit*	ADJ **user-friendly**
accessibility [əkˌsesə'bɪləti]	*Zugänglichkeit, Barrierefreiheit*	ADJ **accessible** → *Siene auch Kasten S. 78*

Web 2.0 (2000s)

The term 'Web 2.0' was first used in 1999. It signified a number of changes which increased the usability of the web for end users. These changes happened gradually, rather than being a sudden revolution in web design.

Rather than being static, web 2.0 sites are dynamic: they change in response to the user's needs. Pages may even be created in real time from database information in response to users' requests. Examples include e-commerce websites, where the shopper is presented with one or more pages of items which match the search terms he or she typed in.

On many sites, users can interact and work with each other, e.g. by posting reviews or comments. Many news websites have this facility. Many e-commerce and tourism websites encourage users to post reviews.

Users can personalize their experience online. What we see when we access a news website often depends on the preferences and settings in our user account. It may also depend on our browsing history and geographical location.

Web 2.0 websites use rich media including lots of images, streaming audio and video, and interactivity.

Expressions with 'user'

end user Anwender/in, Benutzer/in
user friendly anwender-/benutzer-freundlich
user-friendliness Nutzerfreundlichkeit
user account Benutzerkonto
user interface Benutzeroberfläche

Word family 'access'

access (to sth) Zugriff (auf etw), Zugang (zu etw)
to access sth auf etw zugreifen, etw (Datei usw.) öffnen
accessible zugänglich, barrierefrei
accessibility Zugänglichkeit, Barrierefreiheit

CHECKPOINT — *In English, please!*

a Für unsere Firma benötigen wir eine dynamische, interaktive Website.
b Können die Nutzer Kommentare in Echtzeit posten?
c Ja, außerdem können sie sich die Website individuell anpassen.
d Sie können leicht die Einstellungen ändern.

usability [ˌjuːzəˈbɪləti]	Benutzerfreundlichkeit, Nutzbarkeit	ADJ **usable** brauchbar ≈ **ease of use**
dynamic [daɪˈnæmɪk]	dynamisch	ADV **dynamically**
in real time [ɪn ˌrɪəl ˈtaɪm]	in Echtzeit	ADJ **real-time**
database [ˈdeɪtəbeɪs]	Datenbank	vgl. **data !** gewöhnlich im Singular
to **interact** [ˌɪntərˈækt]	miteinander kommunizieren	ADJ **interactive**
to **post** [pəʊst]	(etw im Internet) posten	N **post** Beitrag, Posting
review [rɪˈvjuː]	Rezension, Bewertung	V to **review**
e-commerce [ˈiː kɒmɜːs]	Internethandel, E-Commerce	vgl. **commerce** Handel, Geschäftsverkehr
to **personalize sth** [ˈpɜːsnəlaɪz]	(sich) etw individuell anpassen/einrichten	N **personalization**
to **access sth** [ˈækses]	auf etw zugreifen, etw (Datei usw.) öffnen	→ Kasten links
preferences pl [ˈprefrənsɪz]	Voreinstellungen	V to **prefer** vorziehen, bevorzugen
settings pl [ˈsetɪŋz]	Einstellungen	V to **set**
account [əˈkaʊnt]	Konto, Account	≈ **profile**
browsing history [ˈbraʊzɪŋ hɪstri]	Browserverlauf	V to **browse**
to **stream** [striːm]	streamen	ADJ + N **streaming**
interactivity [ɪntərækˈtɪvɪti]	Interaktivität	vgl. **interaction** Interaktion

Web 3.0 and beyond

It is difficult to predict the future development of any technology, particularly one which is developing as fast as the internet and the World Wide Web. However, we can be fairly confident about a few things.

In the near future, most end users are unlikely to have much awareness that the web even exists. Connectivity will be built into all electronic communication devices, even most household technology such as light switches and washing machines.

It will also be completely normal that most or all content is stored online or 'in the cloud' (on private online servers). As a result of these developments, the idea of having a separate software application called a web browser may soon seem strange and old-fashioned.

The devices we use to access online information may change beyond recognition. Touchscreens may become obsolete because of their limitations. Already virtual assistants support natural language and respond to voice commands. The rise of the Internet of Things means that most of the appliances in our homes will be connected to the internet.

CHECKPOINT   *In English, please!*

a Ich verstehe nicht, weshalb Haushaltsgeräte Internetanschluss benötigen.
b Sind die Fotos auf deinem Tablet? – Nein, sie sind online gespeichert.
c Moderne Handys haben sich bis zur Unkenntlichkeit verändert.
d Sie haben keine Tasten (*buttons*) und unterstützen natürliche Sprache.

in the near future [ɪn ðə ˌnɪə ˈfjuːtʃə]	*in naher Zukunft*	≈ **soon**
		◀)) **in the distant future** *in ferner Zukunft*
connectivity [ˌkɒnekˈtɪvəti]	*Anschlüsse, Anschlussmöglichkeit(en), Verbindung(en)*	**v** to **connect sth to / with sth**
to **build sth into sth** [ˈbɪld ɪntə]	*etw in etw einbauen*	**ADJ in-built**
to **store** [stɔː]	*speichern*	**N storage**
software application [ˈsɒftweər æplɪkeɪʃn]	*Programm, Software-Anwendung*	*vgl.* **software platform**
web browser [ˈweb braʊzə]	*Browser*	**v** to **browse**
old-fashioned [ˌəʊld ˈfæʃnd]	*antiquiert, altmodisch*	≈ **out-dated, out of date**
to **change beyond recognition** [ˌtʃeɪndʒ bɪˌjɒnd rekəgˈnɪʃn]	*nicht mehr wiederzuerkennen sein, sich bis zur Unkenntlichkeit verändern*	**N recognition** *Wiedererkennen*
obsolete [ˈɒbsəliːt]	*veraltet, überholt*	*vgl.* **planned obsolescence** *gewollte Produktalterung, geplanter Verschleiß*
limitation [ˌlɪmɪˈteɪʃn]	*Einschränkung, Grenze(n)*	→ *Kasten links*
to **support** [səˈpɔːt]	*unterstützen*	**N support**
natural language [ˌnætʃrəl ˈlæŋgwɪdʒ]	*natürliche Sprache*	*vgl.* **programming language** *Programmiersprache*
to **respond to sth** [rɪˈspɒnd tə]	*auf etw reagieren*	**N response**
voice command [ˈvɔɪs kəmɑːnd]	*Sprachbefehl(e), Sprachsteuerung*	**v** to **command (sb to do sth)**
Internet of Things [ˈɪntənet əf ˈθɪŋz]	*Internet der Dinge*	**ABBR IoT**
appliance [əˈplaɪəns]	*Elektrogerät*	≈ **household appliance** *(elektrisches) Haushaltsgerät*

What does social media do?

Online <u>social media</u> allows us to share information, ideas and opinions with virtual communities and networks. Through social media we can connect with individuals and join groups that share our interests.

Social media began with forums which allowed members to discuss topics which interested them, using simple text-only questions and answers.

As social media became more complex and started to use Web 2.0 technology, special platforms were created, e.g. Facebook, Instagram or LinkedIn. Most or all of the content there is user-generated. Other users can respond to the content (e.g. like or upvote it, link to and share it). This enables content to spread rapidly – to 'go viral'.

A social media platform provides its users with a range of services. These differ from platform to platform, but they generally include the following: disk space on its online servers, a user interface with a set of functions (e.g. write a post, upload images) and content moderation, so that offensive or illegal material can be removed and abusive users (e.g. trolls and spammers) blocked.

'Media'

The plural noun 'media' (meaning 'radio', 'TV', 'internet', etc.) is often used with a singular verb:
*Social media **has changed** the way we communicate.*

Expressions with 'media'

media literacy Medienkompetenz
digital media digitale Medien
<u>**social media**</u> soziale Medien
in the media in den Medien
mass media Massenmedien
the news media Nachrichten-
    medien, Informationsmedien

CHECKPOINT   *In English, please!*

a Quora ist eine virtuelle Gemeinschaft, wo Mitglieder Fragen stellen und beantworten können.
b Bislang haben 1400 Personen meinen Post positiv bewertet und 15 haben ihn geteilt.
c Die Benutzeroberfläche ist gut, benötigt aber noch mehr Funktionen.

to **share** [ʃeə]	teilen, weitergeben	N sharing, share
virtual ['vɜːtʃuəl]	virtuell	vgl. virtual reality
community [kə'mjuːnəti]	Gemeinde, Gemeinschaft, Community	≈ group
network ['netwɜːk]	Netz, Netzwerk	v to network (with sb)
to **join sth** [dʒɔɪn]	einer Sache beitreten, bei etw mitmachen	◆ to leave
user-generated [ˌjuːzə 'dʒenəreɪtɪd]	von Nutzern gestaltet, nutzergeneriert	vgl. computer-generated
to **respond to sth** [rɪ'spɒnd tə]	auf etw reagieren	N response
to **upvote** [ʌp'vəʊt]	positiv bewerten	◆ to downvote
to **link to sth** ['lɪŋk tə]	etw verlinken	N link
to **spread** [spred]	sich verbreiten, sich ausbreiten	vgl. to **spread sth** etw verbreiten (z. B. Gerüchte), to **disseminate sth** etw verbreiten (z. B. Ideologien)
to **go viral** [ˌgəʊ 'vaɪrəl]	sich rasend schnell aus-/verbreiten	vgl. viral marketing
disk space ['dɪsk speɪs]	Speicherplatz	≈ storage space
user interface [ˌjuːzər 'ɪntəfeɪs]	Benutzeroberfläche	ABBR UI
to **upload** [ˌʌp'ləʊd]	hochladen	◆ to download
moderation [ˌmɒdə'reɪʃn]	Moderation	v to moderate moderieren
offensive [ə'fensɪv]	anstößig, beleidigend	N offensiveness, offence
to **remove** [rɪ'muːv]	entfernen	N removal
abusive [ə'bjuːsɪv]	beleidigend, missbräuchlich, betrügerisch	N abuse [ə'bjuːs] Beleidigung(en), Missbrauch v to abuse [ə'bjuːz] beleidigen, missbrauchen
to **block** [blɒk]	sperren, blockieren	≈ to bar, to ban

Effects of social media

Social media has not just made communication easier; it has also changed how we communicate and socialize. Nowadays, we are much more likely to multitask, e.g. carry on a conversation with family face-to-face at the same time as we are browsing web pages or posting on Instagram.

We use social media to stay in touch with distant friends, to share experiences with friends back home while we're on holiday, and to expand our circle of friends to include people we might never meet in person. None of these social possibilities were available to previous generations.

It is increasingly difficult to have a full social life without some form of online social media. As a result, around 70 % of US teenagers have at least one social media account, and figures across the EU are similar.

Users of social media increasingly share information about themselves online. This can be problematic when the information is sensitive. Privacy settings allow us to control who can see the material we post, but social media tracks us across the internet, gathering data about us from all our online behaviour.

'effect' – 'affect'

effect on sth Auswirkung(en) auf etw
to **affect** sth etw betreffen, etw beeinflussen, sich auf etw auswirken

Word family 'use'

to **use** gebrauchen, benutzen, verwenden
use/usage Gebrauch, Nutzung, Verwendung
user Nutzer/in, Anwender/in
useful nützlich
useless nutzlos

'sensitive' – 'sensible'

sensitive sensibel, empfindlich, heikel, vertraulich
sensible vernünftig, praktisch

CHECKPOINT   *In English, please!*

a Hör auf, im Internet zu surfen, während wir uns unterhalten!
b Die sozialen Medien sind nützlich, um in Kontakt zu bleiben.
c Deshalb habe ich jetzt einen viel größeren Freundeskreis.

to **multitask** [ˈmʌltɪtɑːsk]	*mehrere Tätigkeiten gleichzeitig ausführen, multitasken*	N **multitasking**
to **carry on a conversation** [ˌkærɪ ˌɒn ə kɒnvəˈseɪʃn]	*ein Gespräch führen, sich unterhalten*	≈ to **converse**
face-to-face [ˌfeɪs tə ˈfeɪs]	*persönlich*	≈ **in person**
to **browse** [braʊz]	*surfen, browsen*	
to **stay in touch with sb** [ˌsteɪ ɪn ˈtʌtʃ wɪð]	*mit jdm in Verbindung/Kontakt bleiben*	◖ to **lose touch with sb**
distant [ˈdɪstənt]	*(weit) entfernt*	N **distance** ◖ **nearby**
circle of friends [ˌsɜːkl əf ˈfrendz]	*Freundeskreis*	≈ **social network, social circle**
figures *pl* [ˈfɪɡəz]	*Zahlen*	≈ **statistics**
problematic [ˌprɒbləˈmætɪk]	*problematisch*	≈ **troublesome**
sensitive [ˈsensətɪv]	*vertraulich*	N **sensitivity** *Vertraulichkeit (von Informationen)*
privacy settings *pl* [ˈprɪvəsi setɪŋz]	*Privatsphäreeinstellungen*	ADJ **private**
to **control** [kənˈtrəʊl]	*kontrollieren*	N **control**
to **track** [træk]	*verfolgen, folgen*	N **tracking**
to **gather** [ˈɡæðə]	*sammeln*	≈ to **collect**

B Media power and control

Advertising

We have so much entertainment and information available to us that we often take it for granted. It includes websites, TV channels, radio stations and other media. While in some countries, a licence fee for television and radio must be paid, in many other countries, viewers and listeners pay nothing. However, little of this media content is really free. Media companies broadcast it in return for the right to show us advertising. In fact, it is probably fair to say that the primary aim of the content we watch, read and listen to is to influence our consumption: to persuade us to buy something, not to inform us. This is an uncomfortable truth that we often forget when we complain about the poor quality of the media.

Print advertising is included in newspapers and magazines. Direct mail advertising such as leaflets is delivered to our letterboxes or handed to us in the street. Most TV channels have commercial breaks between and during the programmes. In addition, there is advertising in the world around us, on billboards, in shop windows and on public transport.

Expressions with 'television/TV'

TV channel Fernsehsender
TV licence Fernsehgebühren
TV news Fernsehnachrichten
TV programme Fernsehsendung
TV series Fernsehserie
TV set Fernsehgerät, Fernseher
TV show Fernsehserie, Fernseh-sendung
TV star Fernsehstar
TV station Fernsehsender
to **be on TV** im Fernsehen (zu sehen) sein
to **turn on/off the TV** den Fernseher ein-/aussschalten
to **watch TV** fernsehen

Word family 'persuade'

to **persuade sb to do sth** jdn dazu überreden, etw zu tun; jdn dazu bringen, etw zu tun
persuasion Überredung, Überzeu-gung
persuasive überzeugend
persuasiveness Überredungskünste, Überzeugungskraft

entertainment [ˌentəˈteɪnmənt]	*Unterhaltung*	v to **entertain**, ADJ **entertaining**
to **take sth for granted** [ˌteɪk fə ˈgrɑːntɪd]	*etw als selbstverständlich ansehen*	≈ to **assume sth is true**
TV channel [ˌtiː ˈviː ˈtʃænl]	*Fernsehsender*	≈ **television station**
licence fee [ˈlaɪsns fiː]	*Fernsehgebühren*	v to **license**
media company [ˈmiːdiə kʌmpəni]	*Medienunternehmen*	≈ **media corporation**
to **broadcast** [ˈbrɔːdkɑːst]	*senden, (Sendungen) ausstrahlen*	≈ to **transmit**
advertising [ˈædvətaɪzɪŋ]	*Werbung, Reklame*	v to **advertise** → *Siehe auch Kasten S. 88*
primary [ˈpraɪməri]	*vorrangig, primär*	*vgl.* **secondary** *nebensächlich, sekundär*
to **influence** [ˈɪnfluəns]	*beeinflussen*	N **influence**
consumption [kənˈsʌmpʃn]	*Konsum*	v to **consume**
to **persuade sb to do sth** [pəˈsweɪd]	*jdn dazu bringen, etw zu tun*	→ *Kasten links*
print advertising [ˈprɪnt ædvətaɪzɪŋ]	*Printwerbung*	N **advertiser** *(Person, Firma)*
newspaper [ˈnjuːzpeɪpə]	*Zeitung*	≈ **paper**, *bes. pl* **the papers** *die Zeitungen, die Presse*
magazine [ˌmægəˈziːn]	*Zeitschrift*	INFML **mag**
direct mail [dəˌrekt ˈmeɪl]	*per Post, Postwurfsendung(en)*	≈ **junk mail** *(pejorativ)*
leaflet [ˈliːflət]	*Prospekt, Werbezettel*	*vgl.* **handout** *Arbeitsblatt,* **flyer** *Handzettel, Werbezettel*
commercial break [kəˌmɜːʃl ˈbreɪk]	*Werbeblock, (TV-/Radio-)Werbung*	INFML **ad break**
programme [ˈprəʊgræm]	*(TV-/Radio-)Sendung*	AE **program**
billboard [ˈbɪlbɔːd]	*Plakatwand, Werbetafel*	≈ **hoarding** BE
shop window [ˈʃɒp wɪndəʊ]	*Schaufenster*	*vgl.* **window display** *Schaufensterauslage*

Advertisers vs viewers

Viewers who find advertising excessive and intrusive can use modern technology to avoid it. Hard disk recorders allow us to skip or fast-forward through TV ads. However, advertisers have found other ways to promote their products on TV. These include product placement, where a product and its brand name or logo are shown prominently during a programme.

Pay TV channels and streaming services have little or no advertising. After all, the viewer has paid to watch the show, so he or she shouldn't have to 'pay' again by watching advertising.

The web is a different matter. Many websites only exist to promote the company and its products, but most others also have advertisements. These may include banner ads, pop-up ads and videos. Sometimes they are welcome entertainment and information, but they can distract the internet user and make it difficult to concentrate on the main content of the page. Users can fight back with ad blocking software. However some websites retaliate to the use of an ad blocker by denying access until it is disabled, or requiring users to watch a short video advertisement before they can use the website.

Word family 'advertise'

to **advertise** werben, (etw) bewerben, (für etw) Werbung machen
advertiser Werber/in
advertising Werbung, Reklame
advertisement Anzeige, Werbespot
ad(vert) Anzeige, Werbespot

Word family 'produce'

to **produce** produzieren, herstellen
produce (landwirtschaftliche) Erzeugnisse
producer Produzent/in, Hersteller/in
production Produktion, Herstellung
product Produkt, Erzeugnins
(un)productive (un)produktiv
productivity Produktivität

CHECKPOINT *In English, please!*

a Wenn Sie Werbung störend finden, sollten Sie sich Pay-TV besorgen.
b O nein, noch ein Werbeblock! Können wir vorspulen?
c Diese blöden Werbebanner lenken mich von dem Artikel ab!
d Dann solltest du Werbefilter benutzen!

viewer [ˈvjuːə]	(Fernseh-)Zuschauer/in	ν to **view** ansehen, betrachten
excessive [ɪkˈsesɪv]	zu viel, übermäßig	≈ INFML **over-the-top**
intrusive [ɪnˈtruːsɪv]	störend, aufdringlich	N **intrusion** Störung, Eindringen
to **avoid** [əˈvɔɪd]	vermeiden	N **avoidance**
hard disk recorder [ˌhɑːd dɪsk rɪˈkɔːdə]	Festplattenrecorder	ν to **record** [rɪˈkɔːd] vgl. N **recording** [rɪˈkɔːdɪŋ] Aufnahme, Aufzeichnung vgl. N **record** ! [ˈrekɔːd] Schallplatte
to **skip** [skɪp]	überspringen	≈ to **avoid**
to **fast-forward** [ˌfɑːst ˈfɔːwəd]	vorspulen	vgl. to **rewind** zurückspulen
to **promote** [prəˈməʊt]	werben für, Werbung machen für	≈ to **advertise**, to **publicize** N **promotion**
product placement [ˈprɒdʌkt pleɪsmənt]	Produktplatzierung	ν to **place**
brand name [ˈbrænd neɪm]	Markenname	≈ **brand**
banner ad [ˈbænər æd]	Bannerwerbung, Werbebanner	vgl. **pop-up ad** Popup-Werbung
welcome [ˈwelkəm]	willkommen	≈ **desirable**, **agreeable**
to **distract** [dɪˈstrækt]	ablenken	N **distraction**
to **concentrate on sth** [ˈkɒnsntreɪt]	sich auf etw konzentrieren	N **concentration**
ad blocking software [ˈæd blɒkɪŋ sɒftweə]	Werbeblocker, Werbefilter	ν to **block ads**
to **retaliate** [rɪˈtalɪeɪt]	kontern, Vergeltung üben	≈ to **fight back**
to **deny access** [dɪˌnaɪ ˈækses tə]	(den) Zugang zu etw verweigern	◊ **allow access**
to **disable** [dɪsˈeɪbl]	deaktivieren, abschalten	≈ to **deactivate**

Freedom of expression (freedom of speech)

Democratic countries guarantee their citizens' right to freedom of expression: to express their opinions and ideas through the spoken word or in writing, in artworks or through any other medium. This is a basic principle of democracy: without this protection, democracy cannot exist. Freedom of expression is a universal human right and recognized in international law. A related right is the right to peaceful political protest.

Nevertheless, there are some circumstances in which it may be necessary to limit free expression. To stop abuses of free expression, it may be necessary to resort to censorship. Both governments and private organizations may use censorship. For example, a company may tell its employees not to communicate company information to anyone outside the company. Government censorship attempts to protect society against harmful or highly offensive material.

Democratic countries limit censorship, as excessive censorship is harmful to democracy. However, many countries are not fully democratic, and have strict censorship of political or religious opinions.

CHECKPOINT   *In English, please!*

a Redefreiheit ist ein grundlegendes Menschenrecht.
b Ist es gesetzeswidrig, anstößige politische Meinungen zu äußern?
c Das hängt von den Umständen ab.
d Staatliche Zensur kann der Demokratie schaden.

freedom [ˈfriːdəm]	*Freiheit*	v to **free sb from sth**
expression [ɪkˈspreʃn]	*Meinungsäußerung*	v to **express**
speech [spiːtʃ]	*Rede*	*vgl.* **freedom of speech** *Redefreiheit*
democratic [ˌdeməˈkrætɪk]	*demokratisch*	N **democracy**
to **guarantee** [ˌgærənˈtiː]	*garantieren, gewährleisten*	N **guarantee**
citizen [ˈsɪtɪzn]	*Bürger/in*	*vgl.* **citizenship**
right (to sth) [ˈraɪt]	*Recht (auf etw)*	ADJ **rightful**
artwork [ˈɑːtwɜːk]	*Kunstwerk*	≈ **work of art**
protection [prəˈtekʃn]	*Schutz*	v to **protect**
universal [ˌjuːnɪˈvɜːsl]	*allgemein*	N **universality** *Allgemeingültigkeit*
to **recognize** [ˈrekəgnaɪz]	*anerkennen*	N **recognition**
law [lɔː]	*Recht, Gesetz(e)*	ADJ **legal**
related [rɪˈleɪtɪd]	*verwandt*	≈ **connected**
political [pəˈlɪtɪkl]	*politisch*	N **politics** ! *Plural*
circumstances *pl* [ˈsɜːkəmstənsɪz]	*Umstände*	ADJ **circumstantial**
to **limit** [ˈlɪmɪt]	*einschränken*	N **limit** ADJ **limited**
abuse [əˈbjuːs]	*Missbrauch*	ADJ **abusive** v to **abuse** [əˈbjuːz]
to **resort to sth** [rɪˈzɔːt]	*zu etw greifen, auf etw zurückgreifen*	*vgl.* **as a last resort**
censorship [ˈsensəʃɪp]	*Zensur*	v to **censor**
harmful (to sb/sth) [ˈhɑːmfl]	*schädlich (für jdn/etw)*	◊ **harmless, innocuous**
offensive [əˈfensɪv]	*anstößig, beleidigend, aggressiv*	v to **offend**

Defamation, intellectual property theft and hate speech

Defamation is making false and negative statements about a person, organization, religion or nation. These 'statements' may be spoken, in writing or in images. Laws against defamation are designed to protect the reputations of individuals and groups. There is potential conflict between the concept of defamation on the one hand, and an individual's right to free speech on the other. As a result, applying these laws is often difficult.

If a person or a group of people creates an original text, image, piece of music, etc., or invents a machine or a new drug, then this new creation is their intellectual property. Other people cannot copy, share or sell it without the permission of the creator. Illegal copying is sometimes called piracy. There is disagreement about the extent to which basic scientific discoveries can be treated as intellectual property.

Hate speech is intended to incite hatred or violence towards a person or group, for example followers of a religion or members of an ethnic minority. Again, it is sometimes difficult to distinguish hate speech from legitimate political and social commentary.

Word family 'create'

to **create** erschaffen, erzeugen, produzieren, schöpfen
creator Urheber/in, Schöpfer/in
creation Schöpfung
creative schöpferisch, kreativ
creativity Schöpfungskraft, Kreativität

Prefix 'il-'

illegal rechtswidrig, ungesetzlich, illegal
illegible unlesbar
illegitimate unzulässig, unrechtmäßig
illogical unlogisch
illiterate des Lesens und Schreibens unkundig

CHECKPOINT   *In English, please!*

a Das ist Verleumdung – alles, was Sie gesagt haben, ist völlig falsch!
b Der Fernsehstar sorgt sich um seinen Ruf.
c Teilen Sie dieses Bild nicht ohne die Genehmigung des Urhebers/der Urheberin.
d Mit seiner Rede wollte er zu Hass und Gewalt aufstacheln.

theft [θeft]	*Diebstahl*	v to **steal**
defamation [ˌdefəˈmeɪʃn]	*Verleumdung, Rufmord, Diffamierung*	v to **defame**
false [fɔːls]	*unwahr, falsch*	v to **falsify**
reputation [ˌrepjuˈteɪʃn]	*(guter) Ruf, Reputation*	*vgl.* to **bring sb into ill-repute** *jdn in Verruf bringen*
individual [ˌɪndɪˈvɪdʒuəl]	*Einzelperson*	
to **create** [kriˈeɪt]	*erschaffen, erzeugen, produzieren, schöpfen*	→ *Kasten links*
to **invent** [ɪnˈvent]	*erfinden*	N **invention** ADJ **inventive**
intellectual property [ɪntəˌlektʃuəl ˈprɒpəti]	*geistiges Eigentum*	*vgl.* **copyright** *Urheberrecht*
permission [pəˈmɪʃn]	*Genehmigung, Erlaubnis*	v to **permit**
illegal [ɪˈliːgl]	*rechtswidrig, ungesetzlich, illegal*	◆ **legal** N **illegality**
piracy [ˈpaɪrəsi]	*Produktpiraterie, Raubkopieren*	v to **pirate** *illegal nachahmen, raubkopieren*
hate speech [ˈheɪt spiːtʃ]	*Hetzerei, Volksverhetzung*	*vgl.* **hate post**
to **incite** [ɪnˈsaɪt]	*aufstacheln zu, aufhetzen zu, (an)stiften*	N **incitement** (e.g. to **commit a crime**)
hatred [ˈheɪtrɪd]	*Hass*	≈ **hate** v to **hate**
violence [ˈvaɪələns]	*Gewalt*	ADJ **violent**
ethnic minority [ˌeθnɪk maɪˈnɒrəti]	*ethnische Minderheit*	N **ethnicity** *ethnische Zugehörigkeit*
to **distinguish** [dɪˈstɪŋgwɪʃ]	*unterscheiden*	v to **differentiate**
legitimate [lɪˈdʒɪtəmət]	*zulässig, rechtmäßig*	◆ **illegitimate**

Fake news

Although the term 'fake news' is relatively recent, the phenomenon itself is not new: governments and other political organizations have used defamatory rumours and false news stories to manipulate public opinion for thousands of years.

What is new is the use of online social media to spread misleading and untruthful 'news reports'. The viral effect of social media ensures that rumours, innuendo and outright lies spread quickly and widely – more so than later retractions. All that is required is for the false claims to be sufficiently scandalous, and to support the bias of a section of the community. 'A lie can travel halfway around the world while the truth is putting on its shoes,' as American author Mark Twain is claimed to have said. (Ironically, Twain probably never said this.)

In many cases, the 'fake news' doesn't even have to be believed: it is enough to sow doubt. For example, unsubstantiated claims in social media about a political candidate, carefully targeted at uncertain voters, can be sufficient to persuade them not to vote.

CHECKPOINT | *In English, please!*

a Dies ist eine Fake-News-Story: Sie ist irreführend und unwahr.
b Dank des viralen Effekts verbreitete sich die Behauptung weit.
c Die Nachrichtenmeldung war eine glatte Lüge.
d Schon, aber niemand hat dem Widerruf Glauben geschenkt.

fake news [ˌfeɪk ˈnjuːz]	*(gezielte) Falschmeldung(en), Fake News*	v to fake
phenomenon [fəˈnɒmɪnən]	*Phänomen*	! *Plural:* phenomena
political [pəˈlɪtɪkl]	*politisch*	N politics *(Plural)*
defamatory [dɪˈfæmətri]	*verleumderisch, diffamierend*	N defamation
rumour [ˈruːmə]	*Gerücht*	*vgl.* it is rumoured that … *Gerüchten zufolge soll …*
false [fɔːls]	*unwahr, falsch*	N falsehood *Unwahrheit*
to manipulate [məˈnɪpjuleɪt]	*manipulieren*	N manipulation
public opinion [ˌpʌblɪk əˈpɪnɪən]	*öffentliche Meinung*	*vgl.* the public → *Siehe auch Kasten links*
misleading [ˌmɪsˈliːdɪŋ]	*irreführend*	≈ deceptive
untruthful [ʌnˈtruːθfl]	*unwahr, wahrheitswidrig*	*vgl.* fraudulent *betrügerisch, falsch*
viral effect [ˌvaɪrəl ɪˈfekt]	*virale Wirkung, viraler Effekt, rasend schnelle Ausbreitung (im Internet)*	*vgl.* to go viral *sich rasend schnell (im Internet) ausbreiten*
innuendo [ˌɪnjuˈendəʊ]	*Anspielung(en), Andeutung(en)*	≈ insinuation
outright lie [ˌaʊtraɪt ˈlaɪ]	*glatte Lüge*	v to lie, to tell a lie
retraction [rɪˈtrækʃn]	*Widerruf, Zurücknahme*	v to retract
claim [kleɪm]	*Behauptung*	v to claim
scandalous [ˈskændələs]	*skandalös*	N scandal
bias [ˈbaɪəs]	*Vorurteil(e), (ideologische) Ausrichtung*	ADJ biased
to sow doubt [ˌsəʊ ˈdaʊt]	*Zweifel säen*	ADJ doubtful, doubting
unsubstantiated [ˌʌnsəbˈstænʃɪeɪtɪd]	*unbegründet, haltlos*	*vgl.* unverified *ungeprüft*
to target sth at sb [ˈtɑːɡɪt]	*etw an jdn richten*	N target, targeting

C Print media

Newspapers in the UK

The UK has national, regional and local newspapers. Many of them are owned by the same large media groups, but have varying degrees of editorial independence. Local newspapers often appear on a weekly cycle, but most regional and national newspapers are dailies.

The national dailies are separated into two groups: tabloids and broadsheets. These names are historical: they refer to the original formats (dimensions) of the newspapers, even though most newspapers today are published in a compact, tabloid format. Differences in content and layout remain, reflecting a difference in target readership.

The tabloids are image-led newspapers. They feature large headlines and highly-illustrated, short articles in simple language. They report on politics and current affairs, but focus on celebrity gossip and human interest stories. Their take on national and international politics is often sensationalist and contentious.

Features of a newspaper

article Artikel
breaking news Eilmeldung(en)
business section Wirtschaftsteil
byline Verfasserangabe
classified ads Kleinanzeigen
column Spalte
commentary and analysis Kommentar und Analyse
editorial Leitartikel
film and book reviews Film- und Buchbesprechungen
front page Titelseite
headline Überschrift, Schlagzeile
letters to the editor Leserbriefe
sports section Sportteil

Word family 'edit'

to **edit** redigieren, bearbeiten, herausgeben, *(Film:)* schneiden
edit N Bearbeitung
editor Herausgeber/in, Redakteur/in, *(Film:)* Cutter/in
edition Ausgabe, Auflage
editing N Redaktion, Lektorat, Bearbeitung *(Film:)* Schnitt
editorial N Leitartikel
editorial ADJ redaktionell

CHECKPOINT   *In English, please!*

a Die Zeitung verlor ihre redaktionelle Unabhängigkeit, als der Medienkonzern sie kaufte.
b Die Leserschaft einer Zeitung läßt sich daran erkennen, auf welche Art und Weise über aktuelle Themen berichtet wird.
c Ich mag Promi-Klatsch, selbst wenn er reißerisch ist.

media group [ˈmiːdiə gruːp]	*Medienkonzern, Mediengruppe*	≈ media corporation
editorial [ˌedɪˈtɔːriəl]	*redaktionell*	→ Kasten links
independence [ˌɪndɪˈpendəns]	*Unabhängigkeit*	ADJ independent
daily [ˈdeɪli]	*Tageszeitung*	≈ daily newspaper
tabloid [ˈtæblɔɪd]	*Boulevardzeitung, Klatschpresse*	vgl. gutter press (pejorativ)
broadsheet [ˈbrɔːdʃiːt]	*seriöse/große Tageszeitung*	≈ quality newspaper
to **publish** [ˈpʌblɪʃ]	*veröffentlichen, publizieren*	N publication
content [ˈkɒntent]	*Inhalt*	! Aussprache vgl. ADJ content [kɒnˈtent] zufrieden
target readership [ˌtɑːgɪt ˈriːdəʃɪp]	*Zielgruppe, Leserschaft*	V to target
image-led [ˈɪmɪdʒ led]	*bildlastig, bildorientiert*	vgl. text-led (→ S. 99)
headline [ˈhedlaɪn]	*Überschrift, Schlagzeile*	vgl. to make the headlines in die Schlagzeilen geraten
highly-illustrated [ˌhaɪli ˈɪləstreɪtɪd]	*reich bebildert*	V to illustrate
to **report on sth** [rɪˈpɔːt ɒn]	*über etw berichten*	N report, reporting
politics [ˈpɒlətɪks]	*Politik*	ADJ political
current affairs [ˌkʌrənt əˈfeəz]	*aktuelle Themen, Zeitgeschehen*	≈ news, current events
celebrity gossip [səˌlebrəti ˈgɒsɪp]	*Promiklatsch*	V to gossip (about)
human interest story [ˌhjuːmən ˈɪntrəst stɔːri]	*ergreifende Alltagsgeschichte*	vgl. soft news Infotainment
take (on sth) [teɪk]	*Herangehensweise (an etw), Sicht (auf etw)*	≈ interpretation
sensationalist [senˈseɪʃənəlɪst]	*reißerisch, sensationslüstern*	N sensationalism
contentious [kənˈtenʃəs]	*provokativ*	≈ controversial

Newspapers in the UK (continued)

Broadsheets are text-led newspapers which pride themselves on the quality of their news content. They feature in-depth reporting, analysis and commentary. The style of writing is more sophisticated than in the tabloids, with longer sentences and paragraphs. The journalists' and editors' political bias are less obvious than in the tabloids.

Both broadsheets and tabloids publish weekend editions with supplements, which are additional sections with a focus on topics such as finance, culture, fashion and lifestyle. Some of them are highly illustrated and resemble glossy magazines. The idea is that newspaper readers have more time at the weekends for a long read.

Most UK newspapers have a strong web presence. Their content may be either free or mostly behind a paywall. The *Independent* is a quality newspaper which went online entirely in 2016 and no longer has a print edition. The circulation of print newspapers has fallen steeply in recent decades because of competition from online news, so other newspapers may one day follow the example of the *Independent*.

Newspaper roles

columnist Kolumnist/in
correspondent Korrespondent/in
designer Grafiker/in
editor Herausgeber/in, Redakteur/in
journalist/reporter Journalist/in, Reporter/in
photographer Fotograf/in
printer Drucker/in
production manager Produktions-leiter/in
publisher Verleger/in
sub-editor Redakteur/in

Word family 'analyse'

to **analyse** analysieren
analysis (*pl* **analyses**) Analyse
analyst Analytiker/in, Analyst/in
analytical analytisch

CHECKPOINT

In English, please!

a Ich lese diese Zeitung wegen ihrer gründlichen Berichterstattung.
b Ich lese gern den Kulturteil und die Modebeilage.
c Die ideologische Ausrichtung der Journalistin ist offensichtlich.
d Die Auflage der Zeitung sinkt.

text-led ['tekst led]	textlastig, textorientiert	vgl. image-led (→ S. 97)
quality ['kwɒləti]	Qualität	≈ excellence
news content ['njuːz kɒntent]	Nachrichteninhalte, Informationsgehalt	vgl. newsworthy berichtenswert, aktuell
in-depth [ˌɪn 'depθ]	ausführlich, gründlich	◑ superficial
analysis [əˈnæləsɪs]	Analyse	→ Kasten links
commentary ['kɒməntri]	Kommentar	v to comment on sth
style [staɪl]	Stil	ADJ stylistic
sophisticated [səˈfɪstɪkeɪtɪd]	anspruchsvoll, differenziert	N sophistication
journalist ['dʒɜːnəlɪst]	Journalist/in	N journalism
bias ['baɪəs]	Vorurteil(e), Tendenz, (ideologische) Ausrichtung	ADJ biased ◑ impartiality, fairness
obvious ['ɒbviəs]	offensichtlich	≈ clear, apparent
supplement ['sʌplɪmənt]	Beilage	vgl. insert Werbebeilage
finance ['faɪnæns]	Wirtschaft, Finanzwesen	ADJ financial
culture ['kʌltʃə]	Kultur	ADJ cultural
fashion ['fæʃn]	Mode	ADJ fashionable
glossy magazine [ˌglɒsi mægəˈziːn]	Hochglanzmagazin	
web presence ['web prezns]	Internetauftritt, Webpräsenz	≈ online presence
paywall ['peɪwɔːl]	Bezahlschranke, Paywall	vgl. subscription Abonnement
print edition ['prɪnt ɪdɪʃn]	gedruckte Ausgabe	vgl. digital edition digitale Ausgabe
circulation [ˌsɜːkjəˈleɪʃn]	Auflage	v to circulate
competition [ˌkɒmpəˈtɪʃn]	Konkurrenz	→ Siehe Kasten S. 52

TEST YOURSELF

You can check your answers on p. 209.

1 Our company needs a professional _____, but the
   _____ of our present site is poor.

   Webpräsenz; Gestaltung

2 It is largely _____ and looks a little _____.

   textbasiert; dilettantisch

3 What do you think of the web designer's choice of _____ and
   _____?

   Schriften; Bilder

4 How can we improve the website's _____ and
   _____?

   Zugänglichkeit; Nutzerfreund-lichkeit

5 Dear customer, please _____ a _____ of your
   recent purchase on our website.

   posten Sie; Bewertung

6 Go into the _____ page to _____ your
   online experience.

   Einstellungen; individuell anzupassen

7 Please delete your _____ so that the next user of this
   computer cannot _____ it.

   Browserverlauf; zugreifen auf

8 Many of the _____ in smart homes _____
   voice commands.

   Elektrogeräte; werden auf … reagieren

9 _____, we will expect internet _____
   from all our electronic devices.

   In naher Zukunft; Verbindung

10 Your phone's operating system is _____ and can't _____
   the latest apps.

   veraltet; unterstützen

Programm; werden gespeichert	**11** This _____ requires an internet connection, as its data _____ in the cloud.
Benutzeroberfläche; Gemeinde	**12** I like the _____ in this new social media app, but its online _____ is still very small.
sperren; anstößig	**13** I'm going to _____ this troll: I've had enough of his _____ posts.
haben … weitergegeben; verbreitete sich rasend schnell	**14** A lot of people _____ that video, so it soon _____.
verlinkt hast; haben … entfernt	**15** I can't find the article that you _____: maybe the moderators _____ it.
in Verbindung mit … bleiben; persönlich	**16** I find social media essential for _____ people whom I rarely see _____.
problematisch; vertraulich	**17** I find it _____ that my social media activity reveals _____ information about me.
Fernsehgebühren; Fernsehsender	**18** The _____ helps to pay for the content on the free-to-air _____.
Werbeblöcke; Sendungen	**19** There are so many _____ that it's difficult to watch the _____.
beeinflusst; Konsum	**20** Do you think that what you see on TV really _____ your _____?
Produktplatzierung; Marken-namen	**21** I've noticed a lot of _____ and prominent use of _____ in this show recently.

22 I don't find the _____ on this website _____
   or _____; in fact I like it.

   Werbung; zu viel; aufdringlich

23 Don't you find that it _____ you and makes it difficult
   _____ the main content?

   lenkt ... ab; sich auf ... zu konzentrieren

24 Our laws _____ our right to _____.

   gewährleisten; Recht auf freie Meinungsäußerung

25 It is a _____ human right and _____ in
   international law.

   allgemein; wird ... anerkannt

26 Peaceful _____ protest is a necessary part of
   _____ society.

   politisch; demokratisch

27 Your comment could be interpreted as _____ rather than
   _____ commentary.

   Verleumdung; rechtmäßig

28 We will not tolerate _____ or any material which might
   _____.

   Hetzerei; zu Gewalt anstiften

29 This image is the artist's _____, so copying
   it is _____.

   geistiges Eigentum; Raub-kopieren

30 This is clearly fake news, intended to _____.

   die öffentliche Meinung zu manipulieren

31 The story is basically true, but the way it is presented is _____ and
   even _____.

   irreführend; verleumderisch

Gerüchte; Anspielungen	**32** The newspaper article is just _____ and _____ : what are the facts?
virale Wirkung; skandalös	**33** Thanks to the _____ , the _____ news spread quickly.
Widerruf; unwahr	**34** The website published a _____ when the report turned out to be _____ .
Schlagzeile; reißerisch	**35** The _____ is quite _____ , don't you think?
aktuelle Themen; seriöse Tages-zeitungen	**36** For _____ , I always read one of the _____ .
Leitartikel; Sicht auf; provokativ	**37** I enjoy reading the _____ because its _____ politics is amusing and often _____ .
Qualität; Kommentare	**38** What do you think of the _____ of the political _____ in British newspapers?
offensichtliche (ideologische) Ausrichtung; ausführlich; Analyse(n)	**39** I think there is _____ , however there also good, _____ articles with interesting _____ .
Nachrichteninhalte; gedruckte Ausgabe	**40** Does the website have the same _____ as the _____ ?
Bezahlschranke; anspruchsvoll	**41** Yes, but only behind a _____ ; the free articles are much less _____ .

4 Technology and the environment

A Environmental issues

Feeding the world

In 1960 the Earth's human population was 3 billion; by 2050 it will be 9 billion. How can our planet feed that many people? This is a difficult question to answer. With a global population of 7 billion, we are already depleting our natural resources at an alarming rate. Deforestation is accelerating, farmland is being degraded and our oceans are being overfished.

Some see intensive farming methods as our best hope. Through the use of automation, synthetic chemicals and genetic engineering, the aim is to make agricultural production ever more efficient. Factory farms can produce more meat on less land. Others claim that organic, non-intensive methods are best, as they can produce healthier, more nutritious food and can regenerate ecosystems, rather than destroying them.

We may have to find new solutions. Large-scale livestock farming is one of the most damaging forms of food production. Will we satisfy consumers' demand for meat with farmed insects or artificial meat grown in the laboratory?

Expressions with 'farm(ing)'

to **farm** Landwirtschaft treiben, bebauen, züchten
farm Bauernhof, Farm, Zucht
farm animal Nutztier
farmer Landwirt/in, Bauer/Bäuerin
farmland Ackerland, Agrarflächen
factory farm Massentierhaltungs-betrieb, Mastbetrieb
intensive farming Intensivlandwirt-schaft, Intensivtierhaltung
livestock farming Tierhaltung, Viehwirtschaft
organic farming Öko-Landwirtschaft

CHECKPOINT *In English, please!*

a Unsere natürlichen Ressourcen werden abgebaut.
b Wie können wir die Entwaldung stoppen?
c Öko-Landwirtschaft ist gesünder, aber weniger effizient.
d Intensivlandwirtschaft zerstört Ökosysteme.

population [ˌpɒpjuˈleɪʃn]	*Bevölkerung*	v to **populate**
to **feed** [fiːd]	*ernähren*	≈ to **nourish**
to **deplete** [dɪˈpliːt]	*(Ressourcen) abbauen, erschöpfen*	N **depletion**
natural resources *pl* [ˌnætʃrəl rɪˈsɔːsɪz]	*Rohstoffe, natürliche Ressourcen*	≈ **raw materials**
at an alarming rate [əˈlɑːmɪŋ]	*in erschreckendem Tempo*	≈ **alarmingly fast**
deforestation [diːˌfɒrɪˈsteɪʃn]	*Entwaldung, Rodung, Abholzung*	v to **deforest**
to **accelerate** [əkˈseləreɪt]	*zunehmen, (schnell) ansteigen*	≈ to **speed up**
farmland [ˈfɑːmlænd]	*Ackerland, Agrarflächen*	≈ **agricultural land**
to **degrade** [dɪˈgreɪd]	*zerstören, erodieren*	N **degradation**
automation [ˌɔːtəˈmeɪʃn]	*Automatisierung*	v to **automate**
genetic engineering [dʒəˌnetɪk ˌendʒɪˈnɪərɪŋ]	*Gentechnik*	v to **engineer sth** *etw manipulieren*
agricultural [ægrɪˈkʌltʃərəl]	*landwirtschaftlich*	N **agriculture**
organic [ɔːˈgænɪk]	*biologisch angebaut, Bio-, Öko-*	ADV **organically**
nutritious [njuˈtrɪʃəs]	*nahrhaft*	N **nutrition**
to **regenerate** [rɪˈdʒenəreɪt]	*regenerieren*	N **regeneration**
ecosystem [ˈiːkəʊsɪstəm]	*Ökosystem, Umwelt-*	*vgl.* **ecology** *Ökologie*
to **destroy** [dɪˈstrɔɪ]	*zerstören*	N **destruction**
		ADJ **destructive**
to **satisfy** [ˈsætɪsfaɪ]	*befriedigen*	N **satisfaction**
demand [dɪˈmɑːnd]	*Nachfrage*	≈ **requirement**
artificial [ˌɑːtɪˈfɪʃl]	*künstlich*	◄► **natural**
laboratory [ləˈbɒrətri]	*Labor*	ABBR **lab**

Protecting biodiversity

From time to time, life on Earth undergoes a mass extinction, when almost all life forms die out. So far, there have been five such events in the history of our planet. Scientists believe that a sixth mass extinction may be happening right now. This time, the cause is not a natural disaster, but the actions of one species: homo sapiens.

The world's last great biodiversity hotspots are under threat – tropical rainforests are being cut down, coral reefs are dying. While a few invasive plant and animal species benefit from human activity, the overall diversity in the world around us is decreasing measurably.

This is a problem not just for 'the environment', but for human beings as well. The hundreds of millions of types of living organism on our planet perform vital ecosystem services which provide us with food, breathable air and drinkable water.

How can we conserve these other organisms? Does the answer lie in better protection for endangered species, in more national parks and stricter fishing quotas? Or are more fundamental changes required?

Expressions with 'environmental'

environmental awareness Umwelt-
bewusstsein
environmental conservation
Umweltschutz
environmental law Umweltrecht
environmental preservation
Umweltschutz
environmental protection Umweltschutz

Word family 'invade'

to **invade** eindringen
invader Eindringling, Invasor
invasion Eindringen, Ausbreitung
invasive invasiv

biodiversity [ˌbaɪədaɪˈvɜːsɪti]	*Artenvielfalt, Biodiversität*	ADJ **biodiverse**
mass extinction [ˌmæs ɪkˈstɪŋkʃn]	*Massensterben (von Arten)*	*vgl.* to **become extinct** *aussterben*
life form [ˈlaɪf fɔːm]	*Lebensform*	≈ **living creature**
natural disaster [ˌnætʃrəl dɪˈzɑːstə]	*Naturkatastrophe*	ADJ **disastrous**
species [ˈspiːʃiːz]	*Art*	
to **be under threat** [ˈθret]	*bedroht sein*	≈ to **be threatened**
rainforest [ˈreɪnfɒrɪst]	*Regenwald*	
coral reef [ˌkɒrəl ˈriːf]	*Korallenriff*	
to **benefit from sth** [ˈbenɪfɪt]	*von etw profitieren*	◆◗ to **be damaged by sth**
diversity [daɪˈvɜːsəti]	*Vielfalt*	◆◗ **lack of diversity**
measurably [ˈmeʒərəbli]	*deutlich, messbar*	V to **measure**
environment [ɪnˈvaɪrənmənt]	*Umwelt*	ADJ **environmental**
human being [ˌhjuːmən ˈbiːɪŋ]	*Mensch*	≈ **human**
to **perform a service** [pəˌfɔːm ə ˈsɜːvɪs]	*einen Dienst leisten, eine Leistung erbringen*	N **performance**
vital [ˈvaɪtl]	*wichtig, unverzichtbar*	≈ **essential**
breathable air [ˈbriːðəbl]	*Atemluft*	V to **breathe**
to **conserve sth** [kənˈsɜːv]	*etw bewahren, etw schützen*	N **conservation**
endangered [ɪnˈdeɪndʒəd]	*(vom Aussterben) bedroht*	V to **endanger**
fishing quota [ˈfɪʃɪŋ kwəʊtə]	*Fangquote*	*vgl.* **fishing** *Fischerei*, **trawling** *Schleppnetzfischerei*
fundamental [ˌfʌndəˈmentl]	*grundsätzlich, grundlegend*	◆◗ **superficial, minor**

The **greenhouse effect** and **climate change**

The Earth has a natural temperature control system, which we call the greenhouse effect. The greenhouse gases, including carbon dioxide and methane, are an important part of this control system.

About one third of the solar radiation which reaches the Earth's surface is reflected back into space. Of the rest, most is absorbed by the land and oceans, which warm as a result. Some of this heat is emitted as infrared radiation. However, much of this infrared radiation cannot escape into space, as the greenhouse gases trap it, warming the atmosphere. That's a good thing for life on Earth: without the greenhouse effect, the Earth's average global temperature would be -18°C – too cold for life.

In recent centuries, however, human activities have caused the concentration of greenhouse gases to increase, e.g. through burning fossil fuels. This is enhancing the greenhouse effect, causing global warming. Predictions indicate that by the mid-21st century the Earth's global temperature may be 2–3°C warmer than at the beginning of the Industrial Age.

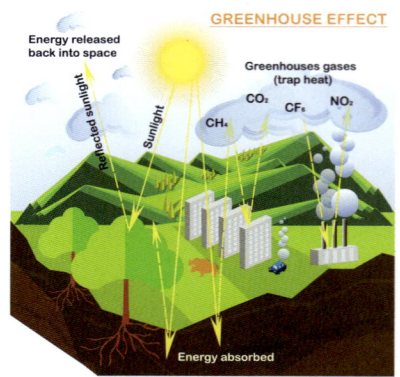

GREENHOUSE EFFECT

Energy released back into space

Greenhouses gases (trap heat)

CO_2 CF_4 NO_2

Reflected sunlight

Sunlight

CH_4

Energy absorbed

CHECKPOINT   *In English, please!*

a Der Treibhauseffekt ist das natürliche Temperaturregelungssystem der Erde.
b Die Treibhausgasemissionen steigen weiter an.
c Die Erderwärmung wird durch menschliches Handeln verursacht.
d Fossile Brennstoffe verstärken den Treibhauseffekt.

greenhouse effect ['gri:nhaʊs ɪfekt]	*Treibhauseffekt*	
climate change ['klaɪmət tʃeɪndʒ]	*Klimawandel*	v to **change the climate**
greenhouse gas [ˌgri:nhaʊs 'gæs]	*Treibhausgas*	
carbon dioxide [ˌkɑ:bən daɪ'ɒksaɪd]	*Kohlendioxid*	ABBR CO_2 vgl. **carbon footprint** *CO_2-Bilanz*
methane ['mi:θeɪn]	*Methan*	ABBR CH_4
solar radiation [ˌsəʊlə reɪdi'eɪʃn]	*Sonnen(ein)strahlung*	v to **radiate**
surface ['sɜ:fɪs]	*Oberfläche*	
to **reflect** [rɪ'flekt]	*reflektieren, spiegeln*	N **reflection** ADJ **reflective**
to **absorb** [əb'sɔ:b]	*absorbieren, aufnehmen*	N **absorption**
heat [hi:t]	*Hitze*	v to **heat (up)**
to **emit** [ɪ'mɪt]	*abgeben, emittieren*	N **emission**
infrared [ˌɪnfrə'red]	*infrarot*	◊ **ultraviolet**
to **escape** [ɪ'skeɪp]	*entweichen*	N **escape**
to **trap** [træp]	*einschließen*	≈ to **capture**
to **burn** [bɜ:n]	*verbrennen*	N **burning, combustion**
fossil fuel ['fɒsl fju:əl]	*fossiler Brennstoff*	vgl. **coal** *Kohle*, **oil** *Öl*, **natural gas** *Erdgas*
to **enhance** [ɪn'hɑ:ns]	*verstärken*	N **enhancement**
global warming [ˌgləʊbl 'wɔ:mɪŋ]	*Erderwärmung*	v to **warm** ◊ to **cool**
prediction [prɪ'dɪkʃn]	*Vorhersage, Prognose*	v to **predict**

The war on waste

Sustainable development meets our needs without compromising the ability of future generations to do the same. Unfortunately, many aspects of our society are unsustainable, including how we deal with waste.

Disposal of plastics is difficult because of their persistence – they may break down into smaller pieces, but they remain in the environment. They enter the food chain when animals mistake them for food. Landfill sites fail to contain plastics, which spill out into waterways. Incineration produces toxic gases. Recycling is technically possible but not always economically viable.

E-waste is another growing problem. Electronic devices contain toxic materials, alongside valuable ones such as copper and gold. Recovery of the valuable materials is often left to workers in developing countries, using methods which result in pollution and health problems.

By increasing consumer awareness of the problems and promoting recycling, hopefully it will be possible to change consumption habits and make progress towards a more sustainable way of life.

Expressions with 'pollution'

to **cause pollution** Umwelt-verschmutzung verursachen
to **reduce pollution** Umwelt-verschmutzung verringern
source of pollution Verschmutzungs-quelle
air pollution Luftverschmutzung
light pollution Lichtverschmutzung
noise pollution Lärmbelastung
soil pollution Bodenverschmutzung
water pollution Wasserverschmut-zung

Expressions with 'waste'

waste disposal Müll-/Abfall-entsorgung
waste separation Mülltrennung
to **generate waste** Müll/Abfall erzeugen
biodegradable waste biologisch abbaubarer Abfall, Biomüll
household waste Hausmüll

CHECKPOINT
In English, please!

a Wie können wir mit Plastik- und Elektronikmüll auf nachhaltige Weise umgehen?
b Wir können wertvolle Rohstoffe durch Recycling rückgewinnen.
c Wir müssen unsere Konsumgewohnheiten ändern.

waste [weɪst]	*Müll, Abfall*	V to **waste**, ADJ **wasteful**
sustainable development [sə,steɪnəbl dɪˈveləpmənt]	*nachhaltige Entwicklung*	ADV **sustainably** *nachhaltig, auf nachhaltige Weise*
to **compromise sth** [ˈkɒmprəmaɪz]	*einer Sache schaden, etw kompromittieren*	N **compromise**
to **deal with sth** [ˈdiːl]	*mit etw umgehen, etw bewältigen*	≈ to **handle**
disposal [dɪˈspəʊzl]	*Entsorgung*	V to **dispose of**
plastic [ˈplæstɪk]	*Kunststoff*	ADJ **plastic**
persistence [pəˈsɪstəns]	*Beständigkeit, Langlebigkeit, Persistenz*	ADJ **persistent**
to **break down** [ˈbreɪk]	*zerfallen, sich zersetzen*	≈ to **decompose**
food chain [ˈfuːd tʃeɪn]	*Nahrungskette*	*vgl.* **food web** *Nahrungsnetz*
to **spill out** [ˈspɪl]	*austreten, (aus etw) fließen*	≈ to **be emitted**
incineration [ɪn,sɪnəˈreɪʃn]	*Verbrennung*	V to **incinerate**
toxic [ˈtɒksɪk]	*giftig, toxisch*	≈ **poisonous**
technical(ly) [ˈteknɪkl]	*technisch*	*vgl.* **technological**
economically viable [iːkə,nɒmɪkli ˈvaɪəbl]	*wirtschaftlich tragbar, rentabel*	N **economic viability**
e-waste [ˈiː weɪst]	*Elektronikschrott, Elektromüll*	= **electronic waste**
valuable [ˈvæljuəbl]	*wertvoll*	N **value**
recovery [rɪˈkʌvəri]	*Rückgewinnung*	V to **recover** *rückgewinnen*
pollution [pəˈluːʃn]	*Umweltverschmutzung*	V to **pollute**, N **pollutant**
consumer awareness [kənˈsjuːmər əweənəs]	*Aufmerksamkeit/Bewusstsein der Verbraucher*	V to **be aware of**
consumption habits *pl* [kənˈsʌmpʃn hæbɪts]	*Konsumgewohnheiten*	V to **consume**
to **make progress towards sth** [ˈprəʊgres]	*Fortschritte in Richtung von etw machen*	≈ to **progress towards**

B Technological progress

Privacy vs surveillance

Thanks to the latest technology, governments and other organizations have an unprecedented amount of information about us. We mostly accept this in return for greater safety and convenience.

When we use the internet, it is convenient to have a 'seamless' experience across different websites. Websites install cookies on our devices and track us, so that they can offer us more of the content we like. However, this data can also be used in less innocuous ways, to provide information to organizations about our online activity.

CCTV monitoring in city centres reduces crime. However, face recognition and other biometric technology allows cameras to do more than watch for illegal activity. They could keep track of our movements, and combine this with our online behaviour and all our personal data.

This may seem like science fiction, but China is already using surveillance technology to trial a system which gives citizens points for 'good' behaviour. Fewer points results in fewer privileges, e.g. no internet access.

CHECKPOINT
In English, please!

a Sollen wir Überwachung akzeptieren, um mehr Sicherheit zu erhalten?
b Videoüberwachung reduziert Kriminalität, aber auch die Privatsphäre.
c Gesichtserkennung gestattet der Regierung, unsere Bewegungen zu verfolgen.

Expressions with 'surveillance'

data surveillance Datenüberwachung
electronic surveillance elektronische Überwachung
surveillance technology Überwachungstechnik
video surveillance Videoüberwachung
to **be under surveillance** überwacht werden
to **have/keep sb/sth under surveillance** jdn/etw überwachen

Expressions with 'technology'

latest technology modernste/neueste Technik
cutting-edge technology Spitzentechnologie, zukunftsweisende Technologie
technological progress technischer Fortschritt

privacy ['prɪvəsi]	*Privatsphäre*	ADJ **private**
surveillance [sɜːˈveɪləns]	*Überwachung*	→ *Kasten links*
unprecedented [ʌnˈpresɪdentɪd]	*beispiellos, (noch) nie dagewesen*	
in return for sth [rɪˈtɜːn]	*als Gegenleistung für etw, um etw zu erhalten*	≈ **in exchange for**
safety [ˈseɪfti]	*Sicherheit*	≈ **security**
convenience [kənˈviːniəns]	*Annehmlichkeit(en), Komfort*	ADJ **convenient**
seamless [ˈsiːmləs]	*nahtlos*	
to **track** [træk]	*verfolgen*	≈ to **trace**
innocuous [ɪˈnɒkjuəs]	*unschädlich, harmlos*	≈ **harmless**
CCTV monitoring [ˈmɒnɪtərɪŋ]	*Videoüberwachung*	V to **monitor** (≠ to **control** *regulieren, steuern*)
crime [kraɪm]	*Kriminalität*	ADJ **criminal** N **criminal**
face recognition [ˈfeɪs rekəgnɪʃn]	*Gesichtserkennung*	V to **recognize**
biometric [ˌbaɪəʊˈmetrɪk]	*biometrisch*	N **biometrics**
to **keep track of sb/sth** [ˌkiːp ˈtræk]	*jdn/etw verfolgen, jdn/etw im Auge behalten*	≈ to **track**, to **trace**
to **combine** [kəmˈbaɪn]	*verbinden, kombinieren*	N **combination**
behaviour [bɪˈheɪvjə]	*Verhalten*	V to **behave**
personal data [ˌpɜːsənl ˈdeɪtə]	*persönliche Daten, personenbezogene Daten*	≈ **personal information**
to **trial** [ˈtraɪəl]	*testen, einem Test unterziehen*	N **trial**
privilege [ˈprɪvəlɪdʒ]	*Privileg, Sonderrecht, Recht*	ADJ **privileged**

Robots and automation

Specialized robots perform both <u>repetitive</u> and <u>delicate</u> tasks in industry but have a narrow range of functions and limited mobility. The latest multipurpose robots, on the other hand, can perform most physical activities that humans can. They can run, jump, climb stairs and open doors. Their <u>agility</u>, speed, <u>strength</u> and dexterity will quickly <u>surpass</u> that of human beings. The potential military applications are frightening. However, multipurpose robots can also look after us, filling the gap in aged care, for example, as fewer young people work in care homes.

Flying robots – <u>drones</u> – are widely used in military and civilian applications. Basic drones are now very affordable for the hobbyist and require little <u>skill</u> to fly. Self-driving cars will soon be a common sight on our roads.

Advances in artificial intelligence mean that robots will be able to go about their day-to-day work without human input. When we need to <u>interact with</u> them, we will be able to use natural language as if we are talking to another human being.

CHECKPOINT	*In English, please!*

a Dies ist kein spezialisierter Roboter, sondern ein Mehrzweck-Roboter.
b Er kann sich wiederholende Aufgaben ausführen, die viel Geschicklichkeit verlangen.
c Es erfordert nicht viel Geschick, diese Drohne zu fliegen.

Word family 'repeat'

to **repeat** wiederholen
repetition Wiederholung
<u>**repetitive**</u> sich wiederholend, monoton
repetitiveness Wiederholung, Wiederholbarkeit

Dimensions and 'strength'

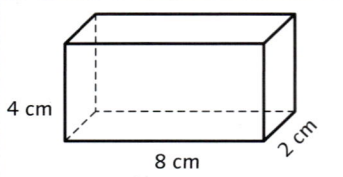

length Länge
8 cm long 8 cm lang
height [hʌɪt] Höhe
4 cm high 4 cm hoch
width/depth Breite/Tiefe
2 cm wide/deep 2 cm breit/tief

strength Stärke
strong stark

robot ['rəʊbɒt]	*Roboter*	ADJ **robotic**
repetitive [rɪ'petətɪv]	*sich wiederholend, monoton*	→ *Kasten links*
delicate ['delɪkət]	*fein, heikel*	N **delicacy**
multipurpose [ˌmʌlti'pɜːpəs]	*Mehrzweck-, Multifunktions-*	⟨⟩ **single-purpose**
agility [ə'dʒɪləti]	*Beweglichkeit*	ADJ **agile**
strength [streŋθ]	*Stärke*	⟨⟩ **weakness** → *Kasten links*
dexterity [dek'sterɪti]	*Geschicklichkeit*	ADJ **dextrous**
to **surpass** [sə'pɑːs]	*übertreffen*	≈ to **exceed**
military ['mɪlətri]	*militärisch, Militär-*	
application [ˌæplɪ'keɪʃn]	*Anwendung*	V to **apply sth to sth**
aged care ['eɪdʒd keə]	*Altenpflege*	*vgl.* **the aged** *alte Menschen*
care home ['keə həʊm]	*Pflegeheim*	≈ **nursing home**
drone [drəʊn]	*Drohne*	
civilian [sə'vɪliən]	*zivil, Zivil-*	N **civilian** *Zivilist/in*
hobbyist ['hɒbɪɪst]	*Laie*	≈ **amateur enthusiast**
skill [skɪl]	*Kenntnisse, Geschick*	ADJ **skilful**
self-driving [ˌself 'draɪvɪŋ]	*selbstfahrend*	
advance [əd'vɑːns]	*Fortschritt*	≈ **progress**
artificial intelligence [ɑːtɪˌfɪʃl ɪn'telɪdʒəns]	*künstliche Intelligenz*	ABBR **AI**
human input [ˌhjuːmən 'ɪnpʊt]	*menschliche Einflussnahme*	V to **input**
to **interact with sb/sth** [ˌɪntər'ækt]	*mit jdm/etw kommunizieren*	N **interaction**, ADJ **interactive**

Industry 4.0

Industry 4.0 is the 'fourth industrial revolution' in manufacturing technologies. It is based on four principles.

- Interconnection: Machines and people connect to and communicate with each other.
- Information transparency: Operators have access to data from all stages in the industrial process.
- Technical assistance: Systems support human decision-making by collecting and visualizing the data. Robots physically support humans by performing tasks that are unpleasant, tiring or unsafe for humans.
- Decentralized decisions: Robots make decisions on their own and work autonomously. Only when exceptions or problems arise are decisions delegated to a higher level.

For industry 4.0 to be successful, advances in supporting technologies are needed: e.g. the Internet of Things, cloud computing and artificial intelligence. Challenges include IT security issues (hacking, bugs, etc.), the potential job losses to automation and the difficulty of democratic oversight and control. There is also the fundamental question: how will society benefit?

The prefix 'inter-'

interactive interaktiv
interchangeable austauschbar
interconnection Kopplung, Vernetzung
to interconnect koppeln, vernetzen
interface Schnittstelle, Verbindung

'principle' – 'principal'

principle Prinzip, Grundsatz
principal Haupt-
principal AE Schulleiter/in

CHECKPOINT   *In English, please!*

a Welche Vorteile wird das Internet der Dinge bringen?
b Roboter werden Aufgaben ausführen, die für Menschen zu ermüdend oder gefährlich sind.
c Sie werden selbstständig arbeiten, ohne Beaufsichtigung durch uns.
d Wird die Automatisierung Sicherheitsprobleme verursachen?

manufacturing [ˌmænjuˈfæktʃərɪŋ]	*Fertigung, Herstellung*	V to **manufacture**
principle [ˈprɪnsəpl]	*Prinzip*	≈ **rule**
interconnection [ɪntəkəˈnekʃn]	*Kopplung, Vernetzung*	ADJ **interconnected**
to **connect to sb/sth** [kəˈnekt]	*sich in Verbindung mit jdm/sth setzen*	N **connection**
to **communicate with sb/sth** [kəˈmjuːnɪkeɪt]	*mit jdm/etw kommunizieren*	N **communication**
transparency [trænsˈpærənsi]	*Transparenz*	ADJ **transparent**
to **have access to sth** [ˈækses]	*Zugang zu etw haben, Zugriff auf etw haben*	→ *Siehe Kasten S. 78*
assistance [əˈsɪstəns]	*Hilfe*	V to **assist**
support [səˈpɔːt]	*Unterstützung, Hilfe*	V to **support**
decision-making [dɪˈsɪʒn meɪkɪŋ]	*Entscheidungsfindung, Entscheidungsprozess(e)*	V to **make/take a decision**
to **visualize** [ˈvɪʒuəlaɪz]	*sichtbar machen, veranschaulichen, visualisieren*	N **visualization**
unpleasant [ʌnˈpleznt]	*unangenehm*	N **unpleasantness**
tiring [ˈtaɪərɪŋ]	*ermüdend*	≈ **exhausting**
decentralized [ˌdiːˈsentrəlaɪzd]	*dezentral*	N **decentralization**
autonomous(ly) [ɔːˈtɒnəməs]	*unabhängig, selbstständig, autonom*	
to **delegate sth to sb/sth** [ˈdelɪgeɪt]	*etw an jdn/etw delegieren*	N **delegation**
security issues *pl* [sɪˈkjuərəti ɪʃuːz]	*Sicherheitsfragen, Sicherheitsprobleme*	ADJ **secure**
job losses *pl* [ˈdʒɒb lɒsɪz]	*Entlassungen, Stellenabbau*	≈ **redundancy, lay-off**
oversight [ˈəʊvəsaɪt]	*Aufsicht, Beaufsichtigung*	≈ **supervision**
to **benefit** [ˈbenɪfɪt]	*(von etw) profitieren*	N **benefit** *Vorteil, Nutzen*

C Energy

Replacing fossil fuels

Fossil fuels are a finite resource, and they are becoming harder and more expensive to find as existing supplies are used up. For this reason, energy companies are seeking to exploit sources which were previously uneconomic, such as fracking oil and gas from rocks and extracting oil from tar sands. Both of these practices bring many environmental risks.

Even more importantly, the search for new sources of oil and gas does nothing to address the main problem with fossil fuels: climate change. Burning fossil fuels emits carbon dioxide and other greenhouse gases into the atmosphere, and that drives climate change.

Fortunately, other technologies can use renewable sources to generate power. Wind turbines are one of the most widely used of these technologies: wind farms are now common in rural areas and offshore. Solar panels on roofs and in large solar farms harvest energy from the sun. Other clean, green technologies include biomass and geothermal, hydroelectric and tidal power generation.

CHECKPOINT	*In English, please!*

a Fracking bringt Umweltrisiken mit sich.
b Das Verbrennen fossiler Brennstoffe treibt den Klimawandel an.
c Solarmodule wandeln die Energie der Sonne in Strom um.

Expressions with 'power'

power plant Kraftwerk, Elektrizitätswerk
power station Kraftwerk, Elektrizitätswerk
power supply Stromversorgung
geothermal power Erdwärme
hydroelectric power Wasserkraft
nuclear power Kernkraft
tidal power Gezeitenkraft
wind power Windkraft

Word family 'replace'

to **replace** ersetzen, austauschen
replacement Ersatz, Austausch
replaceable ersetzbar, austauschbar
irreplaceable unersetzlich, nicht austauschbar

fossil fuel [ˈfɒsl fjuːəl]	fossiler Brennstoff	
finite resource [ˌfaɪnaɪt rɪˈsɔːs]	endliche Ressource	◀▶ renewable resource
to exploit [ɪkˈsplɔɪt]	(Rohstoff) abbauen, verwerten	N exploitation
uneconomic [ˌʌniːkəˈnɒmɪk]	unwirtschaftlich	≈ uneconomical, unprofitable
oil [ɔɪl]	Öl	vgl. crude oil Rohöl
to extract sth from sth [ɪkˈstrækt]	etw aus etw gewinnen, etw aus etw extrahieren	N extraction
tar sands pl [ˈtɑː sændz]	Teersand	≈ oil sands
environmental risk [ɪnvaɪrənˈmentl]	Umweltrisiko	ADJ environmentally risky
to address a problem [əˈdres]	ein Problem angehen	
climate change [ˈklaɪmət tʃeɪndʒ]	Klimawandel	≈ anthropogenic global warming (AGW)
to emit [ɪˈmɪt]	abgeben, ausstoßen, emittieren	N emission
renewable [rɪˈnjuːəbl]	erneuerbar	V to renew
to generate power [ˌdʒenəreɪt ˈpaʊə]	Strom erzeugen	N power generation
wind farm [ˈwɪnd fɑːm]	Windpark	vgl. wind turbine
offshore [ˌɒfˈʃɔː]	vor der Küste, Offshore-	◀▶ onshore
solar panel [ˌsəʊlə ˈpænl]	Solarmodul	≈ photovoltaic (PV) panel
to harvest [ˈhɑːvɪst]	ernten, sammeln	≈ to capture
biomass [ˈbaɪəʊmæs]	Biomasse	vgl. biofuel Biobrennstoff, Biokraftstoff
hydroelectric power [haɪdrəʊɪˌlektrɪk ˈpaʊə]	Wasserkraft	vgl. dam Staumauer, reservoir Stausee
tidal power [ˈtaɪdl paʊə]	Gezeitenkraft	N tide
power generation [ˈpaʊə dʒenəreɪʃn]	Stromerzeugung	N generator

The future of transport

In the 20th century, the car and the internal combustion engine symbolized mobility and freedom. Now new technologies and attitudes are challenging those ideas.

In motor vehicles, quiet, clean and mechanically simple electric motors are fast replacing noisy, polluting and complex petrol and diesel engines. With improvements in battery technology, range is less of a limiting factor. Recharging points are becoming common in our towns and cities, and increasingly also in service stations on motorways. Ideas about vehicle ownership are also changing, driven by ride-share services and self-driving vehicles. Some experts are confidently predicting that car ownership will die out, as self-driving taxis will offer the same convenience without the costs of ownership, maintenance and parking.

Rail transport has long been electrified in many countries. The last remaining fuel-guzzling transportation forms are aircraft and ships, both vital for the movement of freight. Will these also be electrified in the future?

CHECKPOINT   *In English, please!*

a Elektromotoren sind leiser und sauberer als Verbrennungsmotoren.
b Symbolisiert das Auto immer noch Mobilität und Freiheit?
c Selbstfahrende Autos sind dabei, unsere Vorstellungen von Autobesitz zu verändern.
d Ist der Schienenverkehr in diesem Land elektrifiziert?

internal combustion engine [ɪnˌtɜːnl kəmˈbʌstʃn endʒɪŋ]	*Verbrennungsmotor*	v to **combust** *(technisch)*
mobility [məʊˈbɪləti]	*Mobilität*	ADJ **mobile**
freedom [ˈfriːdəm]	*Freiheit*	ADJ **free**
motor vehicle [ˌməʊtə ˈviːəkl]	*Kraftfahrzeug*	
mechanical(ly) [mɪˈkænɪkl]	*mechanisch*	N **mechanics, mechanic** *(Person)*
petrol [ˈpetrəl]	*Benzin*	AE **gas(oline)**
range [reɪndʒ]	*Reichweite*	
limiting factor [ˌlɪmɪtɪŋ ˈfæktə]	*einschränkender Faktor, Einschränkung*	ADJ **limited**
recharging point [ˌriːˈtʃɑːdʒɪŋ pɔɪnt]	*Ladestation, Ladesäule*	v to **recharge**
service station [ˈsɜːvɪs steɪʃn]	*Tankstelle*	AE **gas station**
motorway BE [ˈməʊtəweɪ]	*Autobahn*	AE **highway, freeway, expressway**
ownership [ˈəʊnəʃɪp]	*Besitz, Haltung*	N **owner**
ride-share service [ˈraɪd ʃeə sɜːvɪs]	*Mitfahragentur*	
self-driving vehicle [self ˌdraɪvɪŋ ˈviːəkl]	*selbstfahrendes Fahrzeug*	≈ **autonomous vehicle**
maintenance [ˈmeɪntənəns]	*Wartung, Instandhaltung*	v to **maintain**
rail transport [ˈreɪl trænspɔːt]	*Schienenverkehr*	*vgl.* **train** *Zug, Bahn*
electrified [ɪˈlektrɪfaɪd]	*elektrifiziert*	→ *Kasten links*
fuel-guzzling [ˈfjuːəl gʌzlɪŋ]	*spritfressend*	◆ **economical to run**
aircraft [ˈeəkrɑːft]	*Flugzeug*	≈ **airplane**
vital [ˈvaɪtl]	*unverzichtbar*	≈ **essential**
movement of freight [ˌmuːvmənt əf ˈfreɪt]	*Frachttransport, Güterverkehr*	≈ **movement of goods**

Nuclear energy

Nuclear fission power plants have been generating electricity since the 1950s and are a proven technology, used in over 30 countries around the world. Despite safety concerns, serious accidents have been relatively rare. Nevertheless, a few catastrophic incidents, such as the meltdowns at Chernobyl and Fukushima and the major leak at Three Mile Island, have shaken public confidence in nuclear power.

Nuclear power plants produce no CO_2 and little waste, but critics of nuclear power point out that the highly radioactive waste that the plants produce is very difficult to dispose of safely. Another concern is the cost of decommissioning obsolete plants: it costs billions of euros to remove a single nuclear power plant.

Nuclear fusion is a different matter, as it does not result in highly radioactive byproducts (although a nuclear fusion power plant may result in some radioactive waste). Nuclear fusion is the energy which powers the sun, and has been used in hydrogen bombs, but unfortunately it is difficult to harness it for power generation. There is an old joke that a working nuclear fusion plant is 'always 30 years in the future'.

CHECKPOINT	*In English, please!*

a Kernkraft ist eine bewährte Technologie.
b Es ist sehr schwierig, hochradioaktiven Müll zu entsorgen.
c Das Kraftwerk ist veraltet und muss stillgelegt werden.

Expressions with 'nuclear'

nuclear accident Reaktorunfall
nuclear catastrophe Reaktor-
  katastrophe
nuclear energy Kernkraft
nuclear fission Kernspaltung
nuclear fusion Kernfusion
nuclear power Kernkraft

Big numbers

million ['mɪljən] Million
billion ['bɪljən] Milliarde
trillion ['trɪljən] Billion

Word family 'prove'

to **prove** beweisen, nachweisen
to **disprove** widerlegen
proven bewährt
proof Beweis, Nachweis
proof (against sth) beständig (gegen etw), sicher (vor etw)

122

4

nuclear energy [ˌnjuːkliə ˈenədʒi]	Kernkraft	≈ nuclear power
nuclear fission [ˌnjuːkliə ˈfɪʃn]	Kernspaltung	→ Kasten links
power plant [ˈpaʊə plɑːnt]	Kraftwerk	≈ power station
to generate [ˈdʒenəreɪt]	erzeugen	N generation N generator
proven [ˈpruːvn]	bewährt	◁▷ unproven, experimental → Kasten links
technology [tekˈnɒlədʒi]	Technologie, Technik	! ≠ technique
safety concerns pl [ˈseɪfti kənsɜːn]	Sicherheitsbedenken	≈ safety worry
accident [ˈæksɪdənt]	Unfall	! ADJ accidental zufällig
catastrophic [ˌkætəˈstrɒfɪk]	katastrophal	≈ disastrous
to shake public confidence in sth [ˌpʌblɪk ˈkɒnfɪdəns]	das Vertrauen der Bevölkerung in etw erschüttern	◁▷ to boost public confidence
highly radioactive [ˌhaɪli reɪdɪəʊˈæktɪv]	hochradioaktiv	◁▷ mildly radioactive
to dispose of sth [dɪˈspəʊz əv]	etw entsorgen	N disposal
to decommission [diːkəˈmɪʃn]	stilllegen	N decommissioning
obsolete [ˈɒbsəliːt]	veraltet	N obsolescence
nuclear fusion [ˌnjuːkliə ˈfjuːʒn]	Kernfusion	V to fuse
to result in sth [rɪˈzʌlt ɪn]	etw zur Folge haben	N result
byproduct [ˈbaɪprɒdʌkt]	Nebenprodukt	vgl. waste product Abfallprodukt
to power [ˈpaʊə]	mit Energie versorgen, antreiben	N power
hydrogen bomb [ˈhaɪdrədʒən bɒm]	Wasserstoffbombe	vgl. atom(ic) bomb
to harness (sth for sth) [ˈhɑːnɪs]	(etw für etw) nutzen	≈ to make use of sth

D Biotechnology

Genetic engineering

Genetic engineering is the direct manipulation of an organism's genes using biotechnology. It is not one technology but a set of technologies, which can be used to change the genetic makeup of cells.

Humans have manipulated the genes of animals and plants for thousands of years through selective breeding, but genetic engineering is a new and more targeted approach. It involves either removing or introducing DNA. It can transfer genes both within a species and from one species to another, to produce improved or novel organisms.

Genetic engineering has applications in many fields, including medical research, healthcare, industrial biotechnology and agriculture. It can cure hereditary genetic diseases through gene therapy. Industrial applications of genetic engineering include manufacturing enzymes for detergents and food production.

Genetic engineering has the potential to make industry safer and cleaner. For example, genetically engineered microbes could be used to clean up oil spills and toxic waste, and make biofuels.

Word family 'gene'

gene Gen
genetic(ally) genetisch
genetics Genetik
genome Genom
transgenic transgen

Collocations with 'genetic(ally)'

genetic code genetischer Code
genetic disease Erbkrankheit
genetic disorder genetische Störung
genitic engineering Gentechnik
genetic fingerprint genetischer Fingerabdruck
genetic makeup genetischer Aufbau, genetische Ausstattung
genetically modified (GM) gentechnisch verändert, genmanipuliert

CHECKPOINT *In English, please!*

a Ist Gentechnik dasselbe wie selektive Zucht?
b Wir können Gene von einer Art auf eine andere übertragen.
c Gentechnisch veränderte Mikroben sind neuartige Organismen.
d Gentechnik findet im Gesundheitswesen Anwendung.

genetic engineering [dʒəˌnetɪk ˌendʒɪ'nɪərɪŋ]	*Gentechnik*	N genetic engineer
organism ['ɔːɡənɪzəm]	*Organismus*	≈ living thing
gene [dʒiːn]	*Gen*	→ Kasten links
set [set]	*Menge, Reihe*	≈ group
genetic makeup [dʒəˌnetɪk 'meɪkʌp]	*genetischer Aufbau, genetische Ausstattung*	→ Kasten links
selective breeding [sɪˌlektɪv 'briːdɪŋ]	*selektive Zucht, Zuchtwahl*	V to breed
targeted ['tɑːɡɪtɪd]	*gezielt*	N target
to transfer [trænsˈfɜː]	*übertragen*	N transfer
novel ['nɒvl]	*neuartig*	≈ new
application [ˌæplɪ'keɪʃn]	*Anwendung*	V to apply
medical research [ˌmedɪkl rɪ'sɜːtʃ]	*medizinische Forschung*	V to research
healthcare ['helθkeə]	*Gesundheitswesen*	vgl. medicine
agriculture ['æɡrɪkʌltʃə]	*Landwirtschaft*	ADJ agricultural
to cure [kjʊə]	*heilen*	N cure *Heilmittel, Therapie, Heilung*
hereditary disease [həˌredɪtri dɪ'ziːz]	*Erbkrankheit*	V to inherit
to manufacture [ˌmænju'fæktʃə]	*herstellen*	≈ to make
detergent [dɪ'tɜːdʒənt]	*Reinigungsmittel*	vgl. soap *Seife*
microbe ['maɪkrəʊb]	*Mikrobe*	ADJ microbial
to clean up [ˌkliːn 'ʌp]	*reinigen, säubern, sanieren*	N clean-up
oil spill ['ɔɪl spɪl]	*Ölverschmutzung, Ölpest*	V to spill
toxic waste [ˌtɒksɪk 'weɪst]	*Giftmüll*	vgl. biowaste *Bioabfall, Bioabfälle*
biofuel [ˌbaɪəʊ'fjuːəl]	*Biokraftstoff*	

GMOs

An organism created through genetic engineering is a genetically modified organism (GMO). The first GM animal was created in 1974. Genetically modified food has been sold since the release of a GM tomato in 1994.

GM crops have benefits for food production (e.g. pest resistance), but have also caused controversy. Early field trials were often destroyed by anti-GM activists. Although the scientific consensus is that current GM crops do not pose a risk to human health, GM food safety is still a major concern to many. GM food critics point out that there is still much that we do not know about the human digestive system.

Other concerns around GM crops and animals include the possibility that they will escape into the environment, where their impact is unknown and unpredictable, and the potential control of the global food supply by a small number of multinational companies, which own the intellectual property rights. Different countries have different regulatory systems for GMOs, with large differences between the EU and the USA, for example.

Word family 'active'

active aktiv
activist Aktivist/in
to **activate** aktivieren
activity Aktivität

Word family 'produce'

to **produce** erzeugen, herstellen, produzieren
produce (landwirtschaftliche) Erzeugnisse
producer Hersteller/in, Produzent/in
production Herstellung, Produktion
product Erzeugnis, Produkt
(un)productive (un)produktiv
productivity Produktivität

'safe' – 'save'

safe sicher, unbedenklich
to **save** retten, schützen, sparen

CHECKPOINT
In English, please!

a Finden Sie, dass gentechnisch veränderte Nahrungsmittel unbedenklich sind?
b Aktivisten wollen Feldversuche gentechnisch veränderter Pflanzen stoppen.
c Die Umweltfolgen sind unberechenbar.
d Ich möchte nicht, dass multinationale Konzerne die globale Nahrungsmittelversorgung kontrollieren.

genetically modified [dʒəˌnetɪkli ˈmɒdɪfaɪd]	*gentechnisch verändert, genmanipuliert*	ABBR **GM**
release [rɪˈliːs]	*Veröffentlichung, Freigabe*	v to **release**
crop [krɒp]	*Feldfrucht, Nutzpflanze*	
food production [ˈfuːd prədʌkʃn]	*Nahrungsmittelproduktion*	v to **produce** → *Kasten links*
pest resistance [ˈpest rɪzɪstəns]	*Schädlingsresistenz*	ADJ **pest resistant**
controversy [ˈkɒntrəvɜːsi]	*Auseinandersetzung(en), Streit*	ADJ **controversial**
field trial [ˈfiːld traɪəl]	*Feldversuch, praktische Erprobung*	v to **trial**
activist [ˈæktɪvɪst]	*Aktivist/in*	→ *Kasten links*
scientific consensus [saɪənˌtɪfɪk kənˈsensəs]	*wissenschaftlicher Konsens*	*vgl.* to **reach a consensus**
to **pose a risk to sth** [pəʊz]	*ein Risiko / eine Gefahr für etw darstellen, etw gefährden*	≈ to **endanger**
safety [ˈseɪfti]	*Sicherheit, Unbedenklichkeit*	◑ **danger**
concern [kənˈsɜːn]	*Sorge, Besorgnis*	≈ **worry**
to **escape** [ɪˈskeɪp]	*entweichen*	N **escape**
impact [ˈɪmpækt]	*Auswirkung(en), Folge(n)*	v to **impact on** *sich auf etw auswirken*
unpredictable [ˌʌnprɪˈdɪktəbl]	*unvorhersehbar, unberechenbar*	*vgl.* **unforeseen** *unvorhergesehen*
food supply [ˈfuːd səplaɪ]	*Nahrungsmittelversorgung*	v to **supply sb with sth** *jdn mit etw versorgen*
multinational company [mʌltiˌnæʃnəl ˈkʌmpəni]	*(multinationaler) Konzern*	
intellectual property rights *pl* [ɪntəˌlektʃʊəl ˈprɒpəti raɪts]	*Rechte des geistigen Eigentums*	
regulatory system [ˌregjələtri ˈsɪstəm]	*Kontrollsystem, Aufsicht*	v to **regulate**

Cloning

Cloning is the process of producing genetically identical copies of an organism. It is a process which happens both naturally (in plants, fungi and bacteria), and artificially in the laboratory.

Animals are currently cloned in laboratories (to produce identical organisms for experiments) and in livestock farming (to pass on desirable qualities to future generations of animals). The first and most famous cloned mammal was Dolly the sheep (1996–2003). However, cloned embryos still have a high failure rate.

The possibility of human cloning has raised ethical concerns. Several nations have passed legislation restricting or prohibiting it. On the other hand, therapeutic cloning could be beneficial, allowing laboratories to grow organs for patients who need a transplant and will otherwise die.

There is also the possibility of cloning extinct species from samples of DNA. So far, this is largely science fiction. Not only is it technically very difficult, it is also largely pointless, if the species' native habitat no longer exists.

Unusual plurals

fungus – fungi Pilz
nucleus – nuclei Kern
stimulus – stimuli Reiz
bacterium – bacteria Bakterium – Bakterien
curriculum – curricula Lehrplan
medium – media Medium – Medien

Word family 'benefit'

benefit Vorteil, Nutzen
to **benefit sb** jdm nützen
to **be of benefit to sb/sth** für jdn/etw von Nutzen sein
beneficial vorteilhaft, nützlich, positiv
beneficiary Nutznießer, Begünstigte/r

CHECKPOINT   *In English, please!*

a Die beiden Tiere sind genetisch identisch.
b Haben Sie moralische Bedenken bezüglich des Klonens von Menschen?
c Ich finde, es sollte eingeschränkt, jedoch nicht verboten werden.
d Klonen ist technisch schwierig und hat eine hohe Misserfolgsquote.

cloning ['kləʊnɪŋ]	Klonen	v to clone
genetically identical [dʒəˌnetɪkli aɪ'dentɪkl]	genetisch identisch	
artificially [ˌɑːtɪ'fɪʃli]	künstlich	⟨⟩ naturally
livestock ['laɪvstɒk]	Vieh, Nutztiere	≈ farm animal, domestic animal
mammal ['mæml]	Säugetier	
failure rate ['feɪljə reɪt]	Fehlquote, Misserfolgsquote	⟨⟩ success rate
human cloning [ˌhjuːmən 'kləʊnɪŋ]	Klonen von Menschen	≈ cloning of humans
ethical concerns pl [ˌeθɪkl kən'sɜːnz]	ethische/moralische Bedenken	v to be concerned
to pass legislation [ˌpɑːs ledʒɪs'leɪʃn]	Gesetze erlassen	≈ to pass laws
to restrict [rɪ'strɪkt]	einschränken	N restriction
to prohibit [prə'hɪbɪt]	verbieten	N prohibition
therapeutic [ˌθerə'pjuːtɪk]	therapeutisch	N therapy
N therapist (Person)
beneficial [ˌbenɪ'fɪʃl]	positiv, nützlich, vorteilhaft	→ Kasten links
organ ['ɔːgən]	Organ	vgl. organ donor Organspender/in
transplant ['trænsplɑːnt]	Transplantation	v to transplant
extinct [ɪk'stɪŋkt]	ausgestorben	N extinction
technically ['teknɪkli]	technisch	
pointless ['pɔɪntləs]	sinnlos, zwecklos	≈ useless
native habitat [ˌneɪtɪv 'hæbɪtæt]	natürlicher Lebensraum	≈ natural environment

TEST YOURSELF

You can check your answers on pp. 210–211.

1 How can our planet _____ a _____ of nine billion people?   *ernähren; Bevölkerung*

2 _____ rapidly since the Industrial Revolution.   *Rohstoffe sind abgebaut worden*

3 Farmland _____ thanks to many years of _____ .   *wurde erodiert; Intensivland-wirtschaft*

4 Is _____ food _____ than food which is grown with synthetic chemicals?   *Bio-; nahrhafter*

5 Would you eat _____ meat which had been grown in a _____ ?   *künstliches; Labor*

6 What more can we do to protect _____ hotspots which _____ ?   *Artenvielfalts-; bedroht sind*

7 Five _____ on Earth have been caused by _____ .   *Massensterben; Naturkatastro-phen*

8 _____ depend on the _____ to perform _____ services.   *Menschen; Umwelt; unver-zichtbar*

9 While _____ die out, invasive plants and animals _____ human activity.   *bedrohte Arten; profitieren von*

10 The _____ is natural, but human activities _____ it.   *Treibhauseffekt; verstärken*

Kohlendioxid und Methan;
Klimawandel

11 Increased levels of _____ in
the atmosphere are causing _____.

fossile Brennstoffe zu
verbrennen; Erderwärmung

12 We need to stop _____ if we want to control
_____.

mit Müll umgeht; nachhaltig

13 The way our society _____ is not _____.

Kunststoffe; Beständigkeit

14 _____ are a problem because of their _____
in the environment.

Rückgewinnung; wertvoll;
technisch

15 _____ of _____ materials from e-waste is
_____ possible.

Bewusstsein der Verbraucher;
Konsumgewohnheiten

16 Hopefully by increasing _____ we can change
_____.

verfolgen; Verhalten

17 I don't want my electronic devices to _____ my online
_____.

Gesichtserkennungs-; harmlos

18 Do you think that the use of _____ technology is
_____?

Videoüberwachung; Sicherheit;
Kriminalität

19 _____ may increase our _____ and
reduce _____.

Überwachung; beispiellos

20 The level of _____ in today's society is _____
in democratic societies.

Roboter; monoton

21 _____ have replaced human workers for many _____ tasks.

22 This _____ has impressive _____ and _____.

Mehrzweckroboter; Beweglichkeit; Stärke

23 Will it be used in _____ or in _____ applications?

militärisch; zivil

24 Thanks to _____, _____ cars won't need _____.

künstliche Intelligenz; selbstfahrende; menschliche Einflussnahme

25 Will automation lead to _____ and IT _____?

Stellenabbau; Sicherheitsprobleme

26 The system functions _____ and _____ its human operators.

selbstständig; kommuniziert mit

27 Advanced _____ systems support human _____ by collecting and visualizing data.

Fertigungs-; Entscheidungsprozesse

28 There are offshore _____ which can _____ many gigawatts of _____.

Windparks; erzeugen; Strom

29 We need to replace _____ in order to _____ of climate change.

fossile Brennstoffe; das Problem anzugehen

30 _____ are a relatively clean, green technology but their manufacture brings _____.

Solarmodule; Umweltrisiken

31 Oil companies want to _____ new sources of oil and gas which used to be _____.

verwerten; unwirtschaftlich

32 Will electric motors completely replace the _____ in _____?

Verbrennungsmotor; Kraftfahrzeuge

Ladestationen; Tankstellen	**33**	We need more _____ in motorway _____ .
Flugzeuge; unverzichtbar; Frachttransport	**34**	_____ and ships are both _____ for the _____ over long distances.
Reichweite; Einschränkung	**35**	As battery technology improves, _____ won't be a _____ for electric cars.
Sicherheitsbedenken; Kernkraft	**36**	There are a lot of serious _____ about _____ .
Kernfusion zu nutzen	**37**	It is proving difficult to _____ for power generation.
genetischen Aufbau; übertragen	**38**	Is it safe to alter the _____ of organisms and _____ genes to new species?
Gentechnik; medizinische Forschung	**39**	_____ has important applications in _____ and healthcare.
Nahrungsmittelproduktion; Sicherheit; Sorge	**40**	GM crops promise benefits for _____ but their _____ is still a major _____ to consumers.
wissenschafticher Konsens; stellen keine Gefahr für … dar	**41**	The _____ is that GM crops _____ human health.
ethische Bedenken; Klonen von Menschen	**42**	Are there _____ about the possibility of _____ ?
Organe; Transplantation	**43**	Laboratories could grow _____ for patients who need a _____ .
ausgestorbene; technisch; sinnlos	**44**	Cloning _____ species from DNA samples is both difficult and _____ .

5 Society

A Social challenges

What is a multicultural society?

Most countries today are ethnically and culturally diverse. Yet they deal with that diversity differently. How a society deals with diversity reflects how its citizens and institutions see themselves. Attitudes may change rapidly when the country faces new challenges, e.g. a sudden growth in immigration.

A multicultural society is one which is not just diverse, but treats its various cultures with equal respect and views their diversity as positive. Other societies may be tolerant of diversity, but encourage social integration in line with its core values. Still others may expect assimilation of minorities into the majority culture. Some actively repress minorities.

Countries such as the USA and Australia have traditionally seen themselves as lands of opportunity, which welcomed immigrants. At the same time, there are elements of racism and xenophobia in these (and all) societies, often justified as a love of 'tradition'. Both immigrants and indigenous people have often experienced persecution.

Expressions with 'society'

affluent society Wohlstandsgesellschaft, Überflussgesellschaft
class society Klassengesellschaft
classless society klassenlose Gesellschaft
dog-eat-dog society Ellenbogengesellschaft
ethnically diverse society ethnisch vielfältige/heterogene Gesellschaft
multicultural society multiulturelle Gesellschaft

CHECKPOINT *In English, please!*

a Deutschland ist ethnisch und kulturell vielfältig.
b Toleranz ist einer unserer Grundwerte.
c Gibt es Länder in der EU, die Minderheiten unterdrücken?
d Indigene Menschen erleben oft Rassismus.

multicultural [ˌmʌltiˈkʌltʃərəl]	*multikulturell*	N **multiculturalism**
ethnically [ˈeθnɪkli]	*ethnisch*	ADJ **ethnic**, N **ethnicity** ! ≠ **ethically**
culturally [ˈkʌltʃərəli]	*kulturell*	ADJ **cultural**, N **culture**
diverse [daɪˈvɜːs]	*vielfältig, gemischt, heterogen*	◆▶ **uniform**
diversity [daɪˈvɜːsəti]	*Vielfalt, Diversität*	◆▶ **uniformity**
citizen [ˈsɪtɪzn]	*Bürger/in*	N **citizenship**
attitude [ˈætɪtjuːd]	*Einstellung, Haltung*	≈ **opinion, standpoint**
to **face a challenge** [ˈtʃælɪndʒ]	*eine schwierige Aufgabe zu bewältigen haben*	*vgl.* to **be challenged by sth** *mit etw konfrontiert werden*
to **be tolerant of sb/sth** [ˈtɒlərənt]	*jdn/etw tolerieren*	N **tolerance** *Toleranz*
to **encourage sth** [ɪnˈkʌrɪdʒ]	*etw fördern, etw begünstigen*	◆▶ **discourage**
core values *pl* [ˌkɔː ˈvæljuːz]	*Grundwerte*	V to **value sth**
assimilation [əˌsɪməˈleɪʃn]	*Assimilierung*	V to **assimilate**
minority [maɪˈnɒrəti]	*Minderheit*	ADJ **minor**
majority [məˈdʒɒrəti]	*Mehrheit*	ADJ **major**
to **repress** [rɪˈpres]	*unterdrücken*	N **repression**, ADJ **repressive**
opportunity [ˌɒpəˈtjuːnəti]	*Chance, Möglichkeit*	ADJ **opportune**
racism [ˈreɪsɪzəm]	*Rassismus*	ADJ **racist**
xenophobia [zenəˈfəʊbɪə]	*Fremdenfeindlichkeit*	ADJ **xenophobic**
to **justify** [ˈdʒʌstɪfaɪ]	*rechtfertigen*	N **justification**
indigenous [ɪnˈdɪdʒənəs]	*indigen, autochthon*	≈ **native**
persecution [ˌpɜːsɪˈkjuːʃn]	*Verfolgung*	*vgl.* to **experience persecution**

Are we all 'free and equal'?

According to the Universal Declaration of Human Rights, we are all 'born free and equal'. The Declaration, a historic document adopted by the United Nations in 1948, describes the rights that all human beings have in 30 articles. Articles 1–21 describe our civil and political rights. The rights listed include freedom from slavery and torture, the right to justice, the right to own property and the right to freedom of thought and expression. Articles 22–27 describe our economic, social and cultural rights. They include the right to work, the right to equal pay for equal work, the right to leisure and a standard of living adequate for health and well-being.

The Declaration has become part of international treaties, national constitutions and other legal documents. Yet we seem a long way from fully achieving those rights, even in wealthy, developed, democratic countries. Many people are unemployed and many live in poverty, in conditions which affect their health and well-being. Some are homeless. The distribution of wealth in society is very unequal, and wealth buys privilege – in other words, more 'rights'.

CHECKPOINT
In English, please!

a Obdachlos zu sein hat negativ Auswirkungen auf Gesundheit und Wohlbefinden.
b Meinungsfreiheit ist ein Recht, kein Privileg.
c Was können wir gegen die ungleiche Wohlstandsverteilung in der Gesellschaft tun?

Expressions with 'freedom'

freedom of expression Meinungsfreiheit, Redefreiheit
freedom of religion Religionsfreiheit,
  Glaubensfreiheit
freedom of speech Meinungsfreiheit, Redefreiheit
freedom of the press Pressefreiheit
freedom of thought Gedankenfrei-
  heit

Expressions with 'rights'

civil rights Bürgerrechte
cultural rights kulturelle Rechte
economic rights wirtschaftliche
  Rechte
human rights Menschenrechte
political rights politische Rechte
social rights soziale Rechte

Word family 'political'

political politisch
politics Politik, Politikwissenschaft
politician Politiker/in
apolitical unpolitisch

equal ['iːkwəl]	gleich	N equality
right [raɪt]	Recht	ADJ rightful
civil ['sɪvl]	Bürger-	vgl. civilian Zivilist/in
slavery ['sleɪvəri]	Sklaverei	v to enslave sb
torture ['tɔːtʃə]	Folter	v to torture sb
justice ['dʒʌstɪs]	Recht, Gerechtigkeit, Justiz	ADJ just
property ['prɒpəti]	Grundbesitz, Immobilie	≈ possessions
freedom ['friːdəm]	Freiheit	ADJ free, v to free (sb from sth)
economic [ˌiːkəˈnɒmɪk]	wirtschaftlich, ökonomisch	! ≠ economical sparsam
social ['səʊʃl]	gesellschaftlich, sozial	N society
standard of living [ˌstændəd əv 'lɪvɪŋ]	Lebensstandard	≈ living standards
adequate ['ædɪkwət]	hinreichend	N adequacy
health [helθ]	Gesundheit	ADJ healthy
well-being ['wel biːɪŋ]	Wohlbefinden, Wohl	vgl. welfare Wohlergehen; Sozialhilfe
to achieve sth [əˈtʃiːv]	etw erreichen, etw erlangen	N achievement, ADJ achievable
wealthy ['welθi]	wohlhabend, reich	≈ prosperous, rich
unemployed [ˌʌnɪmˈplɔɪd]	arbeitslos	N unemployment
to live in poverty ['pɒvəti]	in Armut leben	ADJ poor
homeless ['həʊmləs]	obdachlos	N homelessness
distribution of wealth [dɪstrɪˌbjuːʃn əv 'welθ]	Wohlstandsverteilung	v to distribute
privilege ['prɪvəlɪdʒ]	Privileg, Sonderrecht	ADJ privileged

Women's rights

Women have had to fight hard for social equality: the right to vote, the right to follow any career path they choose, equal pay for equal work, adequate legal protection against sexual assault and domestic violence, the right to terminate an unwanted pregnancy, the right to maternity leave.

In the countries of the European Union, these rights are mostly guaranteed, at least in theory, although the right to terminate a pregnancy varies from country to country. In practice, there are still many examples of gender imbalance in our societies. There is still a glass ceiling for women in many professions; women's careers still tend to suffer if they choose to have children; on average, women still do more than their fair share of household chores. The proportion of women who suffer sexual harassment and sexual violence is still distressingly high.

Many feminists (of both sexes) see the root cause as entrenched ideas about gender roles – in the home, in the workplace and in society. They claim that these continue to harm both men and women.

Word family 'equal'

equal ADJ gleich, N Gleichgestellte/r, Ebenbürtige/r
unequal ungleich
equality Gleichheit, Gleichberechtigung
to **equal** ergeben, gleichkommen
to **equalize** angleichen, ausgleichen

Expressions with 'gender'

gender bias geschlechtsspezifische Vorurteile
gender gap Kluft zwischen den Geschlechtern, Geschlechtergefälle
gender identity geschlechtliche Identität
gender imbalance Ungleichgewicht zwischen den Geschlechtern
gender role Geschlechterrolle
gender stereotyping geschlechtsspezifische Rollenklischees

CHECKPOINT   *In English, please!*

a Theoretisch ist das gut, aber in der Praxis gibt es ein Ungleichgewicht zwischen den Geschlechtern.
b In dieser Firma gibt es für weibliche Führungskräfte eine unsichtbare Barriere.
c Sie erledigt mehr als ihren gerechten Anteil an den Hausarbeiten.
d Viele ältere Menschen haben eingefahrene Vorstellungen von Geschlechterrollen.

to **fight for sth** [faɪt fə]	*um etw kämpfen*	**!** to **fight hard** (*nicht:* hardly)
to **vote** [vəʊt]	*wählen*	N **voting, suffrage** (formal)
to **follow a career path** [ˌfɒləʊ ə kəˈrɪə pɑːθ]	*eine berufliche Laufbahn einschlagen*	≈ to **pursue a career**
legal protection [ˌliːgl prəˈtekʃn]	*rechtlicher Schutz*	v to **protect** (sb against sth)
sexual assault [ˌsekʃuəl əˈsɔlt]	*sexuelle Gewalt, sexuelle(r) Übergriff(e)*	v to **assault sb sexually**
domestic violence [dəˌmestɪk ˈvaɪələns]	*häusliche Gewalt*	≈ **violence in the home**
to **terminate a pregnancy** [ˌtɜːmɪneɪt ə ˈpregnənsi]	*eine Schwangerschaft abbrechen*	≈ to **get an abortion**
maternity leave [məˈtɜːnəti liːv]	*Mutterschaftsurlaub*	*vgl.* **paternity leave, parental leave**
in practice [ɪn ˈpræktɪs]	*in der Praxis*	◆ **in theory** *theoretisch*
gender imbalance [ˈdʒendər ɪmˌbæləns]	*Ungleichgewicht zwischen den Geschlechtern*	≈ **sexual inequality**
glass ceiling [ˌglɑːs ˈsiːlɪŋ]	*gläserne Decke, (unsichtbare) Barriere*	
to **tend to do sth** [ˈtend]	*dazu neigen, etw zu tun*	N **tendency**
to **suffer** [ˈsʌfə]	*leiden, in Mitleidenschaft gezogen werden*	◆ to **benefit**
more than one's fair share [ˌfeə ˈʃeə]	*mehr als jds gerechter Anteil*	◆ **less than one's fair share**
household chores *pl* [ˌhaʊshəʊld ˈtʃɔːz]	*Hausarbeiten*	≈ **housework**
sexual harassment [ˌsekʃuəl ˈhærəsmənt]	*sexuelle Belästigung*	v to **harass sb sexually**
distressingly [dɪˈstresɪŋli]	*erschreckend*	N **distress**
root cause [ˈruːt kɔːz]	*Grundursache*	≈ **underlying cause**
entrenched [ɪnˈtrentʃt]	*tief verwurzelt, eingefahren*	≈ **deep-seated, persistent**
workplace [ˈwɜːkpleɪs]	*Arbeitsplatz*	**in the workplace** ≈ **at work**
to **harm sb** [hɑːm]	*jdm Schaden zufügen*	N **harm**

Gender identity and sexuality

Gender identity is an individual's sense of their own gender. It can correlate with their sex at birth, or can differ from it. In most traditional societies, there was a binary distinction between sexes: one could be either male or female.

Science does not support this belief: around one per cent of the population has biological intersex characteristics. Modern society recognizes that people may be transgender or gender fluid. Sex reassignment surgery and other treatment may be available to those that need it, and laws increasingly reflect a more flexible attitude towards gender identity.

Sexuality is a separate, but related issue. Until recently in many countries, heterosexuality was the only permissible sexual orientation. People who entered into homosexual relationships suffered persecution and social exclusion. Anthropologists now believe that there is a spectrum of sexuality, with individuals at different points on the scale. Sexuality may be fluid, i.e. an individual's sexuality may change over time.

Word family 'sex'
sex Geschlecht, Sex
sexual geschlechtlich, sexuell
sexuality Sexualität
bisexual bisexuell
heterosexual heterosexuell
homosexual homosexuell
intersex intersexuell
intersexual intersexuell

Word family 'permit'
to **permit** erlauben, genehmigen
permit Genehmigung, Lizenz, Erlaubnis(schein)
permission Genehmigung, Einverständnis
permissible gestattet, zulässig, erlaubt
impermissible unzulässig

CHECKPOINT
In English, please!

a Die Geschlechtsidentität einer Person entspricht möglicherweise nicht dem Geburtsgeschlecht.
b Operative Geschlechtsumwandlung steht Transgender-Personen zur Verfügung.
c Die sexuelle Orientierung sollte kein Grund für soziale Ausgrenzung sein.

identity [aɪ'dentəti]	*Identität*	v to **identify (with)**
sexuality [ˌsekʃu'æləti]	*Sexualität*	≈ **sexual feelings**
sense (of sth) ['sens]	*Bewusstsein (für etw)*	≈ **perception of**
to **correlate with sth** ['kɒrəleɪt]	*einer Sache entsprechen*	N **correlation** *Entsprechung*
sex at birth [bɜ:θ]	*Geburtsgeschlecht*	≈ **birth gender**
binary distinction [ˌbaɪnəri dɪ'stɪŋkʃn]	*ausschließlicher Gegensatz*	v to **distinguish**
to **support** [sə'pɔːt]	*untermauern, bekräftigen*	◀▶ to **refute**, to **disprove**
intersex characteristics *pl* [ˌɪntəseks ˌkærəktə'rɪstɪks]	*intersexuelle Merkmale*	ADJ **characteristic**
fluid ['fluːɪd]	*fließend*	N **fluidity** *Veränderlichkeit, Instabilität*
sex reassignment ['seks riːəˌsaɪnmnt]	*Geschlechtsumwandlung*	≈ **gender reassignment**
surgery ['sɜːdʒəri]	*Operation(en)*	N **surgeon** *Chirurg/in*
treatment ['triːtmənt]	*Behandlung*	v to **treat**
heterosexuality [ˌhetrəʊˌsekʃu'æliti]	*Heterosexualität*	ADJ **heterosexual**
permissible [pə'mɪsɪbl]	*gestattet, zulässig, erlaubt*	→ *Kasten links*
sexual orientation [ˌsekʃuəl ɔːriən'teɪʃn]	*sexuelle Orientierung*	v to **orient**
homosexual relationship [həʊməˌsekʃuəl rɪ'leɪʃnʃɪp]	*homosexuelle Beziehung*	N **homosexuality**
persecution [ˌpɜːsɪ'kjuːʃn]	*Verfolgung*	v to **persecute**
social exclusion [ˌsəʊʃl ɪk'skluːʒn]	*gesellschaftliche Ausgrenzung*	v to **exclude**
scale [skeɪl]	*Skala*	≈ **spectrum**
over time [ˌəʊvə 'taɪm]	*im Lauf der Zeit*	≈ **with (the passage of) time**

B Crime and terrorism

Capital punishment

Fifty-six countries around the world have the death penalty as a punishment for certain crimes, and 60 % of the world's population lives in those countries, which include the USA, India, Japan, China, Indonesia and most countries in the Middle East. Capital punishment is prohibited in the European Union by the Charter of Fundamental Rights.

The death penalty is a controversial issue. Public opinion varies by country and according to the crime involved. Abolitionists regard capital punishment as inhumane and a violation of human rights. They are also concerned about miscarriages of justice which lead to innocent people being convicted of capital crimes, and argue that a life sentence without parole is adequate punishment. Advocates of the death penalty, on the other hand, may claim that it deters crime and is a morally justified retribution in the case of murder.

In the USA there is a complex appeals process, which can lead to prisoners spending many years on Death Row in isolation and uncertainty.

CHECKPOINT	*In English, please!*

a Kein EU-Staat hat die Todesstrafe.
b Der Häftling erhielt eine lebenslängliche Freiheitsstrafe.
c Die Todesstrafe verhindert keine Straftaten.
d Unschuldige Menschen haben Jahre im Todestrakt verbracht.

'murder' – 'murderer'

murder Mord
murderer Mörder/in

Word family 'prison'

prison Gefängnis
prisoner Gefangene/r, Häftling
to **imprison sb** jdn inhaftieren
imprisonment Haft

capital punishment [ˌkæpɪtl ˈpʌnɪʃmənt]	Todesstrafe	v to punish
death penalty [ˈdeθ penlti]	Todesstrafe, Todesurteil	vgl. execution *Hinrichtung*
crime [kraɪm]	Verbrechen, Straftat(en)	ADJ criminal
to prohibit sth [prəˈhɪbɪt]	etw (gesetzlich) verbieten	N prohibition
controversial [ˌkɒntrəˈvɜːʃl]	umstritten	N controversy
public opinion [ˌpʌblɪk əˈpɪnɪən]	öffentliche Meinung	
abolitionist [ˌæbəˈlɪʃnɪst]	Gegner/in der Todesstrafe	v to abolish
inhumane [ɪnhjuˈmeɪn]	unmenschlich	◑ humane
violation [ˌvaɪəˈleɪʃn]	Verstoß, Verletzung	v to violate
miscarriage of justice [mɪsˌkærɪdʒ əv ˈdʒʌstɪs]	Justizirrtum, Fehlurteil	≈ wrongful conviction
innocent [ˈɪnəsnt]	unschuldig	N innocence
to convict sb of sth [kənˈvɪkt]	jdn wegen etw verurteilen	N conviction / ◑ to acquit, N acquittal
life sentence [ˈlaɪf sentəns]	lebenslängliche Freiheitsstrafe	vgl. to get a life sentence
parole [pəˈrəʊl]	Bewährung	vgl. to be out on parole
advocate [ˈædvəkət]	Befürworter/in	◑ opponent
to deter sth [dɪˈtɜː]	etw (durch Abschreckung) verhindern	N deterence
morally justified [ˌmɒrəli ˈdʒʌstɪfaɪd]	moralisch gerechtfertigt	N justification
retribution [retrɪˈbjuːʃn]	Vergeltung, Strafe	vgl. revenge *Rache*
appeal [əˈpiːl]	Berufung	v to appeal (against) a conviction
prisoner [ˈprɪznə]	Gefangene/r, Häftling	→ *Kasten links*
Death Row [ˌdeθ ˈrəʊ]	Todestrakt, Todeszelle	vgl. to be on Death Row

Gun control

Most democratic countries allow individuals to own <u>guns</u>, but strictly control ownership and use. Legitimate <u>civilian</u> uses of firearms include hunting, pest control, target shooting and in some countries, self-defence. People who want to own a gun must obtain a permit, which usually requires a thorough background check. Guns and ammunition must be stored securely. Police officers in many countries routinely carry guns and private security personnel may also be permitted to do so.

The USA is unusual in the freedom it gives citizens to buy, own, carry and use firearms, and the types of weapon which can legally be bought. The USA is also unusual in its high rate of gun-related crime and fatalities; mass shootings in schools and workplaces are relatively frequent. To observers outside the USA, it may be difficult to understand the resistance to effective gun control. A powerful pro-gun lobby plays a part, as does a strong libertarian tradition. The 'right to bear arms' is guaranteed in US law.

In English, please!

CHECKPOINT

a Schädlingsbekämpfung und Jagd sind legitime Verwendungen von Schusswaffen.
b Man benötigt eine gründliche Zuverlässigkeitsüberprüfung um einen Waffenschein zu bekommen.
c Ich finde nicht, dass private Sicherheitskräfte Waffen haben sollten.
d Warum ereignen sich so viele Amokläufe in den USA?

Expressions with 'gun'

gun Schusswaffe
gun control Reglementierung von Waffenbesitz
gunfight Schießerei, Schusswechsel
gunfire Schüsse
to gun sb down jdn niederschießen

Word family 'civil'

civil zivil, bürgerlich, Bürger-
civilian Zivilist/in, Zivil-
civilization Zivilisation
civilized zivilisiert

gun control [ˌɡʌn kənˈtrəʊl]	*Reglementierung von Waffenbesitz*	v to **control** *reglementieren*
ownership [ˈəʊnəʃɪp]	*Besitz*	N owner
legitimate [lɪˈdʒɪtɪmət]	*rechtmäßig, legitime*	◁▷ illegitimate
firearm [ˈfaɪərɑːm]	*Schusswaffe*	≈ gun
hunting [ˈhʌntɪŋ]	*Jagd, Jagen*	N hunter, v to hunt
pest control [ˈpest kəntrəʊl]	*Schädlingsbekämpfung*	v to **control** *bekämpfen*
target shooting [ˈtɑːɡɪt ʃuːtɪŋ]	*Scheibenschießen*	v to **shoot at a target**
self-defence [ˌself dɪˈfens]	*Selbstverteidigung, Selbstschutz*	v to **defend (oneself)**
(gun) permit [ˈpɜːmɪt]	*(Waffen-)Schein*	v to **permit** ! [pəˈmɪt]
background check [ˈbækɡraʊnd tʃek]	*Zuverlässigkeitsüberprüfung*	v to **check sb's background**
ammunition [ˌæmjuˈnɪʃn]	*Munition*	≈ **ammo** (informal)
securely [sɪˈkjuəli]	*sicher*	v to **secure**
security personnel [sɪˈkjuərəti pɜːsənel]	*Sicherheitskräfte, -personal*	≈ **security guards**
citizen [ˈsɪtɪzn]	*Bürger/in*	◁▷ non-citizen
fatality [fəˈtæləti]	*Todesfall, Todesopfer*	≈ death
mass shooting [ˈmæs ˈʃuːtɪŋ]	*Massenerschießung, Amoklauf*	≈ **gun massacre**
observer [əbˈzɜːvə]	*Außenstehende/r, Beobachter/in*	v to **observe**
resistance (to sth) [rɪˈzɪstəns]	*Widerstand (gegen etw), Resistenz (gegen etw)*	ADJ **resistant (to sth)**
lobby [ˈlɒbi]	*Lobby, Interessengruppe(n)*	v to **lobby sb**
libertarian [ˌlɪbəˈteːrɪən]	*liberal*	N libertarianism
to **bear arms** [ˈbeər ˈɑːmz]	*Waffen tragen*	≈ to **carry a weapon**

Terrorism

Terrorism is the use of indiscriminate violence to create fear in a society. The terrorists' aims may be financial, political, religious or ideological. Terrorist organizations are usually small groups of individuals; however dictatorships may use state terror in a similar way. If violence is directed only against military personnel, guerrilla war may be a more appropriate term.

Terrorists' objectives may be stated in a manifesto, or may be vague. Bombings and other atrocities may be perpetrated by organized cells, using paramilitary equipment, organization and methods, or they may be carried out by 'lone wolf' attackers without material support, using improvised weapons. Social media makes this kind of loosely organized terrorism easier.

In some cases, the strategy behind seemingly meaningless acts of violence may be to provoke the authorities into reducing civil liberties and society into becoming less tolerant and pluralistic, in order to increase alienation within minority groups and make them easier to radicalize.

Expressions with 'terror'

terror attack Terroranschlag
terror suspect Terrorverdächtige/r
state terror Staatsterror
war on terror Krieg gegen den Terror
wave of terror Terrorwelle

Word family 'radical'

radical ADJ radikal, N Radikale/r
radicalism Radikalität, Radikalismus
radicalization Radikalisierung
to **radicalize** radikalisieren

CHECKPOINT	*In English, please!*

a Willkürliche Gewalt ist keine gute Art, politische Ziele zu erreichen.
b Die von der Gruppe begangenen Gräueltaten waren nichts als sinnlose Gewaltakte.
c Die Behörden schränkten die Bürgerrechte ein.
d Die Entfremdung von Minderheiten nahm zu.

indiscriminate violence [ˌɪndɪˌskrɪmɪnət ˈvaɪələns]	willkürliche Gewalt	◀ᐅ selective, systematic violence ADJ **violent**
fear [fɪə]	Angst	v to **fear**
aim [eɪm]	Zweck, Ziel	≈ objective
ideological [ˌaɪdɪəˈlɒdʒɪkl]	ideologisch	N ideology
dictatorship [dɪkˈteɪtəʃɪp]	Diktatur	N dictator
state terror [ˌsteɪt ˈterə]	Staatsterror	v to **terrorize**
military personnel [ˌmɪlətri pɜːsəˈnel]	Militärangehörige	vgl. **armed forces** pl Streitkräfte
guerrilla war [gəˈrɪlə wɔː]	Guerillakrieg	vgl. **guerrilla fighter** Guerillakämpfer/in
vague [veɪg]	verschwommen, undeutlich, vage	◀ᐅ precise, exact
bombing [ˈbɒmɪŋ]	Bombardierung, Bombenanschlag	vgl. **suicide bombing** Selbstmordanschlag
atrocity [əˈtrɒsəti]	Gräueltat	ADJ **atrocious**
to **perpetrate** [ˈpɜːpɪtreɪt]	(eine Tat) begehen	N **perpetrator** Täter/in
'lone wolf' attacker [ləʊn ˌwʊlf əˈtækə]	Einzeltäter/in	vgl. **terror cell** Terrorzelle
to **improvise** [ˈɪmprəvaɪz]	improvisieren	N improvisation
meaningless [ˈmiːnɪŋləs]	unsinnig, sinnlos	◀ᐅ meaningful
act of violence [ˌækt əv ˈvaɪələns]	Gewalttat, Gewaltakt	vgl. **act of terrorism**
to **provoke sb into doing sth** [prəˈvəʊk]	jdn zu etw provozieren	N provocation, ADJ provocative
the authorities pl [ɔːˈθɒrətiz]	die Behörden	≈ the government, the state
civil liberties pl [ˌsɪvl ˈlɪbəti]	bürgerliche Freiheitsrechte	≈ personal freedoms
alienation [eɪlɪəˈneɪʃn]	Entfremdung	v to **alienate**
to **radicalize** [ˈrædɪklaɪz]	radikalisieren	N **radical** (Person) vgl. **extremist, fundamentalist**

C Globalization

The growth of globalization

Since the Industrial Revolution in the 18th century there has been increased interaction and integration between people, companies and governments around the world, and the rate of integration has increased rapidly since World War II. This phenomenon is what we call globalization.

Advances in transportation and communications technology have made globalization possible. International standards and free trade agreements have made international trade in goods and services more efficient. The growth of multinational companies and outsourcing has facilitated global cooperation in industry. Globalization is not just an economic and political phenomenon: ideas and culture are also becoming globalized.

On the other hand, there has also been a reaction against globalization. People may attribute job losses and unemployment to competition from cheap imports or to uncontrolled immigration. Political leaders sometimes respond to these concerns by implementing protectionist measures such as trade barriers and stricter border controls.

CHECKPOINT

In English, please!

a Die Globalisierung ist ein wirtschaftliches und kulturelles Phänomen.
b Freihandelsabkommen erleichtern den internationalen Handel.
c Handelsschranken tragen nicht unbedingt dazu bei, die Arbeitslosigkeit zu senken.
d Führende Politiker wollen strengere Grenzkontrollen.

✗ **growth** [grəʊθ]	*Zunahme, Wachstum*	v to **grow**
globalization [ˌgləʊbəlaɪˈzeɪʃn]	*Globalisierung*	→ *Kasten links*
interaction [ˌɪntərˈækʃn]	*Zusammenwirken, Beeinflussung*	v to **interact (with)**
advance (in sth) [ədˈvɑːns]	*Fortschritt(e) (in/bei etw)*	ADJ **advanced**
transportation [ˌtrænspɔːˈteɪʃn]	*Transport*	≈ **transport**
communications technology [kəmjuːnɪˌkeɪʃnz tekˈnɒlədʒi]	*Kommunikationstechnik*	*vgl.* **information and communications technology (ICT)**
standards *pl* [ˈstændədz]	*Normen, Richtlinien*	*vgl.* **standardization**
free trade agreement [ˌfriː treɪd əˈgriːmənt]	*Freihandelsabkommen*	*vgl.* to **sign an agreement**
goods and services *pl* [ˌgʊdz ən ˈsɜːvɪsɪz]	*Waren und Dienstleistungen*	
to **facilitate** [fəˈsɪlɪteɪt]	*ermöglichen, erleichtern*	N **facilitation**
to **attribute sth to sth** [əˈtrɪbjuːt]	*etw einer Sache zuschreiben*	≈ to **ascribe sth to sth**
job losses *pl* [ˈdʒɒb lɒsɪz]	*Stellenabbau*	≈ **job cuts**
unemployment [ˌʌnɪmˈplɔɪmənt]	*Arbeitslosigkeit*	ADJ **unemployed**
competition [ˌkɒmpəˈtɪʃn]	*Konkurrenz*	ADJ **competitive**
uncontrolled [ˌʌnkənˈtrəʊld]	*ungeregelt, unkontrolliert*	≈ **out-of-control**
political leader [pəˌlɪtɪkl ˈliːdə]	*(führende/r) Politiker/in*	N **leadership**
to **implement** [ˈɪmplɪmənt]	*(Maßnahme) einleiten*	N **implementation**
protectionist measures *pl* [prəˌtekʃnɪst ˈmeʒəz]	*protektionistische Maßnahmen*	N **protectionism**
trade barrier [ˈtreɪd bæriə]	*Handelshemmnis, Handelsschranke*	≈ **trade restriction**
strict [strɪkt]	*streng*	◀▶ **lenient**
border controls *pl* [ˈbɔːdə kəntrəʊl]	*Grenzkontrollen*	

A **fair deal** for <u>developing countries</u>

Developing countries often have higher economic and population growth rates than <u>developed countries</u>. Many have other characteristics in common: unsafe drinking water, high levels of pollution, inadequate healthcare and sanitation. Often there is widespread poverty, poor access to education, high gender inequality, corruption in government and political instability. Many are vulnerable to climate change.

The developed world has helped to create this situation, through colonialism, and has benefited from exploitation of weaker countries. It seems only fair to give something back. <u>Development</u> aid supports the economic and social development of poorer countries. It focuses on long-term goals, unlike humanitarian aid, which is usually a short-term response to disasters. The term 'development cooperation' is sometimes <u>preferred</u>, as it indicates a partnership, rather than a one-way transfer of wealth and expertise.

Individuals can play a part through ethical consumerism. This may help producers in developing countries to achieve better trading conditions.

CHECKPOINT	*In English, please!*

a Das Land hat eine hohe Bevölkerungswachstumsrate.
b Ausreichende medizinische Versorgung ist ohne sauberes Trinkwasser unmöglich.
c Länder mit weit verbreiteter Armut sind oft politisch instabil.
d Ethischer Konsum hilft Erzeugern in den Entwicklungsländern.

Expressions with 'country'

country of origin Ursprungsland
<u>**developed country**</u> Industrieland
<u>**developing country**</u> Entwicklungs-land
foreign country Ausland, fremdes Land
home country Heimatland
host country Gastland, Aufnahme-land
industrialized country Industrieland
neighbouring country Nachbarland

Word family 'prefer'

to **prefer** vorziehen
<u>**preferred**</u> bevorzugt
preferable wünschenswert, besser
preferably vorzugsweise, möglichst
preference Vorliebe, Wunsch, Priorität

Word family 'develop'

to <u>**develop**</u> (sich) entwickeln
<u>**developed**</u> entwickelt
<u>**undeveloped**</u> unentwickelt
<u>**development**</u> Entwicklung
<u>**developer**</u> Entwickler/in

fair deal [ˌfeə ˈdiːl]	*faires Angebot, faires Geschäft*	*vgl.* **equity**
population [ˌpɒpjuˈleɪʃn]	*Bevölkerung*	*vgl.* **overpopulation**
growth rate [ˈɡrəʊθ reɪt]	*Wachstumsrate*	≈ **rate of growth**
pollution [pəˈluːʃn]	*Umweltverschmutzung*	v to **pollute**
inadequate [ɪnˈædɪkwət]	*unzureichend*	N **inadequacy**
healthcare [ˈhelθkeə]	*medizinische Versorgung, Gesundheitswesen*	*vgl.* **medicine**
sanitation [ˌsænɪˈteɪʃn]	*Kanalisation, Abwasseraufbereitung*	≈ **sewerage**
poverty [ˈpɒvəti]	*Armut*	◀▶ **prosperity**
access (to sth) [ˈækses]	*Zugang (zu etw), Zugriff (auf etw)*	v to **access**
gender inequality [ˈdʒendər ɪnɪkwɒləti]	*Ungleichbehandlung der Geschlechter*	*vgl.* **sexual discrimination**
political instability [pəˌlɪtɪkl ɪnstəˈbɪləti]	*politische Instabilität*	ADJ **politically unstable**
to **be vulnerable to sth** [ˈvʌlnərəbl]	*einer Sache ausgesetzt sein*	N **vulnerability**
to **benefit from sth** [ˈbenɪfɪt]	*von etw profitieren*	N **benefit**
exploitation [ˌeksplɔɪˈteɪʃn]	*Ausbeutung*	v to **exploit**, ADJ **exploitative**
development aid [dɪˈveləpmənt eɪd]	*Entwicklungshilfe*	≈ **development assistance, foreign aid**
humanitarian aid [hjumænɪˌteərɪən ˈeɪd]	*humanitäre Hilfe*	*vgl.* **disaster relief**
disaster [dɪˈzɑːstə]	*Katastrophe*	≈ **catastrophe**
one-way transfer [wʌn ˌweɪ ˈtrænsfɜː]	*einseitiger Transfer*	◀▶ **exchange**
expertise [ˌekspəˈtiːz]	*Know-how, Fachwissen*	ADJ **expert**
ethical consumerism [ˌeθɪkl kənˈsjuːmərɪzm]	*ethischer Konsum*	v to **consume**
trading conditions *pl* [ˈtreɪdɪŋ kəndɪʃnz]	*Handelsbedingungen*	≈ **terms of trade**

Migration

We tend to associate <u>migration</u> with the movement of people across national borders. However internal migration from one part of a country to another is more common. For example, urbanization occurs when people move from rural areas to urban areas. People may <u>migrate</u> as individuals, as families or in larger groups. The move they make may be temporary or permanent.

Economic migration occurs when people move in search of employment and improved living standards. Seasonal workers may move to areas where tourism or agriculture provides work. <u>Migrant</u> workers may not plan to settle permanently in their new host country or region, and may send part of their earnings back home to support their families.

<u>Refugees</u> move because it has become unsafe for them to stay in their homelands. The cause may be social, political or religious tensions and persecution, war or a natural disaster. Often they may spend months or years in refugee camps with only the most basic facilities. They may travel to another country as asylum seekers.

Word family 'migrate'

to **migrate** (ab-/zu-)wandern, migrieren
migrant Migrant/in
migration Migration
to **immigrate** einwandern, immigrieren
immigration Einwanderung, Immigration
to **emigrate** auswandern, emigrieren
emigration Auswanderung, Emigration

Expressions with 'refuge'/'refugee'

refuge Zuflucht
to **seek/take refuge** Zuflucht suchen
refugee Flüchtling
influx of refugees Zustrom von Flüchtlingen, Flüchtlingsstrom
refugee camp Flüchtlingslager
refugee hostel Flüchtlingsheim

CHECKPOINT   *In English, please!*

a Viele Menschen sind von ländlichen in Stadtgebiete gezogen.
b Sind diese Menschen Flüchtlinge oder Wirtschaftsmigranten?
c Sie wollen sich dauerhaft in ihrem neuen Gastland niederlassen.
d Die Asylsuchenden haben ihr Heimatland aufgrund religiöser Verfolgung verlassen.

national border [ˌnæʃnəl ˈbɔːdə]	*Landesgrenze, Staatsgrenze*	*vgl.* **border patrol, border guard**
urbanization [ɜːbnaɪˈzeɪʃn]	*Verstädterung, Urbanisation*	*vgl.* **urban development**
rural [ˈrʊərəl]	*ländlich*	≈ **country**
urban [ˈɜːbən]	*städtisch, Stadt-*	*vgl.* **suburban** *Vorort-, am Stadtrand*
to **migrate** [maɪˈgreɪt]	*(ab-/zu-)wandern, migrieren*	→ *Kasten links*
economic migration [iːkəˌnɒmɪk maɪˈgreɪʃn]	*Wirtschaftsmigration*	N **economic migrant**
employment [ɪmˈplɔɪmənt]	*Arbeit, Beschäftigung*	V to **employ**
living standard [ˈlɪvɪŋ stændəd]	*Lebensstandard*	≈ **standard of living**
seasonal worker [ˌsiːzənl ˈwɜːkə]	*Saisonarbeiter/in*	*vgl.* to **do seasonal work**
agriculture [ˈægrɪkʌltʃə]	*Landwirtschaft*	ADJ **agricultural**
migrant worker [ˌmaɪgrənt ˈwɜːkə]	*Wanderarbeiter/in*	
to **settle** [ˈsetl]	*sich niederlassen*	≈ to **settle down**
host country [ˈhəʊst kʌntri]	*Gastland, Aufnahmeland*	≈ **host nation**
earnings *pl* [ˈɜːnɪŋz]	*Einkünfte*	≈ **pay**
to **support sb** [səˈpɔːt]	*jdn (finanziell) unterstützen*	N **support**
homeland [ˈhəʊmlænd]	*Heimatland*	≈ **home country**
tension [ˈtenʃn]	*Spannung*	ADJ **tense**
persecution [ˌpɜːsɪˈkjuːʃn]	*Verfolgung*	V to **persecute**
natural disaster [ˌnætʃrəl dɪˈzɑːstə]	*Naturkatastrophe*	◂▸ **manmade disaster**
with only the most basic facilities [ˌbeɪsɪk fəˈsɪlətiz]	*nur mit dem absolut Nötigsten ausgestattet*	≈ **with only rudimentary facilities**
asylum seeker [əˈsaɪləm siːkə]	*Asylsuchende/r*	V to **seek asylum**

Consumerism

Consumerism is an economic model that depends on the continual acquisition of goods and services. We tend to think of consumerism as the 'normal' pursuit of material comfort and enjoyment, but it is a relatively recent development. Consumerism is only possible in a society where a large number of people have more wealth than is required to satisfy their basic needs.

Advertising, branding and planned obsolescence are used to artificially stimulate demand and boost economic activity. Fashions and trends are created, so that older goods, although still functional, are no longer considered useful or desirable as they are 'out of fashion'. Consumption becomes a recreational activity: people refer to a shopping trip as 'retail therapy' – a way to forget their problems.

Consumerism and the unnecessary consumption it brings are difficult to justify in terms of sustainability. Production and delivery of goods and services is energy intensive, and consumerism generates a lot of waste, as older items are discarded. Consumerism is a major driver of climate change. It is also connected with social problems such as excessive debt.

Word family 'consume'
to **consume** konsumieren **consumer** Konsument/in <u>**consumerism**</u> Konsum **consumerist** Konsum- <u>**consumption**</u> Konsum

Word family 'shop'
to **shop** kaufen, einkaufen **shop** Laden **shopaholic** Kaufsüchtige/r **shopper** Käufer/in,   (Laden-)Kunde/-in <u>**shopping**</u> Einkauf, Einkäufe

CHECKPOINT   *In English, please!*

a Die ständige Anschaffung von Waren ist nicht nachhaltig.
b Es ist wichtig, die Konjunktur anzukurbeln.
c Konsum ist energieintensiv und verschwenderisch.

economic model [iːkəˌnɒmɪk ˈmɒdl]	Wirtschaftsmodell, ökonomisches Modell	vgl. economic theory
continual [kənˈtɪnjuəl]	ständig, kontinuierlich	≈ constant
acquisition [ˌækwɪˈzɪʃn]	Anschaffung, Erwerb	v to acquire
pursuit (of sth) [pəˈsjuːt]	Streben (nach etw), Jagd (nach etw)	v to pursue
material comfort [məˌtɪəriəl ˈkʌmfət]	materieller Wohlstand	ADJ comfortable
branding [ˈbrændɪŋ]	Markenbildung	vgl. brand Marke
planned obsolescence [ˌplænd ɒbsəˈlesns]	geplante Produktalterung	ADJ obsolete veraltet
artificial(ly) [ˌɑːtɪˈfɪʃl]	künstlich	◀▶ natural(ly)
to stimulate demand [ˌstɪmjuleɪt dɪˈmɑːnd]	Nachfrage anregen, Nachfrage schaffen	N stimulus, stimulation
to boost sth [buːst]	etw ankurbeln, etw steigern	N boost
economic activity [ˌiːkənɒmɪk ækˈtɪvəti]	Konjunktur, Wirtschaftstätigkeit	
out of fashion [fæʃn]	altmodisch	≈ unfashionable
recreational activity [rekriˌeɪʃənl ækˈtɪvəti]	Freizeitbeschäftigung	≈ pastime
retail therapy [ˌriːteɪl ˈθerəpi]	Shoppingtherapie	ADJ therapeutic
in terms of sth [tɜːmz]	hinsichtlich einer Sache, was etw angeht	≈ from the point of view of
sustainability [səˌsteɪnəˈbɪləti]	Nachhaltigkeit	ADJ sustainable nachhaltig
delivery [dɪˈlɪvəri]	Lieferung, Zustellung	v to deliver
energy intensive [ˈenədʒi ɪˈtensɪv]	energieintensiv	◀▶ energy saving
waste [weɪst]	Abfall, Müll	ADJ wasteful verschwenderisch
to discard sth [dɪsˈkɑːd]	etw wegwerfen	≈ to throw away
major driver [ˌmeɪdʒə ˈdraɪvə]	wichtiger Motor, wichtige Triebfeder	≈ main cause
debt [det]	Schuld(en)	vgl. to get/go into debt sich verschulden

TEST YOURSELF

You can check your answers on p. 212.

1 The European Union is _____ and culturally _____ .

ethnisch; vielfältig

2 The EU _____ of a sudden growth in immigration.

hatte die schwierige Aufgabe … zu bewältigen

3 They welcomed _____ but expected immigrants to respect their _____ .

Diversität; Grundwerte

4 _____ and _____ seemed to grow in the UK during the Brexit discussions.

Rassismus; Fremdenfeindlichkeit

5 Have you read the Universal Declaration of _____ ?

Menschenrechte

6 There can be little _____ in a country which allows _____ .

Gerechtigkeit; Folter

7 Does everyone have a _____ which is _____ for their basic needs?

Lebensstandard; hinreichend

8 Many people in our _____ society still _____ .

wohlhabend; leben in Armut

9 She couldn't decide _____ .

welche berufliche Laufbahn sie einschlagen wollte

10 She was worried that her career would _____ if she accused her boss of _____ .

leiden; sexuelle Belästigung

11 What is the _____ of _____ in the workplace?

Grundursache; Ungleichgewicht zwischen den Geschlechtern

12 Nobody gave us _____ : we had to _____ .

Gleichberechtigung; darum kämpfen

Geschlechtsidentität; Geburtsgeschlecht	**13** We don't choose our _____: like our _____, we're born with it.
Verfolgung; sexuelle Orientierung	**14** Nobody should suffer _____ for their _____.
ausschließlicher Gegensatz; Sexualität	**15** There isn't a _____ between homosexuality and heterosexuality: _____ is a spectrum.
operative Geschlechtsumwandlung	**16** Should _____ be freely available to everyone?
Todesstrafe; Mord	**17** The politician wanted to bring back _____ for the most serious cases, such as _____.
Todesstrafe; Verletzung	**18** The _____ is considered a _____ of the most basic human rights.
Fehlurteil; unschuldig	**19** If there is a _____, an _____ person could be killed.
(durch Abschreckung) verhindern; Vergeltung	**20** Does it really _____ crime, or is it just a form of _____?
Schusswaffe; Selbstverteidigung	**21** Is it legal to carry a _____ for _____ in this country?
Munition; sicher	**22** Gun owners must store their weapons and _____.
Amokläufe	**23** Why are _____ more common in the USA than in Switzerland, for example?

24 Farmers often have guns for _____ and _____ _____. *Jagd; Schädlingsbekämpfung*

25 _____ of minority groups makes them easier to _____. *Entfremdung; radikalisieren*

26 The terrorists' _____ were _____ and their atrocities were seemingly _____. *Ziele; undeutlich; sinnlos*

27 It is impossible for the _____ to provide complete protection against _____. *Behörden; Einzeltäter*

28 _____ creates confusion and _____, even if the attacks are relatively ineffective. *willkürliche Gewalt; Angst*

29 Would globalization have been possible without _____ in _____? *Fortschritte; Kommunikationstechnik*

30 Globalization isn't just about _____ international trade in _____. *ermöglichen; Waren und Dienstleistungen*

31 Will the latest _____ give even more power to big business? *Freihandelsabkommen*

32 _____ is often associated with nations that have widespread _____. *politische Instabilität; Armut*

33 Most _____ have benefited directly or indirectly from _____ of _____. *Industrieländer; Ausbeutung; Entwicklungsländer*

humanitäre Hilfe; Entwicklungs-hilfe	**34** _____ may be needed as a response to disasters, but _____ is more important in the long term.
Zugang zu; Bevölkerungswachstum(srate)	**35** Improving girls' _____ education has been shown to slow the _____ .
Verstädterung; ländlich	**36** Many European countries are experiencing _____ , as people leave _____ areas.
abwandern; Lebensstandarde	**37** It is natural that people _____ in search of improved _____ _____ .
Spannungen; Flüchtlinge	**38** Social and political _____ grew as the number of _____ increased.
Wanderarbeiter; unterstützen; Heimatländer	**39** _____ may have families to _____ back in their _____ .
Konsum; Wirtschaftsmodell	**40** _____ is only one possible _____ .
geplante Produktalterung; Nachhaltigkeit	**41** _____ is hard to justify in terms of _____ .
Shoppingtherapie; Schulden	**42** His use of _____ led him to acquire a lot of _____ .
Lieferung; wichtiger Motor	**43** The production and _____ of consumer goods is a _____ of climate change.
wegzuwerfen	**44** We shouldn't be so quick _____ older goods which are still functional.

6 English-speaking countries

A The United Kingdom

Physical geography and demographics of the British Isles

The total area of the British Isles is 315,159 square kilometres – about 90 % of the size of Germany. They include the island of Great Britain, the island of Ireland and over six thousand smaller islands. The British Isles lie between the Atlantic Ocean and the North Sea and are separated from continental Europe by the narrow English Channel.

The islands are mostly low lying, and their mountainous regions are not very high: Ben Nevis is the highest mountain at 1345 metres. Less than 10 % of the landmass is wooded, and over 80 % is used for agriculture or pasture. The climate is temperate with rainfall all year round. The weather is often unpredictable.

The population of the United Kingdom is 66 million and that of the Republic of Ireland is just under 5 million. The Scottish Highlands and Islands, North Wales and the West of Ireland are sparsely populated, but parts of England, South Wales and the Scottish Lowlands are highly urbanized and have a high population density. Industry is also concentrated in those areas.

Physical geographical features

beach Strand
coast Küste
forest Wald
hill Hügel
lake See
mountain Berg
mountain range Gebirge, Gebirgszug
river Fluss

Expressions with 'sea'

at sea auf See
at the seaside am Meer
by sea auf dem Seeweg, zu Wasser
by the sea am Meer
Baltic Sea Ostsee
Mediterranean Sea Mittelmeer
North Sea Nordsee

CHECKPOINT   *In English, please!*

a Die Britischen Inseln umfassen über sechstausend Inseln.
b Der Ärmelkanal trennt Großbritannien von Kontinentaleuropa.
c Viele Briten träumen davon, am Meer zu wohnen.

physical [ˈfɪzɪkl]	physisch	ADJ geographic(al)
geography [dʒiˈɒgrəfi]	Geographie	≈ demography
demographics [ˌdeməˈgræfɪks]	Demographie	ABBR km²
square kilometres [ˈskweə kɪləmiːtəz]	Quadratkilometer	≈ isle [ʌɪl] (poetisch, gehoben)
island [ˈaɪlənd]	Insel	N separation
to separate [ˈsepəreɪt]	trennen	≈ mainland Europe
continental Europe [kɒntɪˌnentl ˈjʊərəp]	Kontinentaleuropa	vgl. Channel Tunnel
English Channel [ˌɪŋglɪʃ ˈtʃænl]	Ärmelkanal	
low lying [ˈləʊ laɪɪŋ]	tiefliegend, niedrig gelegen	vgl. hilly hügelig
mountainous [ˈmaʊntənəs]	gebirgig, Gebirgs-, bergig, Berg-	≈ land area
landmass [ˈlændmæs]	Landmasse	≈ forested
wooded [ˈwʊdɪd]	bewaldet	ADJ agricultural
agriculture [ˈægrɪkʌltʃə]	Landwirtschaft	≈ grazing land
pasture [ˈpɑːstʃə]	Weideland	ADJ climatic
climate [ˈklaɪmət]	Klima	≈ mild
temperate [ˈtempərət]	gemäßigt	vgl. precipitation Niederschlag
rainfall [ˈreɪnfɔːl]	Regenfälle	vgl. variable unbeständig
unpredictable [ˌʌnprɪˈdɪktəbl]	unberechenbar, unvorhersehbar	vgl. inhabitants pl Einwohner
population [ˌpɒpjuˈleɪʃn]	Bevölkerung	◑ densely populated
sparsely populated [ˌspɑːsli ˈpɒpjuleɪtɪd]	dünn besiedelt	◑ rural
highly urbanized [ˌhaɪli ˈɜːbənaɪzd]	stark verstädtert	ADJ dense
population density [ˌpɒpjuˈleɪʃn densəti]	Bevölkerungsdichte	

Political institutions

The United Kingdom is a union of three nations and one province: England, Scotland, Wales and Northern Ireland. The UK is a constitutional monarchy with the King or Queen as its head of state. The monarch and the Royal Family have ceremonial and diplomatic duties, but their political power is largely symbolic.

The UK's head of government is the Prime Minister. The UK parliament meets in the Palace of Westminster and has two houses: an elected House of Commons and an appointed House of Lords.

Devolution in recent decades has given more autonomy to Scotland, Wales and Northern Ireland. As a result of these political reforms, Scotland, Wales and Northern Ireland each have their own government or executive, which is led by a First Minister. England does not have its own government, however.

In general elections, each of the UK's 650 constituencies elects a single member of parliament (MP). The Prime Minister is usually the leader of the party or coalition which has the largest number of MPs.

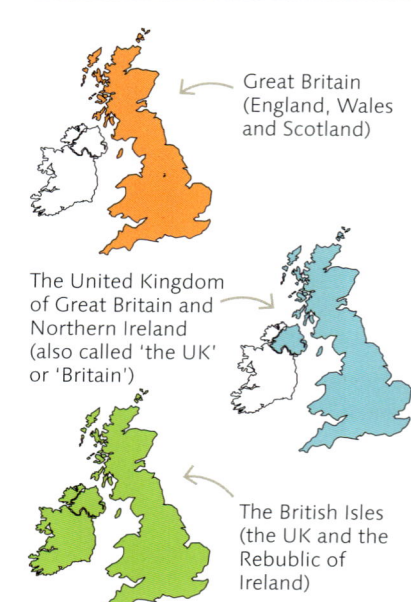

Great Britain
(England, Wales
and Scotland)

The United Kingdom
of Great Britain and
Northern Ireland
(also called 'the UK'
or 'Britain')

The British Isles
(the UK and the
Rebublic of
Ireland)

CHECKPOINT   *In English, please!*

a Obwohl die Königin das Staatsoberhaupt ist, ist ihre Macht nur symbolisch.
b Nach der Parlamentswahl wird unser Wahlkreis einen neuen Abgeordneten haben.
c Wird die Dezentralisierung Schottland und Wales zukünftig weiterhin mehr Autonomie gewähren?

political [pə'lɪtɪkl]	politisch	N politician (Person), politics
kingdom ['kɪŋdəm]	Königreich	vgl. monarchy Monarchie
constitutional monarchy [ˌkɒnstɪtjuːʃənl 'mɒnəki]	konstitutionelle Monarchie	vgl. constitution Verfassung
head of state [ˌhed əf 'steɪt]	Staatsoberhaupt	vgl. head of government Regierungschef/in
ceremonial [ˌserɪ'məʊnɪəl]	zeremoniell	N ceremony
diplomatic [ˌdɪplə'mætɪk]	diplomatisch	N diplomacy
duties pl ['djuːtiz]	Aufgaben, Pflichten	vgl. to do one's duty seine Pflicht tun
power ['paʊə]	Macht	ADJ powerful ◆ powerless
symbolic [sɪm'bɒlɪk]	symbolisch	v to symbolize
Prime Minister [ˌpraɪm 'mɪnɪstə]	Premierminister/in	ABBR PM
parliament ['pɑːləmənt]	Parlament	vgl. member of parliament (MP) Abgeordnete/r
house [haʊs]	(Parlaments-)Kammer	
to elect [ɪ'lekt]	wählen	vgl. to vote for sb für jdn stimmen
to appoint [ə'pɔɪnt]	ernennen	N appointment
devolution [ˌdiːvə'luːʃn]	Regionalisierung, Dezentralisierung	v to devolve (to sth)
autonomy [ɔː'tɒnəmi]	Autonomie, Selbständigkeit	ADJ autonomous
government ['gʌvənmənt]	Regierung	v to govern
executive [ɪg'zekjətɪv]	Exekutive	v to execute (an order)
general election [ˌdʒenrəl ɪ'lekʃn]	Parlamentswahlen	vgl. electorate Wahlvolk, Wähler
constituency [kən'stɪtjuənsi]	Wahlkreis	vgl. constituent Wähler/in

British Empire to British Commonwealth

In the 15th and 16th centuries, Portugal and Spain explored the world and established overseas empires. England, France and the Netherlands competed with these major powers to establish their own colonies and trade networks. A series of wars eventually saw England (later Great Britain) become the dominant imperial power.

The Industrial Revolution started in Britain; the British Empire opened up new markets for British goods and new sources of raw materials. After defeating France in the Napoleonic Wars, for over a century Britain was the world's greatest military and trading power.

World War I overstretched British military, financial and industrial resources, and World War II damaged Britain's reputation as a colonial power. India, Britain's most valuable colony, achieved independence in 1947, followed quickly by most other colonies and territories. Fifteen former colonies joined the British Commonwealth, an association of independent states which have the Queen as head of state.

Word family 'colony'

colony Kolonie
colonist Siedler/in, Kolonist/in
to colonize besiedeln, kolonisieren
colonial kolonial
colonialist Kolonialist/in
colonialism Kolonialismus

Expressions with 'trade'

to **trade (in sth, with sb)** (mit etw, mit jdm) handeln, Handel treiben
trade Handel, Gewerbe
domestic trade Binnenhandel
free trade Freihandel
trader Händler/in, Gewerbetreibende/r
trading power Handelsmacht

CHECKPOINT

In English, please!

a Europäische Länder haben die Welt erforscht und Kolonien gegründet.
b Die Kolonialmächte konkurrierten miteinander, um Handelsnetze zu etablieren.
c Großbritannien ist keine große Militär- und Handelsmacht mehr.
d Das britische Commonwealth ist ein Zusammenschluss unabhängiger Staaten.

century ['sentʃəri]	*Jahrhundert*	*vgl.* **millennium**
to **explore** [ɪk'splɔː]	*erforschen, erkunden*	N **explorer** *(Person)*, **exploration**
to **establish** [ɪ'stæblɪʃ]	*gründen, etablieren*	≈ to **set up**, to **found**
overseas [ˌəʊvə'siːz]	*Übersee-*	≈ **foreign**
empire ['empaɪə]	*Reich*	ADJ **imperial**
to **compete with sb** [kəm'piːt]	*mit jdm konkurrieren*	→ *Kasten S. 52*
colony ['kɒləni]	*Kolonie*	ADJ **colonial**
trade network ['treɪd netwɜːk]	*Handelsnetz*	→ *Kasten links*
dominant ['dɒmɪnənt]	*vorherrschend, dominierend*	V to **dominate**
imperial power [ɪmˌpiːrɪəl 'paʊə]	*Kolonialmacht*	
goods *pl* [gʊdz]	*Waren*	*vgl.* **services** *pl Dienstleistungen*
source [sɔːs]	*Quelle*	V to **source sth** *etw (Ware usw.) beziehen*
raw material [ˌrɔː mə'tɪəriəl]	*Rohstoff*	
to **defeat** [dɪ'fiːt]	*besiegen, schlagen*	N **defeat**
military ['mɪlətri]	*militärisch, Militär(-)*	N **militarism**
trading power ['treɪdɪŋ paʊə]	*Handelsmacht*	≈ **mercantile power**
to **overstretch** [əʊvə'stretʃ]	*überfordern, überstrapazieren*	≈ to **strain**
resources *pl* [rɪ'sɔːs]	*Mittel, Ressourcen*	ADJ **resource-rich** *ressourcenreich*
valuable ['væljuəbl]	*wertvoll*	N **value**
independence [ˌɪndɪ'pendəns]	*Unabhängigkeit*	ADJ **independent**
association [əˌsəʊsi'eɪʃn]	*Vereinigung, Zusammenschluss*	≈ **union, federation, league**

The UK and the EU

The UK joined the European Community in 1972, after unsuccessful applications in 1963 and 1967. In 1975, the UK held a national referendum on membership and there was a clear majority in favour of remaining in the European Community. In 1993 the European Community or 'Common Market' became the European Union, signifying the change from an economic union to a political one.

Eurosceptic voices in British politics could soon be heard, making various complaints: that the UK had signed up for free trade, not a 'United States of Europe'; that the UK was paying more than its fair share; that the EU was bureaucratic and insufficiently democratic; that the UK was being swamped with migrant workers. The British tabloid press often supported these complaints.

Nevertheless, Eurosceptic parties such as UKIP (the United Kingdom Independence Party) did poorly in elections. It was not clear that there was a real and powerful popular wish to leave the EU, rather than just general dissatisfaction, until the 2016 'Brexit' referendum, when a narrow majority voted in favour of leaving.

CHECKPOINT   *In English, please!*

a Die Europäische Gemeinschaft war nie nur eine Wirtschaftsunion.
b Gibt es große Unzufriedenheit mit den Arbeitsmigranten?
c In der Boulevardpresse gibt es viele Klagen über die Europäische Union.

to **join sth** [dʒɔɪn]	einer Sache beitreten	◁▷ to leave
community [kə'mju:nəti]	Gemeinschaft	N member
membership ['membəʃɪp]	Mitgliedschaft	◁▷ minority
majority [mə'dʒɒrəti]	Mehrheit	◁▷ against sb/sth
in favour of sb/sth ['feɪvər]	für jdn/etw	vgl. to have sth in common
Common Market [ˌkɒmən 'mɑːkɪt]	Gemeinsamer Markt, EU-Binnenmarkt	N significance
to **signify** ['sɪgnɪfaɪ]	bedeuten	v to unify, ADJ unified, united
economic union [iːkəˌnɒmɪk 'juːniən]	Wirtschaftsunion	◁▷ Europhile
Eurosceptic ['jʊərəskeptɪk]	euroskeptisch, Euroskeptiker/in	v to complain (about sth)
complaint [kəm'pleɪnt]	Klage, Beschwerde	≈ to commit oneself to
to **sign up for sth** [ˌsaɪn 'ʌp]	sich für etw anmelden, sich an etw beteiligen	◁▷ trade protectionism
free trade [ˌfriː 'treɪd]	Freihandel	
more than one's fair share [ˌfeə 'ʃeə]	mehr als den gerechten Anteil	◁ bureaucrat (Person), bureaucracy
bureaucratic [ˌbjʊərə'krætɪk]	bürokratisch	◁ democrat (Person), democracy
democratic [ˌdemə'krætɪk]	demokratisch	≈ to overrun
to **swamp** [swɒmp]	überschwemmen	vgl. economic migrant
migrant worker [ˌmaɪgrənt 'wɜːkə]	Wanderarbeiter/in, Arbeitsmigrant/in	≈ popular press
tabloid press [ˌtæblɔɪd 'pres]	Boulevardpresse	◁▷ to oppose
to **support** [sə'pɔːt]	unterstützen	≈ autonomy
independence [ˌɪndɪ'pendəns]	Unabhängigkeit	◁▷ to do well
to **do poorly** [ˌduː 'pʊəli]	schlecht abschneiden	ADJ dissatisfied
dissatisfaction [ˌdɪsˌsætɪs'fækʃn]	Unzufriedenheit	

B The United States of America

Physical geography and demographics

The United States of America is part of the North American continent. It is a huge country which is only slightly smaller in area than the whole of Europe. As a result of its size, it has extremely diverse geography, climate and wildlife. The landscapes of the USA range from arid deserts and fertile prairies to high mountain ranges, from the tropical volcanic islands of Hawaii to the arctic tundra of northern Alaska. The Mississippi and Missouri Rivers make up the world's fourth longest river system. There are 59 national parks and many other protected wilderness areas in the USA.

The USA is the world's third-most populous country, with over 325 million inhabitants. It is ethnically very diverse. German Americans are the largest ethnic group (more than 50 million). However, Spanish is spoken at home by 12 % of the population, making it the country's second most common language after English, and Black Americans are the nation's largest racial minority. Over 80 % of US Americans live in urban areas.

CHECKPOINT
In English, please!

a Wenn du viele Wildtiere sehen willst, dann besuche einen der Nationalparks.
b Meine amerikanische Lieblingslandschaft ist die trockene Wüste von Arizona.
c Ich bevorzuge die hohen Gebirgszüge der Rockies.
d Obwohl die USA ein sehr bevölkerungsreiches Land sind, gibt es viele Naturschutzgebiete.

United States / USA / US

'United States', 'USA' and 'US' are used with a singular verb.
*The United States **is** the world's third-most populous country.*
The use of 'America' to mean just the USA is common, but many people from other parts of the American continent dislike it.

Compound nouns with 'national'

national anthem Nationalhymne
national currency Landeswährung
national dish Nationalgericht
national holiday Nationalfeiertag
national identity nationale Identität
national language Landessprache
national park Nationalpark

Word family 'race'

race Rasse
racial rassisch, Rassen-
racism Rassismus
racist N Rassist/in
racist ADJ rassistisch

diverse [daɪˈvɜːs]	*vielfältig, unterschiedlich*	N **diversity**
wildlife [ˈwaɪldlaɪf]	*Tierwelt, Wildtiere*	≈ **wild animals, fauna**
landscape [ˈlændskeɪp]	*Landschaft*	≈ **countryside**
arid [ˈærɪd]	*trocken, arid*	≈ **dry**
desert [ˈdezət]	*Wüste*	*vgl.* to **desert** ! [dɪˈzɜːt] *verlassen*
fertile [ˈfɜːtaɪl]	*fruchtbar*	◀▶ **barren, infertile**
prairie [ˈpreəri]	*Grassteppe*	*vgl.* **plain** *Ebene*
mountain range [ˈmaʊntən reɪndʒ]	*Gebirge, Gebirgszug*	≈ **mountain chain**
tropical [ˈtrɒpɪkl]	*tropisch*	*vgl.* **the Tropics**
volcanic [vɒlˈkænɪk]	*vulkanisch*	N **volcano** (*pl* **volcanoes**)
arctic [ˈɑːktɪk]	*arktisch*	*vgl.* **the Arctic/Antarctic**
river system [ˈrɪvə sɪstəm]	*Flusssystem*	*vgl.* **river basin, river delta**
protected [prəˈtektɪd]	*geschützt*	N **protection**
wilderness area [ˈwɪldənəs eərɪə]	*Naturschutzgebiet*	≠ **wildness** *Wildheit*
populous [ˈpɒpjələs]	*bevölkerungsreich*	◀▶ **sparsely populated**
inhabitant [ɪnˈhæbɪtənt]	*Einwohner/in*	V **to inhabit**
ethnically [ˈeθnɪkli]	*ethnisch*	ADJ **ethnic**
ethnic group [ˈeθnɪk gruːp]	*Ethnie, Volksgruppe*	*vgl.* **ethnicity** *Volkszugehörigkeit, Ethnizität*
racial minority [ˌreɪʃl maɪˈnɒrəti]	*rassische Minderheit*	*vgl.* to **be in the minority**
urban area [ˌɜːbən ˈeərɪə]	*Stadtregion, Ballungsgebiet*	≈ **built-up area**

Political institutions

The United States of America is a federal republic which is made up of 50 states. The states share sovereignty with the federal government, so US Americans are citizens of both the USA and their state. Both the federal government and the states collect taxes. The states have responsibility for law enforcement, education, health and transport. They are divided into counties, which have local governments.

The federal legislature of the USA is the US Congress. Congress has two chambers, the Senate and the House of Representatives. Each state appoints a number of electors (equal to its total number of representatives and senators) to vote in the Electoral College, which elects the President of the United States. Congressional and presidential elections take place every four years.

The Constitution is the supreme law of the United States. It has seven articles and 27 amendments. The amendments include the Bill of Rights, which guarantees citizens' personal freedoms and rights and limits the government's power.

German 'wählen'

to **elect sb** jdn *(in ein Amt)* wählen
to **choose sb/sth** jdn/etw aus-
   wählen, sich etw aussuchen
to **vote** wählen (gehen), abstimmen,
   seine Stimme abgeben

Expressions with 'tax'

tax Steuer
to **tax** besteuern
income tax Einkommensteuern
sales tax AE/**VAT (value added
   tax)** BE Mehrwertsteuer
tax evasion Steuerhinterziehung
taxation Besteuerung
taxpayer Steuerzahler/in

CHECKPOINT   *In English, please!*

a Die USA sind eine Bundesrepublik, also teilen sich die Bundesstaaten die Hoheitsgewalt mit der Bundesregierung.
b Erfahren die Kinder in der Schule etwas über die Verfassung?
c Sie ist uns wichtig, weil sie unsere persönlichen Freiheiten und Rechte garantiert.

federal republic [ˌfedərəl rɪˈpʌblɪk]	Bundesrepublik	vgl. federation, federalism
state [steɪt]	Staat, Bundesstaat/-land	
sovereignty [ˈsɒvrənti]	Souveränität, Hoheitsgewalt	ADJ sovereign
citizen [ˈsɪtɪzn]	Bürger/in	N citizenship Staatsbürgerschaft
to collect taxes [kəˌlekt ˈtæksɪz]	Steuern einziehen	N tax collection
responsibility [rɪˌspɒnsəˈbɪləti]	Verantwortung	V to be responsible for
law enforcement [ˌlɔː ɪnˈfɔːsmənt]	Gesetzesvollzug	V to enforce the law
county [ˈkaʊnti]	(Verwaltungs-)Bezirk	
local government [ˌləʊkl ˈɡʌvənmənt]	Kommunalverwaltung	BE local council
legislature [ˈledʒɪsleɪtʃə]	Gesetzgeber	ADJ legislative gesetzgebend
chamber [ˈtʃeɪmbə]	Kammer	≈ house
to appoint [əˈpɔɪnt]	ernennen	N appointment
elector [ɪˈlektə]	Wahlmann/-frau	vgl. electorate
representative AE [ˌreprɪˈzentətɪv]	Mitglied des Repräsentantenhauses	V to represent
to vote [vəʊt]	abstimmen, seine Stimme abgeben	N vote, voting, voter (Person)
election [ɪˈlekʃn]	Wahl	V to elect
constitution [ˌkɒnstɪˈtjuːʃn]	Verfassung	ADJ constitutional
supreme law [suːˌpriːm ˈlɔː]	höchstes/oberstes Gesetz	vgl. Supreme Court
article [ˈɑːtɪkl]	Artikel	vgl. paragraph
amendment AE [əˈmendmənt]	Zusatzartikel (zur US-Verfassung)	V to amend
personal freedom [ˌpɜːsənl ˈfriːdəm]	persönliche Freiheit	
to limit [ˈlɪmɪt]	begrenzen, einschränken	N limitation

Colony to superpower

Mainland North America was colonized by European settlers from the early 16th century. The colonial population grew quickly, settling new lands and conquering and displacing Native Americans. By 1732, the 13 colonies which later became the USA had been established. The colonists declared independence from Britain on 4 July 1776. Britain recognized US independence in 1783 after a series of military defeats.

Americans' desire for more territory provoked the American Indian Wars. The government implemented an Indian Removal Policy that resettled Native Americans on reservations. The discovery of gold in California in 1848 encouraged western migration and the creation of more states. After the Civil War (1861–65), new transcontinental railroads accelerated this movement.

Rapid economic development during the late 19th and early 20th centuries made the USA into a world power. Tycoons led the booms in the oil, steel and automobile industries. The USA ended World War II as the world's largest military power.

Word family 'settle'

to settle siedeln, besiedeln, sich niederlassen
to resettle umsiedeln, sich neu niederlassen
settler Siedler/in
settlement Siedlung

Native peoples of North America

Although 'American Indian' is used in the USA, including by some Native American groups, it is safer to use 'Native American' to avoid causing offence. In Canada, use 'Indigenous North Americans' or 'Aboriginal Canadians'.

CHECKPOINT

In English, please!

a Die Kolonien erklärten ihre Unabhängigkeit von Großbritannien.
b Die amerikanischen Ureinwohner wurden von den Siedlern vertrieben.
c Die Reservate waren eine Folge der Politik der Vertreibung der Indianer.
d Die wirtschaftliche Entwicklung während des frühen 20. Jahrhunderts war rasant.

colony [ˈkɒləni]	Kolonie	→ *Kasten S. 164*
mainland [ˈmeɪnlænd]	Festland	*vgl.* **island** *Insel*
to **settle** [ˈsetl]	besiedeln	→ *Kasten links*
to **conquer** [ˈkɒŋkə]	besiegen	≈ to **defeat**
to **displace** [dɪsˈpleɪs]	vertreiben	≈ to **push out**
to **declare independence** [dɪˌkleər ɪndɪˈpendəns]	die Unabhängigkeit erklären	N **declaration of independence**
military defeat [ˌmɪlətri dɪˈfiːt]	militärische Niederlage	v to **defeat militarily**
territory [ˈterətri]	(Hoheits-)Gebiet, Territorium	ADJ **territorial**
to **provoke** [prəˈvəʊk]	auslösen, provozieren	N **provocation**, ADJ **provocative**
to **implement** [ˈɪmplɪmənt]	(ein politisches Programm) umsetzen	N **implementation**
removal [rɪˈmuːvl]	Umsiedlung, Ausweisung	v to **remove**
policy [ˈpɒləsi]	(politisches) Programm, Politik	≈ **strategy**
reservation [ˌrezəˈveɪʃn]	Reservat	
discovery [dɪˈskʌvəri]	Entdeckung	v to **discover**
civil war [ˌsɪvl ˈwɔː]	Bürgerkrieg	
transcontinental railroad [ˌtrænzkɒntɪˌnentl ˈreɪlrəʊd]	transkontinentale Eisenbahn	BE **railway**
to **accelerate** [əkˈseləreɪt]	beschleunigen, vorantreiben	N **acceleration**
economic development [iːkəˌnɒmɪk dɪˈveləpmənt]	wirtschaftliche Entwicklung	v to **develop economically**
tycoon [taɪˈkuːn]	Magnat, Industrieboss	≈ **business magnate**
military power [ˌmɪlətri ˈpaʊə]	Militärmacht	*vgl.* **economic, industrial power**

Slavery to presidency

The early USA was economically dependent on the export of cash crops such as tobacco and cotton. African slaves provided a large part of the labour force in the southern states. As a consequence, when the federal government prohibited the slave trade in 1808 and northern US states made slave ownership illegal, reliance on slave labour continued in the south. The Civil War was partly fought over this issue, and the defeat of the Confederacy by the Union led to the abolition of slavery in 1865.

However, emancipation did not automatically lead to equality. When African Americans no longer had the protection of US troops, whites imposed laws to prevent them from voting and restrict their movement, and found other ways to deny black workers' rights and to practise racial discrimination and segregation.

The African-American civil rights movement (1896–1954) was a long series of nonviolent campaigns and protests which eventually won full civil rights for all Americans. The USA elected its first African-American President, Barack Obama, in 2009.

CHECKPOINT
In English, please!

a Die Südstaaten waren von Sklavenarbeit abhängig.
b Die Sklaverei wurde nach dem Sieg der Unionsstaaten abgeschafft.
c Die Emanzipation verhinderte nicht die Rassendiskriminierung.
d Die Bürgerrechtsbewegungen erstritten gleiche Rechte für alle US-Amerikaner.

Expressions with 'labour' (BE)/ 'labor' (AE)

labour force Arbeitskräfte, Arbeiterschaft
cheap labour billige Arbeitskraft/-kräfte
child labour Kinderarbeit
foreign labour ausländische Arbeitskräfte
skilled labour qualifizierte Arbeitskräfte, Facharbeiter/innen
unskilled labour ungelernte Arbeitskräfte, Hilfsarbeiter/innen
slave labour Sklavenarbeit

Hyphenated Americans

Martin Luther King Jr. was an **African-American** civil rights activist. Barack Obama is an **African American**.

Word family 'slave'

slave Sklave/Sklavin
slavery Sklaverei
slaveholder Sklavenhalter/in
to enslave versklaven
enslavement Versklavung

slavery [ˈsleɪvəri]	Sklaverei	→ *Kasten links*
presidency [ˈprezɪdənsi]	Präsidentschaft, Präsidentenamt	ADJ **presidential**
dependent (on sth) [dɪˈpendənt]	(von etw) abhängig	N **dependency**
cash crop [ˈkæʃ krɒp]	für den Verkauf bestimmte Anbaufrucht, Marktfrucht	◊ **subsistence crop** *Anbaufrucht für den Eigenbedarf*
labour force [ˈleɪbə fɔːs]	Arbeitskräfte, Arbeiterschaft	→ *Kasten links*
to **prohibit** [prəˈhɪbɪt]	(gesetzlich) verbieten	N **prohibition**
slave trade [ˈsleɪv treɪd]	Sklavenhandel	N **slave trader** *(Person)*
ownership [ˈəʊnəʃɪp]	Besitz	V **to own**
defeat [dɪˈfiːt]	(militärische) Niederlage	◊ **victory**
abolition [æbəˈlɪʃn]	Abschaffung	V **to abolish**, N **abolitionist** *(Person)*
emancipation [ɪˌmænsɪˈpeɪʃn]	Befreiung, Emanzipation	V **to emancipate**, ADJ **emancipated**
equality [ɪˈkwɒləti]	Gleichheit, Gleichberechtigung	◊ **inequality**
protection [prəˈtekʃn]	Schutz	V **to protect**, ADJ **protective**
to **impose laws** [ɪmˌpəʊz ˈlɔːz]	Gesetze verhängen	N **imposition of laws**
to **restrict sb's movement** [rɪˌstrɪkt ˈmuːvmnt]	jds Freizügigkeit einschränken	N **restriction**, ADJ **restrictive**
to **deny sb sth** [dɪˈnaɪ]	jdm etw verweigern	N **denial**
racial discrimination [ˌreɪʃl dɪˌskrɪmɪˈneɪʃn]	Rassendiskriminierung	→ *Kasten S. 168*
segregation [ˌsegrɪˈgeɪʃn]	Rassentrennung	◊ **desegregation**
civil rights *pl* [ˌsɪvl ˈraɪts]	Bürgerrechte	ADJ **rightful** *rechtmäßig*
nonviolent [ˌnɒnˈvaɪələnt]	gewaltfrei	N **nonviolence**
campaign [kæmˈpeɪn]	Kampagne, Bewegung, Aktion	V **to campaign (for/against)**

Immigration and the American <u>Dream</u>

The USA is a settler colonial society and most Americans trace their ancestry to immigrants. The USA has often been described as a 'melting pot' of world cultures. This refers to the fact that most immigrants to the USA become assimilated into US mainstream culture. The USA understands itself as a land of opportunity, where hard work gives access to the American Dream: prosperity, success and upward social mobility.

However, US immigration policy is selective. From the 1880s to the 1960s, there were strict limits on immigration and naturalization, based on the ethnicity of the migrants. From 1965 these ethnic quotas were replaced by quotas for each country of origin. It is still relatively difficult to obtain a green card (permanent residency card).

There are 11–12 million undocumented immigrants in the USA, many crossing the border from Mexico. They make up around 4 % of the workforce. Many of them are long-term residents and have children born in the USA. Until recently, they were widely tolerated, but deportations have now increased.

Word family 'dream'

to **dream** träumen
dream Traum
dreamer Träumer/in
dreamlike wie im Traum, traumhaft
dreamy verträumt

Expressions with 'border'

border control Grenzkontrolle(n)
border dispute Grenzstreitigkeit(en), Grenzkonflikt
border patrol Grenzschutz, Grenzüberwachung
border town Grenzstadt
to **close a border** eine Grenze schließen
to **cross a border** eine Grenze überschreiten
on the border with … an der Grenze zu …

CHECKPOINT   *In English, please!*

a Viele Amerikaner verfolgen ihre Abstammung bis zu deutschen Einwanderern zurück.
b Der amerikanische Traum verspricht Wohlstand und sozialen Aufstieg.
c Millionen von Einwanderern ohne Papiere haben von Mexiko aus die Grenze überschritten.

to **trace** [treɪs]	*(zurück)verfolgen*	≈ to **track**, to **follow**
ancestry [ˈænsestri]	*Abstammung, Herkunft*	N **ancestor**, ADJ **ancestral**
melting pot [ˈmeltɪŋ pɒt]	*Schmelztiegel*	
to **assimilate** [əˈsɪməleɪt]	*integrieren, eingliedern*	N **assimilation**
opportunity [ˌɒpəˈtjuːnəti]	*Möglichkeit, Chance*	*vgl.* **chance** *Zufall, Gelegenheit*
to **give sb access to sth** [ˈækses]	*jdm Zugang zu etw verschaffen*	≈ to **open the door to**
prosperity [prɒˈsperəti]	*Wohlstand*	V to **prosper**, ADJ **prosperous**
upward social mobility [ˌʌpwəd ˌsəʊʃl məʊˈbɪləti]	*sozialer Aufstieg*	ADJ **socially mobile**
selective [sɪˈlektɪv]	*selektiv*	V to **select**, N **selection**
naturalization [nætʃərəlaɪˈzeɪʃn]	*Einbürgerung*	V to **naturalize**
ethnicity [eθˈnɪsəti]	*Volkszugehörigkeit, Ethnizität*	≈ **ethnic origin**
quota [ˈkwəʊtə]	*Quote, Kontingent*	≈ **fixed share, cap**
country of origin [ˌkʌntri əv ˈɒrɪdʒɪn]	*Herkunftsland*	≈ **home/native country, homeland**
permanent residency card [ˌpɜːmənənt ˈrezɪdnsi kɑːd]	*unbefristete Aufenthalterlaubnis*	V to **reside permanently**
undocumented immigrant [ʌnˌdɒkjumentɪd ˈɪmɪgrənt]	*Einwanderer/-in ohne Papiere*	V to **document**
to **cross the border** [ˌkrɒs ðə ˈbɔːdə]	*die Grenze überschreiten*	N **border crossing** *Grenzübertritt*
workforce [ˈwɜːkfɔːs]	*Erwerbstätige, Erwerbsbevölkerung*	≈ **labour force**
long-term [ˌlɒŋˈtɜːm]	*langfristig*	◀▶ **short-term**
resident [ˈrezɪdənt]	*Ansässige/r*	≈ **inhabitant**
deportation [dɪpɔːˈteɪʃn]	*Abschiebung, Ausweisung*	V to **deport sb**

US global influence and foreign policy

Although the importance of China on the world stage is growing, the USA is still the world's dominant superpower, as it has been since the end of the Second World War.

The influence of the USA around the world continues to be felt in the political, military, economic and cultural spheres. For example, the USA is a founder member of many important international organizations such as the United Nations and the World Bank. The USA is a powerful advocate for democracy and international trade. It is a key member of NATO. The USA has many of the world's top universities and research institutes, museums and galleries. Many of the most powerful corporations and richest individuals in the world have their home in the USA.

While some welcome the role of the USA as a 'global policeman', there is international concern about frequent US military interventions, e.g. in Vietnam, Iraq and Afghanistan. There is also concern about American 'cultural imperialism' and promotion of a particular form of free-market capitalism.

CHECKPOINT   *In English, please!*

a Wird China eines Tages die vorherrschende Supermacht auf der Welt sein?
b Die USA sind einflussreiche Befürworter der Demokratie.
c Die militärische Intervention veranlasste internationale Befürchtungen.
d Der weltweite Einfluss der USA wird viele Jahre lang fortbestehen.

Expressions with 'global'

global economy Weltwirtschaft
global influence weltweiter Einfluss
global market Weltmarkt
global player Weltkonzern, Global Player
global policeman Weltpolizist
global trading Welthandel
global village globales Dorf, Global Village

Political systems and beliefs

capitalism Kapitalismus
communism Kommunismus
democracy Demokratie
dictatorship Diktatur
nationalism Nationalismus
socialism Sozialismus

influence ['ɪnfluəns]	*Einfluss*	ADJ **influential**, V to **influence**
foreign policy [ˌfɒrən 'pɒləsi]	*Außenpolitik*	◀▶ **domestic policy** *Innenpolitik*
on the world stage [ˌwɜːld 'steɪdʒ]	*auf der Weltbühne*	≈ **internationally, in international affairs**
dominant ['dɒmɪnənt]	*beherrschend, dominierend*	V to **dominate**, N **domination**
sphere [sfɪə]	*Sphäre*	*vgl.* **sphere of influence** *Einflussbereich*
founder ['faʊndə]	*Gründer/in*	V to **found**
member ['membə]	*Mitglied*	N **membership**
United Nations *pl* [juˌnaɪtɪd 'neɪʃnz]	*Vereinte Nationen*	ABBR **UN** ! *nicht* UNO
powerful ['paʊəfl]	*mächtig, einflussreich*	◀▶ **weak, powerless**
advocate (for sth) ['ædvəkət]	*Befürworter/in (von etw)*	V to **advocate (for sth)** ! ['ædvəkeɪt]
key [kiː]	*wesentlich, Haupt-*	≈ **vital, essential, highly important**
research institute [rɪ'sɜːtʃ ɪnstɪtjuːt]	*Forschungseinrichtung*	V to **research**
corporation [ˌkɔːpə'reɪʃn]	*Unternehmen, Konzern*	ADJ **corporate** *Unternehmens-*
to **welcome** ['welkəm]	*begrüßen*	≈ **to approve of**
concern [kən'sɜːn]	*Sorge, Befürchtung(en)*	V to **concern sb** *jdn beunruhigen* ADJ **concerning, concerned**
military intervention [ˌmɪlətri ɪntə'venʃn]	*militärische Intervention, militärisches Eingreifen*	V to **intervene militarily**
cultural imperialism [ˌkʌltʃərəl ɪm'pɪəriəlɪzəm]	*Kulturimperialismus*	ADJ **culturally imperialist**
promotion [prə'məʊʃn]	*Propagierung, Förderung*	V to **promote** *propagieren, fördern*
free-market capitalism [friː ˌmɑːkɪt 'kæpɪtəlɪzəm]	*Kapitalismus des freien Marktes*	→ *Kasten links*

C Other countries

Australia and New Zealand

Australia and New Zealand are sometimes called the Antipodes, as they are on the opposite side of the globe to Europe, in the southern hemisphere. Because of their geographical isolation they were discovered and colonized by Europeans relatively recently. Both countries have strong indigenous cultures: the Maori in New Zealand and hundreds of Aboriginal and Torres Strait Islander peoples in Australia.

Australia has 25% of Germany's population in a country the size of Europe. The arid Outback is largely uninhabited, the rural bush is sparsely populated and most Australians live in large coastal cities. New Zealand has 60% of Germany's land area with a population of 5 million.

In both countries, primary industries, e.g. mining and agriculture, are important, but they also have highly developed service economies. Australians and New Zealanders generally enjoy a high quality of life and are known for being laid back, informal and egalitarian. Both countries are important tourist destinations.

Economic sectors

primary primär – retrieval of raw materials, e.g. mining
secondary sekundär – processing of raw materials into goods, e.g. car manufacturing
tertiary tertiär – supply of services to consumers, e.g. retail, banking

Word family 'inhabit'

to **inhabit** bewohnen
(un)inhabited (un)bewohnt
habitat Lebensraum
habitation Wohnung, Siedlung
inhabitant Einwohner/in

CHECKPOINT   *In English, please!*

a Australien wurde im 18. Jahrhundert von Europäern entdeckt.
b Die Maori sind die Ureinwohner Neuseelands.
c Melbourne, Sydney, Perth und Brisbane sind große Küstenstädte.
d Bergbau ist in Australien eine wichtige Industrie.

the Antipodes *pl* [ˈæntɪpəʊdz]	*Antipoden*	ADJ **Antipodean**
southern hemisphere [ˌsʌðən ˈhemɪsfɪə]	*Südhalbkugel*	*vgl.* **northern, eastern, western**
to **discover** [dɪˈskʌvə]	*entdecken*	N **discovery**
to **colonize** [ˈkɒlənaɪz]	*besiedeln, kolonisieren*	N **colonization**
indigenous [ɪnˈdɪdʒənəs]	*indigen, Ureinwohner(-)*	≈ **native**
Aboriginal [ˌæbəˈrɪdʒənl]	*indigen; (australischer) Ureinwohner/in*	! **Aboriginal person** *nicht* Aborigine
islander [ˈaɪləndə]	*Inselbewohner/in, Insulaner/in*	
people [ˈpiːpl]	*Volk*	! **peoples** *(Plural)*
arid [ˈærɪd]	*trocken, arid*	≈ **dry**
uninhabited [ˌʌnɪnˈhæbɪtɪd]	*unbewohnt*	≈ **unoccupied**
rural [ˈrʊərəl]	*ländlich*	◆▶ **urban**
bush [bʊʃ]	*Busch*	*vgl.* **in the (Australian) bush**
sparsely populated [ˌspɑːsli ˈpɒpjuleɪtɪd]	*dünn besiedelt*	◆▶ **densely populated**
coastal [ˈkəʊstl]	*Küsten-*	N **coast**
land area [ˌlænd ˈeərɪə]	*Landfläche, Fläche*	≈ **landmass**
primary industry [ˌpraɪməri ˈɪndəstri]	*Primärindustrie, Grundstoffindustrie*	→ *Kasten links*
mining [ˈmaɪnɪŋ]	*Bergbau*	V to **mine**, N **miner** *(Person)*
agriculture [ˈægrɪkʌltʃə]	*Landwirtschaft*	ADJ **agricultural**
highly developed [dɪˈveləpt]	*hochentwickelt*	◆▶ **underdeveloped**
service economy [ˈsɜːvɪs ɪˈkɒnəmi]	*Dienstleistungswirtschaft*	*vgl.* **service industry**
laid back [leɪd ˈbæk]	*entspannt, lässig*	≈ **relaxed**
egalitarian [iˌgælɪˈteərɪən]	*egalitär*	◆▶ **hierarchical, unequal**

English as a world language

English is the third-most spoken native language in the world, after Chinese and Spanish. It is the most widely learned second language and is an official language in around 60 nations. Most countries in the English-speaking world or the Anglosphere are connected not just by a common language but also by a shared history as part of the former British Empire, which once covered almost a quarter of the globe.

English was first spoken by Germanic settlers in part of the British Isles and is closely related to German, although it has been heavily influenced by French and other languages. Through the worldwide influence of the British Empire and more recently the rise of the USA as a superpower, English has spread around the world.

It has become a global lingua franca – a language which people use to communicate if they do not share a native language. Its importance is particularly wide in professional contexts such as business and commerce, science, law and information technology. At least half of all web content is in English.

Word family 'connect'

to **connect** verbinden, anschließen
connection Verbindung, Anschluss
connector Verbinder, Anschluss
to **disconnect** trennen, abkoppeln, unterbrechen
disconnect Lücke, Kluft

'historic' – 'historical'

historic bedeutendes Ereignis
The Battle of Hastings (AD 1066) was a historic battle.
historical geschichtlicher Bezug
War and Peace is a historical novel.

Word family 'related'

related to bezogen auf, verwandt mit
relation Bezug, Verwandschaft
relationship Beziehung, Verhältnis
relative N Verwandte/r
relative ADJ bezüglich, relativ, entsprechend

CHECKPOINT   *In English, please!*

a Deutsch und Englisch sind eng verwandte Sprachen.
b Englisch ist eine Weltsprache und die am häufigsten erlernte Zweitsprache.
c Englisch ist Amtssprache in vielen Ländern, die einmal Teil des Britischen Weltreichs waren.

world language [ˌwɜːld ˈlæŋgwɪdʒ]	*Weltsprache*	≈ global language
native language [ˌneɪtɪv ˈlæŋgwɪdʒ]	*Muttersprache*	◖◗ foreign language
official language [əˌfɪʃl ˈlæŋgwɪdʒ]	*Amtssprache*	*vgl.* **political office** *politisches Amt*
Anglosphere [ˈæŋgləsfɪə]	*englischsprachige Welt*	*vgl.* **Anglophile, Anglophobe**
to **connect** [kəˈnekt]	*verbinden*	→ *Kasten links*
common [ˈkɒmən]	*gemeinsam*	≈ shared
British Empire [ˌbrɪtɪʃ ˈempaɪə]	*Britisches Weltreich*	
Germanic [dʒəˈmænɪk]	*germanisch*	*vgl.* **Anglo-Saxon** *angelsächsisch*
settler [ˈsetlə]	*Siedler/in*	v to **settle**
closely [ˈkləʊsli]	*eng*	◖◗ distantly
to **be related to sb/sth** [rɪˈleɪtɪd]	*mit jdm/etw verwandt sein*	→ *Kasten links*
to **influence** [ˈɪnfluəns]	*beeinflussen*	ADJ influential, N influence
to **spread** [spred]	*sich ausbreiten*	N spread
particularly [pəˈtɪkjələli]	*besonders, insbesondere*	≈ especially
context [ˈkɒntekst]	*Zusammenhang, Kontext*	≈ situation
business [ˈbɪznəs]	*Wirtschaft, Geschäftsleben*	≈ enterprise
commerce [ˈkɒmɜːs]	*Handel, Handelsverkehr*	ADJ commercial
science [ˈsaɪəns]	*Naturwissenschaft(en)*	N scientist *(Person)*, ADJ scientific
law [lɔː]	*Recht*	ADJ legal
information technology [ɪnfəˌmeɪʃn tekˈnɒlədʒi]	*Informatik, Informationstechnologie*	ABBR IT
web content [ˈweb kɒntent]	*Webinhalt(e)*	≈ online content

TEST YOURSELF

You can check your answers on pp. 213–214.

1 The Scottish Highlands are _____. *dünn besiedelt*

2 The British climate is _____ but often _____. *gemäßigt; unberechenbar*

3 South-eastern England has a high _____. *Bevölkerungsdichte*

4 The British Isles are mostly _____ with few *tiefliegend; bergig*
_____ regions.

5 The _____ is the United Kingdom's _____ *Premierminister/in; Regierungs-chef/in*
_____.

6 Scotland, Wales and Northern Ireland have more _____ now, thanks to *Autonomie; Regionalisierung*
_____.

7 There are 650 _____: one for each *Abgeordnete/r; Wahlkreis*
_____.

8 Which _____ or coalition will win the _____ *Partei; Parlamentswahlen*
_____, do you think?

9 How was little England able to _____ Spain, the great *konkurrieren mit; Kolonialmacht*
_____ of its time?

10 The British Empire was formed through both _____. *Kriege und Handel*

11 Why did the former _____ join the Commonwealth after gaining *Kolonien; Unabhängigkeit*
_____?

12 _____ from the colonies were made into British _____. *Rohstoffe; Waren*

für; beigetreten ist	**13** Were most Britons _____ of European Community membership when the UK _____ in 1972?
Boulevardpresse; Arbeitsmigranten	**14** The _____ frequently complained about _____ _____.
Unzufriedenheit; bürokratisch	**15** There was _____ because the EU was seen as _____.
Euroskeptiker; Mehrheit	**16** The _____ achieved a narrow but important _____ in the 2016 referendum.
Tierwelt; vielfältig	**17** North American _____ is extremely _____.
tropisch; arktisch	**18** The USA stretches from the _____ to the _____ climate zone.
Volksgruppe; rassische Minderheit	**19** German Americans are the country's largest _____ but not its largest _____.
Einwohner; Ballungsgebieten	**20** Most _____ of the USA live in _____.
Bürger; Bundesrepublik; Bundesstaat	**21** US Americans are _____ of the _____ and of their _____.
Kammern; gewählt	**22** Unlike the UK Parliament, both _____ of the US Congress are _____.
seine Stimme abzugeben; Wahlen	**23** How old do you have to be _____ in the presidential _____?
Steuern einzuziehen; Gesetzesvollzug	**24** Who has responsibility for _____ to pay for _____ _____, education and things like that?

25 How quickly _____ | *haben die Siedler ... vertrieben und besiegt*
the Native Americans?

26 Was the settlers' declaration of _____ linked to their desire | *Unabhängigkeit; Territorium*
for more _____?

27 The _____ of gold in California _____ western migration. | *Entdeckung; beschleunigte*

28 Who _____ the American _____, the | *löste aus; Bürgerkrieg*
Confederate or the Union states?

29 When did the _____ take place throughout the USA? | *Abschaffung der Sklaverei*

30 Did _____ of the slaves result in _____ for all US Americans? | *Befreiung; Gleichberechtigung*

31 Southern states found ways to _____ black citizens' _____ | *verweigern; Bürgerrechte*
_____.

32 They _____ laws to _____ the movement of black people. | *verhängten; einzuschränken*

33 Many US Americans seem interested in _____. | *ihre Abstammung zurückzuverfolgen*

34 Is the USA still a _____ | *ein Land der unbegrenzten Möglichkeiten und des sozialen Aufstiegs*
_____ for immigrants?

35 Is _____ justified and fair? | *Abschiebung der Einwanderer ohne Papiere*

36 Do they want to undergo _____ and become | *Einbürgerung; integrieren*
_____ into US culture?

186

weltweiter Einfluss	**37** Is the _____ of the USA a good thing for the world?
Befürworter/in; militärische Interventionen	**38** The USA is _____ democracy, but its _____ haven't always reflected this.
dominierend; wesentliches	**39** As the world's _____ superpower, the USA is a _____ member of NATO.
Befürchtungen; Außenpolitik	**40** Are the _____ about US _____ valid?
trocken; unbewohnt	**41** The Outback is _____ and largely _____.
Primärindustrie(n); Dienstleistungswirtschaft	**42** Both _____ and the _____ are important.
Küsten-; ländliche	**43** Most Australians live in large _____ cities, not in _____ areas.
entspannt; egalitäre	**44** Many Australians seem friendly and _____, perhaps this is because of their _____ culture.
Muttersprache	**45** Although I speak English well, German is my _____.
wurde beeinflusst; ist enger mit ... verwandt	**46** English _____ by French, but it _____ German.
Wirtschaft, Recht und Naturwissenschaften	**47** English is important for professional contexts such as _____ _____.

7 Literature

A Prose fiction

Genres of fiction

Fiction is any literary work which is not presented as fact, though it may be based on a true story or a real-life person. There are many genres of prose fiction, e.g. science fiction, fantasy, historical fiction, realistic fiction and crime fiction. An individual work may be difficult to categorize, for example a science fiction detective story featuring historical characters. A science fiction work need not be set in space, in the future or include aliens: the author may portray an 'alternative reality' e.g. a realistic but dystopian alternative present. Fantasy is a very popular genre. It often involves magic and the supernatural and may feature imaginary creatures and beings.

There are different prose fiction formats: novels (50,000+ words), novellas (7,500–50,000 words), short stories (under 7,500 words), often published as an anthology or collection, and graphic novels. Computer games may have storytelling, plot development and characterization as sophisticated and complex as a graphic novel.

Types of novel

coming-of-age novel Entwicklungs-roman
detective novel Kriminalroman, Detektivroman
epistolary novel Briefroman
gothic novel Schauerroman
graphic novel Comicroman, Graphic Novel
historical novel historischer Roman
mystery novel Kriminalroman
science fiction novel Science-Fiction-Roman
thriller Krimi, Thriller

CHECKPOINT  *In English, please!*

a Die Geschichte ist fiktiv, beruht aber auf einer realen Person.
b Es ist schwierig, diesen Roman einzuordnen: Gehört er zu Science-Fiction oder Fantasy?
c Ich mag Romane, die eine alternative Wirklichkeit darstellen.
d Bevorzugen Sie Romane, Novellen oder Kurzgeschichten?

fiction [ˈfɪkʃn]	*Belletristik*	ADJ **fictional** *fiktiv*
literary work [ˌlɪtərəri ˈwɜːk]	*literarisches Werk, literarische Arbeit*	N **literature**
to **be based on sth** [bi ˈbeɪst ɒn]	*auf etw beruhen, auf etw basieren*	N **basis**
real-life [ˌrɪəl ˈlaɪf]	*real (existierend), aus dem wirklichen Leben*	≈ **real** *vgl.* **in real life** *in der Realität, im wirklichen Leben*
to **categorize** [ˈkætɪgəraɪz]	*kategorisieren, einordnen*	N **categorization**
to **feature sb** [ˈfiːtʃə]	*jdn als Hauptfigur haben*	
character [ˈkærəktə]	*(Roman, Film:) Figur*	≈ **figure**
to **be set in …** [bi ˈset ɪn]	*in … spielen*	N **setting**
to **portray** [pɔːˈtreɪ]	*darstellen, vorstellen, porträtieren*	N **portrayal**
dystopian [dɪsˈtəʊpiən]	*dystopisch*	N **dystopia**
the supernatural [ˌsuːpəˈnætʃrəl]	*das Übernatürliche*	ADJ **supernatural**
imaginary [ɪˈmædʒɪnəri]	*imaginär*	≈ **fantastic**
creature [ˈkriːtʃə]	*Geschöpf, Kreatur*	≈ **animal**
being [ˈbiːɪŋ]	*Wesen*	*vgl.* **human being** *Mensch*
novel [ˈnɒvl]	*Roman*	N **novelist** *Romanautor/in* → *Kasten links*
novella [nəˈvelə]	*Novelle*	
to **publish** [ˈpʌblɪʃ]	*veröffentlichen*	N **publication**
storytelling [ˈstɔːrɪtelɪŋ]	*Geschichten, Erzählen*	N **storyteller**, V to **tell a story**
plot development [ˈplɒt dɪveləpmənt]	*Handlungsdramaturgie*	V to **develop a plot**
characterization [ˌkærəktəraɪˈzeɪʃn]	*Charakterisierung*	V to **characterize**
sophisticated [səˈfɪstɪkeɪtɪd]	*differenziert, niveauvoll*	N **sophistication**

Character, plot and structure

The main characters in a story are the protagonist and antagonist. There may be one or more of each, or no antagonist. They are usually complex, rounded characters. There may also be incidental or minor characters, which may be two-dimensional.

The plot is the sequence of connected events which make up the story. There may also be incidental events which are not critical to the outcome but which add tension or humour, or help to flesh out a character.

Structure refers to how a story is constructed. A story often starts with some kind of exposition, which introduces the characters and situation. However, many stories start in the middle of the action, leaving the reader to work out the situation and who the characters are.

There may then be one or more incidents which cause a conflict between the characters. There is a build-up of tension as further events occur. The story will come to a climax or turning point when the protagonist is forced to take decisive action. After the climax comes the denouement, in which the conflict between the characters is resolved.

Word family 'character'
character Figur *(in einem Roman oder Film)* **characteristic** charakteristisch **characterization** Charakterisierung to **characterize** charakterisieren

Expressions with 'character'
main character Hauptfigur **major character** wichtige Figur, Hauptfigur **minor character** Nebenfigur **out of character** rollenwidrig, untypisch **stock character** typische Figur, Typ, Standardfigur

Story begins

CHECKPOINT
In English, please!

a Welche der Figuren ist der Protagonist?
b Die Gegenspielerin in der Geschichte ist nicht konkret genug ausgestaltet.
c Ein Spannungsaufbau ist wichtig für jeden Kriminalroman.
d Diesen Ausgang habe ich nicht erwartet, er hat mich wirklich überrascht.

character [ˈkærəktə]	*Figur*	→ *Kasten links*
plot [plɒt]	*Handlung*	≈ **storyline**
protagonist [prəˈtægənɪst]	*Hauptfigur, Protagonist/in*	≈ **hero**
antagonist [ænˈtægənɪst]	*Gegenspieler/in, Widersacher/in*	≈ **villain**
complex [ˈkɒmpleks]	*vielschichtig*	N **complexity**
rounded [ˈraʊndɪd]	*ausgewogen, facettenreich*	≈ **three-dimensional**
incidental [ɪnsɪˈdentl]	*wenig bedeutend, Neben-*	≈ **peripheral**
minor [ˈmaɪnə]	*Neben-*	≈ **subsidiary, subordinate**
sequence [ˈsiːkwəns]	*Folge, Abfolge*	≈ **string**
critical (to sth) [ˈkrɪtɪkl tə]	*entscheidend (für etw)*	≈ **vitally important (for/to sth)**
outcome [ˈaʊtkʌm]	*Ausgang*	≈ **result**
tension [ˈtenʃn]	*Spannung*	ADJ **tense** *angespannt*
to **flesh out** [fleʃ ˌaʊt]	*konkret ausgestalten*	
to **construct** [kənˈstrʌkt]	*aufbauen, konstruieren*	≈ to **structure**, to **build**
conflict [ˈkɒnflɪkt]	*Konflikt*	V to **conflict with sb !** [kənˈflɪkt]
build-up [ˈbɪldʌp]	*Aufbau, Zunahme*	V to **build up**
to **come to a climax** [ˈklaɪmæks]	*einen Höhepunkt erreichen*	≈ to **reach a crisis**
turning point [ˈtɜːnɪŋ pɔɪnt]	*Wendepunkt*	≈ **climax**
to **take action** [ˌteɪk ˈækʃn]	*Maßnahmen ergreifen*	≈ to **act**
decisive [dɪˈsaɪsɪv]	*entschlossen, entscheidend*	◑ **indecisive, hesitant**
denouement [deɪˈnuːmõ]	*Auflösung, Ausgang (einer Geschichte)*	≈ **conclusion**
to **resolve** [rɪˈzɒlv]	*auflösen*	N **resolution**

Narrative technique and style

A writer's choice of narrator is crucial for the way the reader perceives a work of fiction. First-person narrative focuses on the feelings, opinions, and perceptions of one character in the story. It can help the reader to feel more personal involvement and empathy. An omniscient third-person narrator can give an overview of events and people, without the need to consider how a particular character could plausibly know certain details. On the other hand, a limited third-person narrator can be the protagonist referring to herself in the third person. An epistolary novel tells a story through documents, e.g. letters, diary entries or newspaper clippings.

Most fiction includes dialogue. It may include passages of interior monologue – the thoughts of one or more characters. It may also include vivid descriptions of places and people and well as reporting events. Some authors pay a lot of attention to world building – creating a believable world as a backdrop to the story, others assume that the context is known to the reader.

Word family 'narrate'

to **narrate** erzählen, schildern
narration Erzählung, Schilderung
narrative ADJ erzählend, narrativ
narrative N Erzählung, Schilderung, Bericht
narrator Erzähler/in

Subdivisions of a novel

part Teil
section Abschnitt
chapter Kapitel
passage Passage
paragraph Absatz
sentence Satz

Narrative perspective

first-person narrator Ich-Erzähler
third-person narrator Erzähler in der 3. Person (auktorial, personal oder neutral)
omniscient narrator allwissender/auktorialer Erzähler
limited narrator personaler/perspektivisch begrenzter Erzähler
in the first/second/third person in der 1./2./3. Person

CHECKPOINT　　　　　　　　　　　*In English, please!*

a Normalerweise bevorzuge ich Geschichten mit einem Ich-Erzähler.
b Mit welcher Figur konntest du am meisten mitfühlen?
c Die Beschreibungen in dieser Passage fand ich nicht anschaulich.
d Was hältst du vom Weltenbau in den Harry-Potter-Romanen?

narrative technique [ˌnærətɪv tekˈniːk]	*Erzählweise, Erzähltechnik*	
narrator [nəˈreɪtə]	*Erzähler/in*	→ *Kasten links*
crucial [ˈkruːʃl]	*entscheidend, ausschlaggebend*	≈ **vital**
to **perceive** [pəˈsiːv]	*wahrnehmen, empfinden*	≈ to **experience**
perception [pəˈsepʃn]	*Wahrnehmung, Empfindung*	ADJ **perceptive**
personal involvement [ˌpɜːsənl ɪnˈvɒlvmənt]	*innere Beteiligung*	V to **become personally involved**
empathy [ˈempəθi]	*Mitgefühl, Einfühlung*	V to **empathize (with sb)**
omniscient [ɒmˈnɪsɪənt]	*allwissend*	≈ **all-knowing**
overview [ˈəʊvəvjuː]	*Überblick*	≈ **outline**
event [ɪˈvent]	*Ereignis*	ADJ **eventful**
limited [ˈlɪmɪtɪd]	*beschränkt*	N **limitation** *Beschränkung*, **limit** *Grenze*
diary entry [ˈdaɪəri entri]	*Tagebucheintrag*	vgl. to **keep a diary** *Tagebuch führen*
clipping [ˈklɪpɪŋ]	*Ausschnitt*	≈ **cutting**
passage [ˈpæsɪdʒ]	*Passage*	→ *Kasten links*
interior monologue [ɪnˌtɪəriə ˈmɒnəlɒg]	*innerer Monolog*	
vivid [ˈvɪvɪd]	*lebendig, anschaulich*	N **vividness** *Lebendigkeit*
world building [ˈwɜːld bɪldɪŋ]	*Weltenbau*	V to **build a world**
backdrop (to sth) [ˈbækdrɒp tə]	*Hintergrund, Kulisse (für etw)*	≈ **background (to sth)**
to **assume** [əˈsjuːm]	*davon ausgehen*	N **assumption** *Annahme*
context [ˈkɒntekst]	*Zusammenhang, Kontext*	≈ **background, situation**

B Drama

Tragedy

Tragedy is one of the two main types of play in Classical drama. A tragedy may be defined as a play in which a sequence of events leads to a catastrophic conclusion. Usually a tragedy concerns the downfall of a person whose character is fundamentally good but imperfect. His or her downfall is usually caused by some flaw or error of judgement. The dramatist generally aims to make the audience empathize with the protagonist's predicament and feel anxiety for him or her.

Adversity may reveal the best aspects of the protagonist's character, as he or she struggles to avoid disaster, then endures it with courage and dignity. Thus, despite its sad subject matter, tragedy is generally uplifting for the audience. Often the play deals with an important issue in society or an aspect of human nature and causes the audience to reflect on this.

Modern journalism often writes about 'tragedies' but these are usually just sad or catastrophic events, and have little in common with tragedy in the dramatic sense.

CHECKPOINT   *In English, please!*

a Was verursacht den Untergang der Hauptfigur?
b Ich konnte mich nicht in ihre missliche Lage hineinversetzen.
c Der Stoff war traurig, aber der Schluss war erhebend.

Word family 'drama'

drama Schauspiel, Theaterstück, Drama
dramatist Bühnenautor/in, Dramatiker/in
dramatic dramatisch, dramaturgisch, Theater-
to **dramatize** dramatisieren, (einen Stoff für TV/Theater/Film) bearbeiten
dramatization Dramatisierung, (TV-/Bühnen-/Kino-)Bearbeitung

German 'Zuschauer', 'Publikum'

audience
*The **audience** was thrilled by the film/concert/play.*
viewers (= TV audience)
***Viewers** can see the whole series on ZDF.*
spectators
***Spectators** cheered as the marathon runner crossed the line.*

German 'Fehler'

defect/fault/flaw
*His personality has a fundamental **defect/flaw/fault**.*
error/mistake
*She made a serious **error/mistake**.*

tragedy ['trædʒədi]	Trauerspiel, Tragödie	ADJ tragic
play [pleɪ]	(Theater-)Stück	≈ theatrical work/piece
sequence of events [ˌsiːkwəns əv ɪ'vents]	Abfolge von Ereignissen	
catastrophic [ˌkætə'strɒfɪk]	verhängnisvoll, katastrophal	N catastrophe
conclusion [kən'kluːʒn]	Ausgang, Ende, Schluss	V to conclude
downfall ['daʊnfɔːl]	Niedergang, Untergang, Sturz	≈ disaster
imperfect [ɪm'pɜːfɪkt]	unvollkommen	N imperfection
flaw [flɔː]	Schwäche, Fehler	ADJ flawed
error of judgement [ˌerər əv 'dʒʌdʒmənt]	falsche Entscheidung, Missgriff	≈ poor decision
to empathize with ['empəθaɪz]	sich jdn hineinversetzen	N empathy, ADJ empathetic
predicament [prɪ'dɪkəmnt]	missliche Lage, Dilemma, Notlage	≈ difficult/precarious situation
anxiety [æŋ'zaɪəti]	Angst, Sorge	ADJ anxious
adversity [əd'vɜːsɪti]	widrige Umstände, Not	ADJ adverse
to reveal [rɪ'viːl]	zum Vorschein bringen	N revelation
to struggle ['strʌgl]	sich (verzweifelt) abmühen	N struggle Kampf
to endure [ɪn'djʊə]	ertragen, aushalten	N endurance
courage ['kʌrɪdʒ]	Mut	ADJ courageous
dignity ['dɪgnəti]	Würde	ADJ dignified
subject matter ['sʌbdʒɪkt mætə]	Inhalt, Stoff, Gegenstand	≈ topic
uplifting [ʌp'lɪftɪŋ]	erbaulich, erhebend	◀▶ depressing, dispiriting
to reflect on sth [rɪ'flekt]	über etw nachdenken	N reflection Nachdenken ADJ reflective nachdenklich

Comedy

Comedy has perhaps changed more than tragedy over the centuries. Classical Greek comedy uses coarse language and deals frankly with sexual themes. It is often heavy-handed satire and parody, and features stock characters to represent social types, with little individualization. Shakespeare's comedies often combine romantic plots with serious themes and exploration of the darker side of human nature. Some of his plays deal with tragic themes but have implausibly happy endings.

Modern comedy on the stage and screen doesn't follow any particular rules. The farces of many British playwrights and screenwriters feature slapstick, improbable situations and exaggerated characters. Oscar Wilde's light-hearted social satires poke fun at society's attitudes and standards of behaviour. Samuel Beckett combines tragedy and comedy in plays which show the absurdity of life, portraying the breakdown of relationships and communication with black humour. In many modern films and plays, comedy is blended with realism in exploring the problems of daily life.

Word family 'comedy'

comedy Komödie
comedian Schauspieler/in, Komödiant/in
comic komödiantisch, komisch
comical komisch, lustig

Prefix 'im-'

immature unreif
impatient ungeduldig
implausible unplausibel, unglaubhaft
impossible unmöglich
improbable unwahrscheinlich

CHECKPOINT   *In English, please!*

a Ich fand, der Humor in dem Theaterstück war eher plump.
b Das Happy End war unglaubhaft.
c Das war ein heiteres Theaterstück: Es sollte gar nicht ernst sein.
d Diese Dramatikerin verbindet gern Realismus mit Satire.

coarse [kɔːs]	*derb*	≈ crude, rude
frankly [ˈfræŋkli]	*offen, offenherzig*	≈ openly
heavy-handed [ˌhevi-ˈhændɪd]	*plump*	≈ clumsy
satire [ˈsætaɪə]	*Satire*	ADJ satirical
parody [ˈpærədi]	*Parodie*	V to parody
stock character [ˈstɒk kærəktə]	*typische Figur, Typ, Standardfigur*	≈ stereotypical figure
individualization [ɪndɪvɪdʒʊəlaɪˈzeɪʃn]	*individuelle Ausprägung, Individualisierung*	V to individualize
romantic [rəʊˈmæntɪk]	*romantisch*	N romance, Romanticism
exploration [ˌekspləˈreɪʃn]	*Erkundung*	V to explore
implausibly [ɪmˈplɔːzəbli]	*unglaubwürdig, unglaubhaft*	≈ unbelievably
happy ending [ˌhæpi ˈendɪŋ]	*Happy End*	◀▶ sad ending
stage [steɪdʒ]	*Bühne*	/gl. a stage actor *Theaterschauspieler/in*
farce [fɑːs]	*Farce*	ADJ farcical
playwright [ˈpleɪraɪt]	*Bühnenautor/in, Dramatiker/in*	≈ dramatist
screenwriter [ˈskriːnraɪtə]	*Drehbuchautor/in*	≈ scriptwriter
exaggerated [ɪgˈzædʒəreɪtɪd]	*übertrieben, überzeichnet*	◀▶ understated
light-hearted [ˌlaɪtˈhɑːtɪd]	*heiter, unbeschwert*	≈ happy, joyful
to **poke fun at sb/sth** [pəʊk ˈfʌn]	*sich über etw/jdn lustig machen*	≈ to laugh at sb/sth, make fun of sb/sth
absurdity [əbˈsɜːdəti]	*Absurdität*	ADJ absurd
to **portray** [pɔːˈtreɪ]	*darstellen, porträtieren*	N portrayal, portrait
realism [ˈriːəlɪzəm]	*Realismus*	ADJ realistic

C Poetry

Features and functions of poetry

Poetry is closely related to music, in that the sound of the words may be as important as, and enhance, their meaning. Poetry may use rhythm, rhyme, assonance, alliteration and onomatopoeia to achieve musical effects. In 2016, a musician and songwriter, Bob Dylan, was awarded the Nobel Prize in Literature 'for having created new poetic expressions within the great American song tradition', illustrating the close link between music and poetry.

Poetry invites the reader or listener to become involved imaginatively in ways that prose often does not. Thus it often encourages multiple interpretations, using ambiguity and symbolism to allude to possible meanings, which readers or listeners must interpret for themselves.

The length and structure of poetry varies widely. Poems may be very short works of one stanza (e.g. haiku) or as long as novels (e.g. epic poems). Drama may be written in poetic form, e.g. the plays of Shakespeare.

One of the earliest functions of poetry may have been to memorize knowledge in societies which had not yet invented writing. To this day, people take pleasure in memorizing and reciting poetry, and of course, singing songs.

feature ['fiːtʃə]	*Charakteristikum, Merkmal*	V to **feature**
poetry ['pəʊətri]	*Dichtung*	→ *Kasten links*
to **enhance** [ɪn'hɑːns]	*verstärken*	◆ to **diminish**
rhythm ['rɪðəm]	*Rhythmus*	N **rhythmic** *vgl.* **metre** *Versmaß*
rhyme [raɪm]	*Reim*	ADJ **rhyming**
assonance ['æsənəns]	*Assonanz*	ADJ **assonant**
alliteration [əˌlɪtə'reɪʃn]	*Alliteration*	V to **alliterate**, ADJ **alliterative**
onomatopoeia [ˌɒnəmætə'piːə]	*Lautmalerei*	ADJ **onomatopoeic**
songwriter ['sɒŋraɪtə]	*Liedtexter und -komponist, Songschreiber/in*	≈ **lyricist**
expression [ɪk'spreʃn]	*Ausdruck*	ADJ **expressive**, V to **express**
multiple ['mʌltɪpl]	*mehrere, mannigfache*	◆ **single**
interpretation [ɪnˌtɜːprɪ'teɪʃn]	*Deutung, Auslegung, Interpretation*	V to **interpret**
ambiguity [ˌæmbɪ'gjuːəti]	*Mehrdeutigkeit*	ADJ **ambiguous**
symbolism ['sɪmbəlɪzm]	*Symbolik, Symbolismus*	ADJ **symbolic**
to **allude to sth** [ə'ljuːd]	*auf etw anspielen*	N **allusion** ! ≠ **illusion** ADJ **allusive** *voller Anspielungen*
to **interpret** [ɪn'tɜːprɪt]	*deuten, auslegen, interpretieren*	N **interpretation**
stanza ['stænzə]	*Strophe*	*vgl.* **verse** *Vers, Dichtung*
epic ['epɪk]	*episch, erzählend*	
to **memorize** ['meməraɪz]	*auswendig lernen*	N **memorization**
to **take pleasure in doing sth** ['pleʒər]	*sich daran erfreuen, etw zu tun; etw gern tun*	≈ to **enjoy**
to **recite** [rɪ'saɪt]	*vortragen, rezitieren*	N **recital**

Figurative language

Figurative language departs from the literal meaning of words.

A simile occurs when one thing is explicitly compared to another thing which, taken literally, is fundamentally different, e.g. 'My blood, it is like light.'[1] This is logically impossible; however the writer is alluding to certain attributes or characteristics of light – bright, swift and weightless. Using these characteristics for 'blood' creates a forceful expression of joy and energy. If the comparison is implicit rather than explicit, then a metaphor is created, e.g. 'Once my heart was a summer rose.'[2]

A literary symbol is both literal and metaphorical. Thus when 'man and shadow meet,'[3] the shadow is both the man's literal shadow, meeting him as he falls to the ground, and a symbol of death. Often a symbol is not clear-cut, but subtle and complex.

Figurative language often makes an impact by comparing an abstract concept to something concrete. When figurative language is used to evoke pictures in the reader's mind, it is also called imagery.

1 Thom Gunn, 'Rites of Passage' **2** Edith Sitwell, 'Song' **3** Keith Douglas, 'How to Kill'

CHECKPOINT

In English, please!

a Die Beschreibung ist nicht wörtlich zu nehmen, sondern bildlich.
b Ich finde, in diesem Kontext scheint dieser Vergleich etwas seltsam.
c Nein, der Vergleich ist hintersinnig und metaphorisch, nicht scharf.
d Ich finde diese Bildsprache sehr plastisch.

German 'Schatten'

shadow = dark shape on a surface when an object blocks the light
*You can see the photographer's **shadow** in the photo.*
shade = lack of sunlight
*Let's sit in the **shade**. It's too hot in the sun.*

Word family 'death'

death Tod
deathly totenähnlich, Toten-, Grabes-, Leichen-
dead tot
deadly tödlich, todbringend
deadliness tödliche Wirkung
to **die** sterben
to **deaden** dämpfen, abtöten, betäuben

figurative ['fɪɡərətɪv]	*übertragen, bildlich*	*vgl.* **figure of speech** *Redefigur*
to **depart from sth** [dɪ'pɑːt]	*von etw abweichen*	N **departure**
literal ['lɪtərəl]	*wörtlich, eigentlich, buchstäblich*	N **literalness**
simile ['sɪmɪli]	*Vergleich*	! *Aussprache*
explicitly [ɪk'splɪsɪtli]	*ausdrücklich, explizit*	◊ **implicitly**
to **take sth literally** ['lɪtərəli]	*etw wörtlich nehmen*	ADJ **literal** *wörtlich (zu nehmen)*
attribute ['ætrɪbjuːt]	*Eigenschaft, Merkmal*	V to **attribute sth to sb/sth**
characteristic [ˌkærəktə'rɪstɪk]	*charakteristisches Merkmal*	≈ **feature**
swift [swɪft]	*schnell, rasch*	≈ **fast**
forceful ['fɔːsfl]	*eindringlich*	≈ **powerful**
implicit [ɪm'plɪsɪt]	*stillschweigend, unausgesprochen, implizit*	V to **imply** *andeuten, unterstellen*
metaphor ['metəfə]	*Metapher*	! *Aussprache*
metaphorical [ˌmetə'fɒrɪkl]	*metaphorisch*	! *Aussprache*

TEST YOURSELF

You can check your answers on p. 214.

1   This collection of short stories _____ country.
    spielt in einem imaginären

2   Many of Margaret Atwood's works _____
    near future.
    stellen eine dystopische … vor

3   Although the _____ of J.K. Rowling's *Harry Potter*
    series is excellent, I sometimes find the _____ weak.
    Handlungsdramaturgie;
    Charakterisierung

4   Who is your favourite _____ in a _____?
    Figur; Kriminalroman

5   The _____ between the main characters arises from a
    _____ of apparently unconnected events.
    Konflikt; Folge

6   I don't agree that Gollum in *The Lord of the Rings* is a _____,
    as he is _____.
    Nebenfigur; entscheidend für den
    Höhepunkt

7   Using _____ makes it a lot easier for the
    author to give an _____ of events and people.
    einen allwissenden Erzähler;
    Überblick

8   I didn't experience much _____ with the characters.
    innere Beteiligung

9   The author's _____ may be poor, but he has
    a good imagination and a talent for _____ descriptions.
    Erzähltechnik; anschauliche

10 I didn't find the _____ believable: the protagonist made too many
    _____.
    Stück; falsche Entscheidungen

11 I'm not sure that she showed much _____
    _____ either.
    Mut oder Würde; angesichts der
    widrigen Umstände

Zuschauer; sich in sie hineinzuversetzen	**12** Maybe the rest of the _____ were able to _____ _____ her, but I just didn't care.
überzeichnet; Bühnenautor/in; Parodie	**13** The characters and their actions are _____, but then the _____ intends the play to be a _____.
porträtiert die Absurdität	**14** It _____ of society's standards of behaviour.
romantische Komödie; Happy End	**15** It's a _____ with an improbable _____.
spielen auf ... an; interpretieren	**16** The poet's notes _____ a number of possible meanings, but readers must _____ the poem for themselves.
Mehrdeutigkeit; Dichtung	**17** I enjoy the _____ of this _____, rather than searching for a single meaning.
verstärkt; vortragen	**18** The sound of the words _____ the poem's dramatic effect, so to understand it you need to _____ it.
episches; Strophen	**19** It is a long _____ poem comprising more than 100 _____.
Eigenschaften; Metapher	**20** Which _____ of darkness is the writer alluding to with this _____?
metaphorisch; eindeutig	**21** I don't think his intention is _____: the meaning seems literal and _____.
konkret; unausgesprochen; Tod	**22** The way I read it, the poet's use of the word 'dark' here isn't _____: there's an _____ allusion to _____.
eindringlich; erzielt eine große Wirkung	**23** This _____ language really _____.

Suggested answers: Checkpoint and Test yourself

1 Young people in society

page 6
a Adults often/frequently criticize today's youth/young people.
b Electronic devices have changed our leisure activities/pursuits.
c We volunteer for a charity in our free time.

page 8
a My favourite activity is using social media.
b I'm too busy to hang out with my friends.
c What are your favourite extracurricular activities?
d I enjoy creative pastimes/hobbies like music and art.
e Far from being active and busy, he leads a sedentary life.

page 10
a We're thinking about doing/taking a gap year when we leave school.
b Working abroad will take us out of our comfort zone/be a challenge for us.
c The volunteers come from many different social backgrounds.
d We will have to learn new skills and adapt to unfamiliar living conditions.

page 12
a Charities like us rely on volunteers like you.
b All participants receive adequate training.
c I'm interested in helping the elderly and people with disabilities.
d She wants to find a voluntary/unpaid position with a non-profit/not-for-profit organization.

page 14
a Adolescents often feel vulnerable when they face unfamiliar social situations.
b Acceptance is important to everyone.
c Peer pressure is sometimes difficult to cope with.
d It's completely natural to feel insecure about our appearance.

page 16
a Most models don't really have flawless skin.
b Even attractive people have imperfections.
c It's important to have ideals to live up to.
d He is preoccupied with his body image.
e Anxiety and depression are serious mental health problems.
f Low self-esteem led her to undergo plastic surgery.

page 18
a This medicine should help you to manage your symptoms.
b However, it may cause psychological changes.
c Can I buy it over the counter/without a prescription?
d No, you need a prescription from your doctor.
e Be careful and don't take too much: an overdose can be dangerous.

page 20
a Did you experience any sensory changes when you took the drug?
b Recreational drug use is pleasurable until it become addictive.
c Some recreational drugs are legal and others are banned.
d Everything is harmful to your health if you take too much of it.

page 22
a There is controversy about the legalization of cannabis.

b Even soft drugs can cause major harm.
c There is no evidence that they are dangerous if they are used in moderation.
d Do harsh penalties for drug possession reduce drug use?

page 24
a Moderate social drinking creates a relaxed atmosphere.
b Binge drinking can have serious consequences.
c He drank an excessive amount of alcohol at the party.
d His loss of self-control was embarrassing to his friends.

page 26
a Drunk driving often leads to fatal accidents.
b Impaired judgement leads to risk taking.
c Even small quantities of alcohol are unsafe for drivers.
d Alcohol use is habit-forming for many people.
e Alcohol abuse is destructive, but prohibition is not the answer.

page 28
a Greg grew up in a small, close-knit community.
b His extended family included many aunts, uncles and cousins.
c Family, friends and neighbours influenced his upbringing.
d He wants a safe, stable environment for his children.

page 30
a Family breakup is disruptive for children.
b Ann had to cope with the separation and divorce of her parents.
c She lived in a blended family with step-siblings and half-siblings.
d She then lived with foster parents.
e Sudden changes in our social networks can be difficult.

page 32
a This country recognizes same-sex marriage(s).

b Homosexual relationships are equal to heterosexual relationships.
c Same-sex couples have stable, committed relationships.
d Social recognition is important for (our) emotional well-being.

page 34
a Bullying does not always involve violence and threats.
b Verbal abuse is distressing for the victim.
c Many people experience cyberbullying on the internet.
d The bully was motivated by low self-esteem.
e Her humour was cruel and insensitive.
f He wanted to intimidate and dominate others.

page 36
a Nobody should have to put up with bullying.
b The victim is never to blame.
c There is nothing shameful in seeking help.
d The school offers support and counselling for victims of bullying.
e We have a zero-tolerance attitude towards bullying here.

pages 38–41 (Test yourself)
1 leisure actitivies; youth – **2** educational; on a regular basis – **3** volunteered – **4** spend a lot of time – **5** taking up a new hobby – **6** lead active lives – **7** taking a gap year – **8** social conscience – **9** took … out of his comfort zone – **10** adapt to; living conditions – **11** Charities; rely on – **12** homeless – **13** meant well – **14** participants; adventures – **15** application process; overseas – **16** vulnerable; adolescence – **17** human; acceptance – **18** peer pressure; insecure – **19** flawless; self-esteem – **20** live up to – **21** are preoccupied with – **22** medicine; with prolonged use – **23** over the counter; prescription – **24** restricted; habit-forming – **25** frightening; disorientating – **26** anti-drug laws; justified – **27** evidence; cause harm – **28** controversy; punishments – **29** drug of choice – **30** social drinking; binge

drinking – **31** drunken; excessive; spirits – **32** Drunk driving; judgement; impaired – **33** was raised by; parents – **34** extended family; safe environment – **35** neighbours; community – **36** relatives; upbringing – **37** family breakup; childhood – **38** looked after; divorce – **39** right of access – **40** gender-neutral – **41** same-sex; gay – **42** bullying; violence – **43** motivated; cruel – **44** stand up for themselves; insensitive – **45** Don't blame the victim – **46** zero-tolerance – **47** suffer; sought help

2 Education and work

page 42
a The British school/education system is different to/from the German system.
b Early years education is optional.
c Most state schools are comprehensive schools.
d Most students go on to further education or higher education.

page 44
a Parents may homeschool their children.
b They do not have to follow a strict curriculum.
c The framework states which subjects schools must teach.
d Students sit/take exams at the end of their school education.
e Have you seen the exam results yet?

page 46
a Is your school government/state-funded?
b No, I attend a private school.
c What grade are you in?
d After the summer break, I will be in 12th grade.

page 48
a German is an elective (subject) in our school.
b Astronomy is my favourite extracurricular activity.
c I need to get a high score in the test.

d I want to enrol/enroll at a good college/university.
e My parents both graduated from college.

page 50
a This company won't take on young people without workplace experience.
b Apprenticeships are available in many technical professions.
c My apprenticeship is a combination of classroom study and on-the-job training.
d Vocational training is comprehensive in Germany.

page 52
a The company offers a graduate programme.
b You complete in-company training and get practical work tasks.
c Competition for paid internships is often fierce.

page 54
a How can I find out about job vacancies?
b Look at careers websites and newspaper advertisements.
c Networking is another important strategy.
d I have written lots of applications and filled in lots of online forms.
e How do I upload my CV and covering letter?

page 56
a Did you use the German format for your CV/résumé?
b No, I included personal details but no photo(graph).
c Tailor/Customize your CV/résumé to the job offered.
d This covering/cover letter has several spelling errors.

page 58
a We want to invite you to a preliminary interview.
b Will it be a video interview or face-to-face?
c The interview will last about an hour.
d There will also be an assessment and a psychometric test.
e You can chat informally with the senior managers.

f There will be a tour of the company.

page 60
a We often take workers' rights for granted.
b In the 19th century, few workers received sick pay.
c The union wants shorter working hours and more annual leave.
d Industrial action is sometimes necessary to protect jobs.
e Our jobs are under threat/threatened because of automation.

page 62
a Will I get a permanent contract?
b No, we want you to work freelance.
c The retail outlet employs a lot of casual staff.
d I have a good work-life balance.
e There is little/isn't much job security if you are self-employed.

page 64
a The employers' ideas are very innovative.
b Workers don't have their own workstations.
c They have to share company resources efficiently.
d The staff are finding the working conditions stressful.

page 66
a The unemployment rate is decreasing/falling/declining/dropping/sinking.
b Demand for goods and services is rising/increasing/climbing/growing.
c There is still a scarcity of good jobs.
d Does your job make good use of your skills?
e No, I feel underemployed in my job.

page 68
a Hamid's qualifications were not recognized in Germany.
b He has a high level of education and several years' experience.
c Access to childcare facilities is a problem for many workers/employees.

d Part-time work is available here in the holiday season.

page 70
a Unemployment is threatening economic growth.
b We're afraid of losing our jobs.
c A universal basic income is a good solution to this problem.
d Unemployment benefit is only available after means testing.
e Would you work if it was your individual lifestyle choice, not a necessity?

pages 72–75 (Test yourself)
1 Primary; compulsory – **2** specializes in – **3** grammar schools; comprehensive schools – **4** curricula; subjects and course content – **5** sit/take a public exam – **6** apprenticeship; leaves school – **7** school year; summer recess/break – **8** grade; (senior) high school – **9** public school; private school – **10** academic progress is assessed – **11** supervise; extracurricular activities – **12** graduate school; have graduated from – **13** professional certification; vocational training – **14** are reluctant to take on – **15** role; on-the-job training – **16** Competition; graduate programme – **17** internship; labour – **18** to get an overview of; departments – **19** recruitment agencies; careers advice – **20** research; application – **21** favourable impression; accomplishments – **22** formal letter; grammatical errors – **23** brief; suitable for – **24** conduct; interview; screening process – **25** tour of the company; impressed me – **26** keen attitude; assessment – **27** working hours; overtime – **28** dismissal; annual leave – **29** minimum wage – **30** show up; won't get paid – **31** casual staff; retail outlets – **32** benefits; freelance – **33** premises; efficiently – **34** had a negative effect on productivity – **35** Office space; resource – **36** underemployment; unemployment – **37** supply; demand – **38** service industries; manufacturing – **39** Overqualification; experience – **40** work full-time; overstaffing – **41** market contracted – **42** unemployment benefit; meet a person's needs – **43** growth; undesirable

3 Media and communication

page 76
a This web page is loading / loads very slowly.
b That's annoying. Does it contain a lot of images?
c No, it's mostly / largely text-based, but my connection is quite slow.
d The poor layout reduces the website's accessibility.

page 78
a We need a dynamic, interactive website for our company.
b Can users post comments in real time?
c Yes, they can also personalize the website.
d They can easily change the (preferences and) settings.

page 80
a I don't see why household appliances need internet connectivity.
b 'Are the photos on your tablet?' – 'No, they're stored online.'
c Modern mobile phones have changed beyond recognition.
d They don't have buttons and they support natural language.

page 82
a Quora is a virtual community where members can ask and answer questions.
b So far, 1,400 people have upvoted my post and 15 have shared it.
c The user interface is good, but needs more functions.

page 84
a Don't browse the internet while we're carrying on a conversation!
b Social media is useful for staying in touch.
c I have a much larger circle of friends now because of it / as a result.

page 86
a The TV shows that we watch influence our consumption.
b I find advertising entertaining but not persuasive.
c I saw these shoes on a billboard and bought them right away.

page 88
a If you find advertising intrusive, you should get pay TV.
b Oh no, another commercial break! Can we fast-forward?
c These stupid banner ads are distracting me from the article.
d You should use ad blocking software then.

page 90
a Freedom of speech is a basic human right.
b Is it against the law to express offensive political opinions?
c It depends on the circumstances.
d Government censorship may be harmful to / can harm democracy.

page 92
a That is defamation – everything you said is completely false!
b The TV star is worried about his/her reputation.
c Do not share this image without the permission of the creator.
d With his speech he wanted to incite hatred and violence.

page 94
a This is a fake news story: it's misleading and untruthful.
b Thanks to the viral effect, the claim spread widely.
c The news story was an outright lie.
d Yes, but nobody believed the retraction.

page 96
a The newspaper lost its editorial independence when the media group bought it.
b You can recognize the target readership of a newspaper from the way it reports on current affairs.
c I like celebrity gossip, even if it's sensationalist.

page 98
a I read this newspaper for its in-depth reporting.
b I like reading the culture section and the fashion supplements.
c The journalist's political bias is obvious.
d The newspaper's circulation is falling.

pages 100–103 (Test yourself)
1 web presence; design – **2** text-based; amateurish – **3** fonts; images – **4** accessibility; user-friendliness – **5** post; review – **6** settings; personalize – **7** browsing history; access – **8** appliances; will respond to – **9** In the near future; connectivity – **10** obsolete; support – **11** software application; is stored – **12** user interface; community – **13** block; offensive – **14** shared; went viral – **15** linked to; have removed – **16** staying in touch with; face-to-face – **17** problematic; sensitive – **18** licence fee; TV channels – **19** commercial breaks; programmes – **20** influences; consumption – **21** product placement; brand names – **22** advertising; excessive; intrusive – **23** distracts; to concentrate on – **24** guarantee; freedom of expression – **25** universal; is recognized – **26** political; democratic – **27** defamation; legitimate – **28** hate speech; incite violence – **29** intellectual property; piracy – **30** manipulate public opinion – **31** misleading; defamatory – **32** rumours; innuendo – **33** viral effect; scandalous – **34** retraction; untruthful – **35** headline; sensationalist – **36** current affairs; broadsheets – **37** editorial; take on; contentious – **38** quality; commentary – **39** obvious bias; in-depth; analysis – **40** news content; print edition – **41** paywall; sophisticated

4 Technology and the environment

page 104
a Our natural resources are being depleted.
b How can we stop deforestation?

c Organic farming is healthier but less efficient.
d Intensive farming destroys ecosystems.

page 106
a Fundamental changes are required to protect biodiversity.
b Which animal and plant species benefit from human activity?
c We need food, breathable air and drinkable water.
d Many species that are vital for our ecosystems are currently under threat.

page 108
a The greenhouse effect is Earth's natural temperature control system.
b Greenhouse gas emissions are still rising / continuing to rise.
c Global warming is caused by human activities.
d Fossil fuels are enhancing / enhance the greenhouse effect.

page 110
a How can we deal with plastic and e-waste sustainably?
b We can recover valuable materials through recycling.
c We need to change our consumption habits.

page 112
a Should we accept surveillance in return for / in order to have more safety?
b CCTV monitoring reduces crime but also privacy.
c Face recognition allows the government to track / keep track of our movements.

page 114
a This isn't a specialized robot, it's a multipurpose robot.
b It can / is able to perform repetitive tasks which require a lot of dexterity.
c It doesn't require much skill to fly this drone.

page 116

a Which kind of benefits will the Internet of Things bring?
b Robots will perform/carry out tasks that are too tiring and unsafe/dangerous for humans.
c They will work autonomously without our oversight.
d Will automation cause security issues?

page 118

a Fracking brings environmental risks.
b Burning/The burning of fossil fuels drives climate change.
c Solar panels turn/convert the sun's energy into electricity.

page 120

a Electric motors are quieter and cleaner than internal combustion engines.
b Does the car still symbolize mobility and freedom?
c Self-driving vehicles are changing our ideas about vehicle ownership.
d Is rail transport electrified in this country?

page 122

a Nuclear power is a proven technology.
b It is very difficult to dispose of highly radioactive waste.
c The plant/power plant is obsolete and must be decommissioned.

page 124

a Is genetic engineering the same as selective breeding?
b We can transfer genes from one species to another.
c Genetically engineered microbes are novel organisms.
d Genetic engineering has applications in healthcare.

page 126

a Do you think that genetically modified food is safe?
b Activists want to stop field trials of GM crops.
c The environmental impact is/impacts are unpredictable.

d I don't want multinational companies to control the global food supply.

page 128

a The two animals are genetically identical.
b Do you have ethical concerns about human cloning/cloning of humans?
c I think it should be restricted but not prohibited.
d Cloning is technically difficult and has a high failure rate.

pages 130–133 (Test yourself)

1 feed; population – 2 Natural resources have been depleted – 3 has been degraded; intensive farming – 4 organic; more nutritious – 5 artificial; laboratory – 6 biodiversity; are under threat – 7 mass extinctions; natural disaster – 8 Human beings; environment; vital – 9 endangered species; benefit from – 10 greenhouse effect; are enhancing – 11 carbon dioxide and methane; climate change – 12 burning fossil fuels; global warming – 13 deals with waste; sustainable – 14 Plastics; persistence – 15 Recovery; valuable; technically – 16 consumer awareness; consumption habits – 17 keep track of; behaviour – 18 face recognition; innocuous – 19 CCTV monitoring; safety; crime – 20 surveillance; unprecedented – 21 Robots; repetitive – 22 multipurpose robot; agility; strength – 23 military; civilian – 24 artificial intelligence; self-driving; human input – 25 job losses; security issues – 26 autonomously; communicates with – 27 manufacturing; decision-making – 28 wind farms; generate; power – 29 fossil fuels; address the problem – 30 Solar panels; environmental risks – 31 exploit; uneconomic – 32 internal combustion engine; motor vehicles – 33 recharging points; service stations – 34 Aircraft; vital; movement of freight – 35 range; limiting factor – 36 safety concerns; nuclear power – 37 harness nuclear fusion – 38 genetic makeup; transfer – 39 Genetic engineering; medical research – 40 food production;

safety; concern – **41** scientific consensus; do not pose a risk to – **42** ethical concerns; human cloning – **43** organs; transplant – **44** extinct; technically; pointless

5 Society

page 134
a Germany is ethnically and culturally diverse.
b Tolerance is one of our core values.
c Are there countries in the EU that/which repress minorities.
d Indigenous people often experience racism.

page 136
a Being homeless/Homelessness affects one's health and well-being.
b Freedom of expression is a right, not a privilege.
c What can we do about the unequal distribution of wealth in society?

page 138
a That's good in theory, but in practice, there is a gender imbalance.
b There is a glass ceiling for female managers in this company.
c She does more than her fair share of household chores.
d Many older people have entrenched/deep-seated/persistent ideas about gender roles.

page 140
a A person's gender identity may not correlate with his or her sex at birth.
b Sex/Gender reassignment surgery is available for transgender people.
c Sexual orientation should not be a reason for social exclusion.

page 142
a No EU country has/countries have the death penalty.
b The prisoner received/got a life sentence.
c Capital punishment/The death penalty does not deter crime.
d Innocent people have spent years on Death Row.

page 144
a Pest control and hunting are legitimate uses of firearms.
b You need a thorough background check to get a gun permit.
c I don't think that private security personnel should have guns.
d Why do so many mass shootings occur in the USA?

page 146
a Indiscriminate violence is not a good way to achieve political aims.
b The atrocities perpetrated by the group were nothing but meaningless acts of violence.
c The authorities reduced civil liberties.
d Alienation of minority groups/minorities increased.

page 148
a Globalization is an economic and cultural phenomenon.
b Free trade agreements facilitate international trade.
c Trade barriers may not (help to) reduce unemployment.
d Political leaders want stricter border controls.

page 150
a The country has a high population growth rate.
b Adequate healthcare s impossible without safe/clean drinking water.
c Countries with widespread poverty are often politically unstable.
d Ethical consumerism helps producers in developing countries.

page 152
a Many people have moved from rural/country to urban areas.

b Are these people refugees or economic migrants?
c They want to settle permanently in their new host country.
d The asylum seekers left their homeland because of religious persecution.

page 154
a The continual acquisition of goods is not sustainable.
b It is important to boost economic activity.
d Consumerism is energy intensive and wasteful.

pages 156–159 (Test yourself)
1 ethnically; diverse – **2** faced the challenge – **3** welcomed diversity; core values – **4** Racism; xenophobia – **5** Human Rights – **6** justice; torture – **7** standard of living; adequate – **8** wealthy; live in poverty – **9** which career path to follow – **10** suffer; sexual harassment – **11** root cause; gender imbalance – **12** equality; fight for it – **13** gender identity; sex at birth – **14** persecution; sexual orientation – **15** binary distinction; sexuality – **16** sex reassignment surgery – **17** capital punishment; murder – **18** death penalty; violation – **19** miscarriage of justice; innocent – **20** deter; retribution – **21** firearm; self-defence – **22** ammunition securely – **23** mass shootings – **24** hunting; pest control – **25** Alienation; radicalize – **26** aims; vague; meaningless – **27** authorities; 'lone wolf' attackers – **28** Indiscriminate violence; fear – **29** advances; communications technology – **30** facilitating; goods and services – **31** free trade agreement – **32** Political instability; poverty – **33** developed countries; exploitation; developing countries – **34** Humanitarian aid; development aid – **35** access to; population growth rate – **36** urbanization; rural – **37** migrate; living standards – **38** tensions; refugees – **39** Migrant workers; support; homelands – **40** Consumerism; economic model – **41** Planned obsolescence; sustainability – **42** retail therapy; debt – **43** delivery; major driver – **44** to discard

6 English-speaking countries

page 160
a The British Isles include over six thousand islands.
b The English Channel separates Great Britain from continental Europe.
c Many British people dream of living by the sea.

page 162
a Although the Queen is the head of state, her power is only symbolic.
b Our constituency will have a new MP after the general election.
c Will devolution continue to give more autonomy to Scotland and Wales in the future?

page 164
a European countries explored the world and established colonies.
b The imperial powers competed with each other to establish trade networks.
c Britain is no longer a great military and trading power.
d The British Commonwealth is an association of independent states.

page 166
a The European Community was never just an economic union.
b Is there much dissatisfaction with migrant workers?
c There are lots of complaints about the European Union in the tabloid press.

page 168
a If you want to see lots of wildlife, go to one of the national parks.
b My favourite American landscape is the arid desert of Arizona.
c I prefer the high mountain ranges of the Rockies.

d Although the USA is a very populous country, there are many wilderness areas.

page 170
a The USA is a federal republic, so the states share sovereignty with the federal government.
b Do children learn (anything) about the Constitution in school?
c It is important to us because it guarantees our personal freedoms and rights.

page 172
a The colonies declared independence from (Great) Britain.
b Native Americans were displaced by the settlers.
c The reservations were a result of the Indian Removal Policy.
d The USA's economic development during the early 20th century was rapid.

page 174
a The southern states were dependent on slave labour.
b Slavery was abolished after the victory of the Union states.
c Emancipation did not prevent racial discrimination.
d The civil rights campaigns won equal rights for all US Americans.

page 176
a Many Americans trace their ancestry to German immigrants.
b The American Dream promises prosperity and upward social mobility.
c Millions of undocumented immigrants have crossed the border from Mexico.

page 178
a Will China one day be the world's dominant superpower?
b The USA is a powerful advocate for democracy.
c The military intervention caused international concern.
d The global influence of the USA will continue for many years.

page 180
a Australia was discovered by Europeans in the 18th century.
b The Maori are the incigenous people of New Zealand.
c Melbourne, Sydney, Perth and Brisbane are large coastal cities.
d Mining is an important industry in Australia.

page 182
a German and English are closely related languages.
b English is a world language and the most widely learned second language.
c English is an official language in many countries that were once part of the British Empire.

pages 184–187 (Test yourself)
1 sparsely populated – 2 temperate; unpredictable – 3 population density – 4 low lying; mountainous – 5 Prime Minister; head of government – 6 autonomy; devolution – 7 members of parliament; constituency – 8 party; general election – 9 compete with; imperial power – 10 wars and trade – 11 colonies; independence – 12 Raw materials; goods – 13 in favour; joined – 14 tabloid press; migrant workers – 15 dissatisfaction; bureaucratic – 16 Eurosceptics; majority – 17 wildlife; diverse – 18 tropical; arctic – 19 ethnic group; racial minority – 20 inhabitants; urban areas – 21 citizens; federal republic; state – 22 chambers; elected – 23 to vote; elections – 24 collecting taxes; law enforcement – 25 cid the settlers displace and conquer – 26 independence; territory – 27 discovery; accelerated – 28 provoked; Civil War – 29 abolition of slavery – 30 emancipation; equality – 31 deny; civil rights – 32 imposed; restrict – 33 tracing the r ancestry – 34 land of opportunity and upward social mobility – 35 deportation of the undocumented immigrants – 36 natura ization; assimilated – 37 global influence – 38 an advocate for; mil tary interventions – 39 dominant; key – 40 concerns; foreign policy – 41 arid; uninhabited – 42 primary

industries; service economy – **43** coastal; rural – **44** laid back; egalitarian – **45** native language – **46** has been influenced; is more closely related to – **47** business, law and science

7 Literature

page 188
a The story is fictional but based on a real-life person.
b It's difficult to categorize this novel: is it science fiction or fantasy?
c I like novels which portray an alternative reality.
d Do you prefer novels, novellas or short stories?

page 190
a Which of the characters is the protagonist?
b The antagonist in this story is not fleshed out enough.
c A build-up of tension is important for any crime novel.
d I didn't expect that denouement: it really surprised me.

page 192
a I usually prefer stories with a first-person narrator.
b Which character were you able to/did you empathize with most?
c I didn't find the descriptions in that passage vivid.
d What do you think of the world building in the Harry Potter novels?

page 194
a What causes the protagonist's downfall?
b I couldn't empathize with her predicament.
c The subject matter was sad, but the conclusion was uplifting.

page 196
a I thought that the humour in the play was heavy-handed.
b The happy ending was implausible.

c It was a light-hearted play: it wasn't supposed to be serious.
d This playwright likes to blend/combine realism with satire.

page 198
a The effect of rhythm and onomatopoeia in this poem is very musical.
b The songwriter likes to use rhyme and assonance in his songs.
c The poem is ambiguous and allusive.
d What is your interpretation of this symbolism?

page 200
a The description isn't literal; it's figurative.
b I think in this context this simile seems a bit strange.
c No, the simile is subtle and metaphorical, not clear-cut.
d I find this imagery very evocative.

pages 202–203 (Test yourself)
1 is set in an imaginary – **2** portray a dystopian – **3** plot development; characterization – **4** character; detective novel – **5** conflict; sequence – **6** minor character; critical to the climax – **7** an omniscient narrator; overview – **8** personal involvement – **9** narrative technique; vivid – **10** play; errors of judgement – **11** courage or dignity in the face of adversity – **12** audience; empathize with – **13** exaggerated; playwright; parody – **14** portrays the absurdity – **15** romantic comedy; happy ending – **16** allude to; interpret – **17** ambiguity; poetry – **18** enhances; recite – **19** epic; stanzas – **20** attributes; metaphor – **21** metaphorical; clear-cut – **22** concrete; implicit; death – **23** forceful; makes an impact

Useful language for your exams

Describing charts and diagrams

Types

The information is presented as …	Die Daten werden dargestellt in …
a pie chart	einem Tortendiagramm
a bar chart	einem Balken-/Säulendiagramm
a histogram	einem Histogramm
a line graph	einer Kurve/einem Liniendiagramm
a timeline	einer Zeitachse
an infographic	einer Infografik
a map	einer Karte

Elements

Graphic elements / Grafikelemente

Looking at …, we can see that	Wenn wir … betrachten, können wir sehen, dass
the x-axis	die X-Achse
the y-axis	die Y-Achse
the bars	die Balken
the columns	die Säulen
the line(s)	die Kurven/die Linien
the segments	die Abschnitte

Text elements / Textelemente

The … tells us that	… sagt uns, dass
title	Der Titel

legend/key	Die Zeichenerklärung
The values are given ...	Die Werte werden angegeben ...
in thousands of units	in tausend Einheiten
in percentages	in Prozent
over a period of 20 years	über einen Zeitraum von 20 Jahren

Evaluating the information

Proportions	Anteile
roughly ten per cent	ungefähr zehn Prozent
more than half	mehr als die Hälfte
exactly a third	genau ein Drittel
nearly a quarter	fast ein Viertel
barely an eighth	kaum ein Achtel
less than a tenth	weniger als ein Zehntel

Developments over time	Zeitliche Entwicklungen
to rise steadily • a steady rise	kontinuierlich steigen/zunehmen • kontinuierliche/r Anstieg/Zunahme
to grow gradually • gradual growth	allmählich wachsen/zunehmen • allmähliche/s Wachstum/Zunahme
to increase suddenly • a sudden increase	sprunghaft ansteigen/zunehmen • sprunghafte/r Anstieg/Zunahme
to fall sharply • a sharp fall	stark zurückgehen • starker Rückgang
to decline slightly • a slight decline	leicht zurückgehen • leichter Rückgang
to decrease rapidly • a rapid decrease	rasch abnehmen / schnell zurückgehen • rasche Abnahme / schneller Rückgang
to end abruptly • an abrupt end	abrupt enden • abruptes Ende
to fluctuate erratically • erratic fluctuations	unberechenbar schwanken • unberechenbare Schwankungen
to level off	sich stabilisieren
to reach a peak	einen Höchstwert/-stand erreichen

Describing pictures and cartoons

Content

The cartoon depicts …	Die Karikatur stellt … dar.
The photo shows …	Das Foto zeigt …
The illustration/picture portrays …	Die Abbildung / Das Bild stellt … dar.
The poster refers to …	Das Plakat bezieht sich auf ..

Arrangement

in the centre	in der Mitte
in the foreground	im Vordergrund
in the background	im Hintergrund
on the left/right	links/rechts
at the very top/bottom	ganz oben/unten
in the bottom left/right corner	in der unteren linken/rechten Ecke

Technique and style

choice of colours	Farbwahl, Farbgestaltung
black-and-white	schwarzweiß
attention to detail	Liebe zum Detail
complex	vielschichtig, komplex
exaggerated	übertrieben
impressionistic	impressionistisch
precise	genau, präzise
simple	einfach, schlicht
stark	krass, schonungslos
vague	vage, schwammig

Reaction

Personally, I find the picture …	Ich für meinen Teil finde das Bild …
Although the picture is … , I also find it …	Obwohl das Bild … ist, finde ich es auch …
effective	wirkungsvoll, effektvoll
enigmatic	geheimnisvoll, rätselhaft
eyecatching	markant, auffällig
humorous	humorvoll, lustig
irritating	irritierend, nervig
persuasive	überzeugend
powerful	beeindruckend, eindringlich
puzzling	verwirrend, rätselhaft
touching	rührend, bewegend

Message and meaning

I take this to mean that …	Ich nehme an, das bedeutet …
The artist seems to be indicating that …	Der/Die Künstler/in scheint andeuten zu wollen, dass …
The cartoonist clearly wants us to …	Der/Die Karikaturist/in will offensichtlich, dass wir …
The viewer is compelled to think of …	Der/Die Betrachter/in wird quasi dazu gezwungen, an … zu denken.
to criticize	kritisieren
to examine	überprüfen, (genau) untersuchen
to idealize	idealisieren
to satirize	persiflieren, satirisch darstellen, verspotten
to symbolize	symbolisieren, versinnbildlichen

Useful expressions for essay writing

Introducing the topic

Stating the opening proposition	Eine Eröffnungsthese aufstellen
It is often claimed/said/asserted/stated that …	Oft wird behauptet/gesagt/beteuert/erklärt, dass …
Today we are often confronted with the problem of …	Heute werden wir oft mit dem Problem des/der … konfrontiert.
We often read in the newspapers that …	Oft lesen wir in der Zeitung dass …
X made the assertion that …	X stellte die Behauptung auf, dass …

Calling the proposition into question	Die These hinterfragen
One must ask oneself whether/why/how …	Man muss sich fragen, ob/weshalb/wie …
This assertion raises a fundamental question/issue: …	Diese Behauptung wirft eine grundsätzliche Frage auf: …
We must examine the truth of this assertion.	Wir müssen den Wahrheitsgehalt dieser Behauptung überprüfen.

Developing the argument

Enumerating the elements	Bestandteile aufzählen
Firstly … secondly … thirdly …	Erstens … zweitens … drittens …
On the one hand … on the other hand …	Einerseits … andererseits …

Adding another point	Einen weiteren Punkt hinzufügen
Furthermore, …	Außerdem … / Darüber hinaus …
In addition to this, …	Außerdem … / Darüber hinaus …
It must also be said that …	Es darf nicht unerwähnt bleiben, dass …
We must also consider …	Wir müssen ebenfalls … betrachten/berücksichtigen.

Introducing an example	Ein Beispiel anführen
For example, …	Zum Beispiel …
Take for example …	Nehmen Sie zum Beispiel …
To illustrate this, …	Um dies zu veranschaulichen, …
… illustrates this point perfectly.	… veranschaulicht deutlich diesen Aspekt.

Introducing a quotation	Ein Zitat anführen
As X said/wrote, …	Wie X sagte/schrieb, …
In the words of X, …	Um es mit den Worten von X zu sagen: …
To quote X, …	Um X zu zitieren: …
Introducing a hypothesis	**Eine Hypothese aufstellen**
It is quite possible that …	Es ist sehr gut möglich, dass …
This leads one to believe that …	Dies veranlasst zu der Annahme, dass …
It may well be that …	Es kann sehr wohl sein, dass …
Expressing certainty	**Gewissheit ausdrücken**
All the indications are that …	Alles deutet darauf hin, dass …
It is certainly true that …	Es ist sicherlich zutreffend, dass …
It is clear/certain that …	Es ist klar/sicher, dass …
The truth is that …	In Wahrheit ist/sind … / Tatsache ist, dass …
… as everyone knows.	…, wie wir alle wissen. / …, wie ja allgemein bekannt ist.
Expressing uncertainty and doubt	**Unsicherheit und Zweifel ausdrücken**
It is difficult to believe that …	Es fällt schwer zu glauben, dass …
It is uncertain whether …	Es ist ungewiss, ob …
This may be true, but …	Das mag wohl stimmen, aber …
… seems probable/possible	… scheint wahrscheinlich/möglich.
… seems likely/unlikely.	… scheint wahrscheinlich/unwahrscheinlich
Emphasizing a point	**Einen Punkt betonen**
It is important/vital/essential to realize that …	Es ist wichtig/unerlässlich/wesentlich zu begreifen, dass …
We must remember that …	Wir dürfen nicht vergessen, dass …
… is an important/vital/essential point.	… ist ein wichtiger/entscheidender/wesentlicher Aspekt.

Considering counter-arguments

Signalling a change of viewpoint	Einen Perspektivwechsel ankündigen
However, this is just one side of the matter.	Das ist jedoch nur eine Seite der Medaille.
On the other hand, …	Andererseits …
Turning to Y for an alternative view, …	Y hat eine andere Sicht der Dinge, und zwar …

Conceding a point	Etwas einräumen
It must be admitted/conceded that …	Man muß zugeben/eingestehen, dass …
There is no denying that …	Es lässt sich nicht leugnen, dass …

Denying a point	Etwas zurückweisen
It would be ridiculous to maintain that …	Es wäre lächerlich, darauf zu bestehen, dass …
On the contrary, …	Im Gegenteil: …

Ending the essay

Summarizing the arguments	Zusammenfassen der Argumente
Let us remind ourselves of the main arguments: …	Rufen wir uns die Hauptargumente in Erinnerung: …
To summarize, …	Zusammenfassend lässt sich sagen, dass …
We have seen/established that …	Wir haben gesehen/festgestellt, dass …

Drawing conclusions	Schlussfolgerungen ziehen
All in all, …	Alles in allem … / Unterm Strich …
All of these considerations lead me to the conclusion that …	Diese Betrachtungen führen mich zu der Schlussfolgerung, dass …
From this I must conclude that …	Daraus muss ich den Schluss ziehen, dass …

Stating one's own point of view	Die eigene Sichtweise vortragen
I am convinced that …	Ich bin überzeugt, dass …
I personally believe that …	Ich persönlich bin der Auffassung, dass …
In my opinion, …	Meiner Meinung nach …
It seems to me that …	Mir scheint, dass …

Index

Acknowledgements

S. 8: Shutterstock.com / Antonio Guillem; S. 10: Shutterstock.com / mangostock; S. 12: Shutterstock.com / Pressmaster; S. 14: Shutterstock.com / Zurijeta; S. 16: Shutterstock.com / Jacob Lund; S. 18: Shutterstock.com / Kwangmoozaa; S. 22: Shutterstock.com / maradon 333; S. 24: Shutterstock.com / runzelkorn; S. 28: Shutterstock.com / DisobeyArt; S. 30: Shutterstock.com / catastrophe_OL; S. 32: Shutterstock.com / Lisa F. Young; S. 34: Shutterstock.com / SpeedKingz; S. 36: Shutterstock.com / Lurin; S. 42: Shutterstock.com / Monkey Business Images; S. 44: Shutterstock.com / Monkey Business Images; S. 46 / flags: Shutterstock.com / Hampus design; S. 46 / bus: Shutterstock.com / MattLphotography; S. 48: Shutterstock.com / Rawpixel.com; S. 50: Shutterstock.com / Monkey Business Images; S. 52: Shutterstock.com / TierneyMJ; S. 56 / photo: Shutterstock.com / Magnetic Mcc; S. 56 / flags: Shutterstock.com / Hampus design; S. 58: Shutterstock.com / Lucky Business; S. 60: Shutterstock.com / SeventyFour; S. 62: Shutterstock.com / Th3lastpeace; S. 64: Shutterstock.com / Monkey Business Images; S. 66 / photo: Shutterstock.com / Paparacy; S. 66 / graphics: Shutterstock.com / KerdaZz; S. 70: Shutterstock.com / Andrew Rybalko; S. 80: Shutterstock.com / Peshkova; S. 82: Shutterstock.com / Evgeniy Yatskov; S. 84: Shutterstock.com / Festa; S. 90: Shutterstock.com / Tero Vesalainen; S. 92: Shutterstock.com / EtiAmmos; S. 94: Shutterstock.com / Georgejmclittle; S. 98: Shutterstock.com / alexsmaga; S. 106: Shutterstock.com / Chinnapong; S. 108: Shutterstock.com / danylyukk1; S. 110: Shutterstock.com / Stephen Gibson; S. 112: Shutterstock.com / Virojt Changyencham; S. 114/1: Shutterstock.com / attaphong; S. 114/2: Shutterstock.com / RedlineVector; S. 118: Shutterstock.com / Nuttawut Uttamaharac; S. 122: Shutterstock.com / jaroslava V; S. 126: Shutterstock.com / machimorales; S. 128: Shutterstock.com / andriano.cz; S. 138: Shutterstock.com / dianameise; S. 140: Shutterstock.com / ADragan; S. 142: Shutterstock.com / Jerry-Rainey; S. 144: Shutterstock.com / Jacob Lund; S. 146: Shutterstock.com / Nadezhda Shoshina; S. 148: Shutterstock.com / Rawpixel.com; S. 152: Shutterstock.com / Fishman64; S. 154: Shutterstock.com / LightField Studios; S. 162: Shutterstock.com / Mark1987; S. 164: Shutterstock.com / Durden Images; S. 166: Shutterstock.com / vasara; S. 170: Shutterstock.com / Vlad G; S. 172: Shutterstock.com / Zack Frank; S. 176: Shutterstock.com / Billion Photos; S. 178: Shutterstock.com / Pla2na; S. 180: Shutterstock.com / Max Niessen; S. 190: Shutterstock.com / IZZ HAZEL; S. 196: Shutterstock.com / jiunn; S. 200: Shutterstock.com / abstract

FOCUS

FOCUS ON VOCABULARY

Focus on Vocabulary wurde geplant und entwickelt von Cornelsen Berufliche Bildung, Berlin.

Verfasser:	Steve Williams, Corio Bay Media, Melbourne
	Oliver Busch, Berlin (deutsche Erläuterungen und Vokabelverzeichnis)
	Peadar Curran, Berlin (interaktive Online-Übungen)
Beraterin:	Alexandra Köpf, Ulm
Projektleitung:	Andreas Goebel
Verlagsredaktion:	Franziska Gräbe, Menemsha MacBain
Außenredaktion:	Janan Barksdale
Redaktionelle Mitarbeit:	Nicola Stebbing, Katarina Hlavata
Layoutkonzept:	Petra Eberhard (designcollective), Berlin; graphitecture book & edition
Umschlaggestaltung:	Matthias Höppener-Fidus (werkstatt für gebrauchsgrafik), Berlin
Technische Umsetzung:	graphitecture book & edition
Bildredaktion:	Janan Barksdale, Gertha Maly

www.cornelsen.de

1. Auflage, 1. Druck 2019

Alle Drucke dieser Auflage sind inhaltlich unverändert und können im Unterricht nebeneinander verwendet werden.

Druck: AZ Druck und Datentechnik GmbH, Kempten

ISBN 978-3-06-451772-1

PEFC zertifiziert
Dieses Produkt stammt aus nachhaltig
bewirtschafteten Wäldern und kontrollierten
Quellen.

www.pefc.de

PEFC/04-31-2260